Hooligan

Also by Geoffrey Pearson

The Deviant Imagination
Working Class Youth Culture
edited with Geoffrey Mungham

Hooligan

A history of respectable fears

Geoffrey Pearson

MACMILLAN

First published 1983
Reprinted 1983, 1985, 1987, 1988, 1990

Published by
MACMILLAN EDUCATION LTD
Houndmills, Basingstoke, Hampshire RG21 2XS
and London
Companies and representatives
throughout the world

Printed in Hong Kong

ISBN 0–333–23400–6 (paperback)

For Saul Edward

Till children sniggering back from Sunday school
Know twenty ways of proving you a fool
Till hooligans have Hegel for their teacher
And every navvy own his pocket Nietzsche.

E. M. FORSTER, 1903

Contents

Sources of illustrations   viii
Preface: English Rose or British Bulldog?   ix

PART ONE: DECLINE AND FALL OF THE
   'BRITISH WAY OF LIFE'   1

1.   Present Tense: Moderates and Hooligans   3
2.   Twenty Years Ago: Teds under the Bed   12
3.   Since the War: Past Perfect   25

PART TWO: THE ORIGINAL HOOLIGANS   51

4.   The Traditional 'Way of Life'   53
5.   Victorian Boys, We Are Here!   74

PART THREE: THE STABLE TRADITIONS   119

6.   A New Variety of Crime   121
7.   The Artful Chartist Dodger   156
8.   Merrie England and its Unruly Apprentice   183

PART FOUR: MAKING SENSE OF
   'LAW-AND-ORDER' MYTH   207

Notes and References   244
Index   276

Sources of Illustrations

These sources are listed in the order the illustrations appear in the book. The author gratefully acknowledges the work of the photography unit at the University of Bradford for reproducing the illustrations.

p. 50   *Daily Graphic*, 5 December 1900
p. 78   *Punch*, 10 September 1898
p. 87   *Daily Graphic*, 2 November 1900
p. 93   *Daily Graphic*, 5 December 1900
p. 95   *Daily Graphic*, 16 November 1900
p. 97   *Daily Graphic*, 16 November 1900
p. 99   *Comic Cuts*, 23 August 1897
p. 118 *Punch*, 8 October 1881
p. 123 *Punch's Almanack for 1882*
p. 125 *Punch*, 30 April 1881
p. 133 *Punch's Almanack for 1863*
p. 135 *Punch*, 3 January 1863
p. 136 *Punch*, 10 January 1863
p. 137 *Punch's Almanack for 1857*
p. 139 *Punch*, 13 December 1862; 20 December 1862;
        23 September 1856
p. 141 *Punch*, 27 December 1856
p. 145 *Punch*, 13 December 1862
p. 147 *Punch's Almanack for 1863*
p. 149 *Punch*, 29 November 1862
p. 151 *Punch*, 21 December 1878
p. 204 *Punch*, 18 October 1856

Preface: English Rose or British Bulldog ?

This book aims to cast some old light on new problems. It is about street crime and violence. But it is also about myth and tradition: the myth of the 'British way of life' according to which, after centuries of domestic peace, the streets of Britain have been suddenly plunged into an unnatural state of disorder that betrays the stable traditions of the past.

What I hope to show, by contrast, is that the real traditions are quite different: that for generations Britain has been plagued by the same fears and problems as today; and that this is something which should require us to reassess the shape of our present difficulties and the prospects for the future.

First, a word of apology may be in order. There is a shady confusion in the English language whereby the words 'British' and 'English' are used as if they were interchangeable. At least, this is what happens when it is the English who are speaking; the people of Wales, Scotland and Ireland usually care to make finer distinctions when talking about themselves or their close neighbours.

Hooliganism touches on a nerve of this confusion. Because, allied to the way in which the British (or do I mean English?) style themselves as the most orderly nation on earth, when trouble and violence visit the streets — as they do — there is a habitual tendency to disown this as 'un-British' or 'un-English'. It is 'not playing the game', 'not cricket', and so on.

At the moment it is black people who stand accused of disrupting the peaceful traditions of the 'British way of life', and it has even been found necessary to import an American word 'mugging' into the vocabulary in order to describe such an unheard-of and un-English crime as street robbery. But the English have been blaming their violence on someone else for a century or more, and in the past street crime and disorderly conduct have been foisted on to any number of alien influences — 'street Arabs', 'hot-blooded' ruffians, the 'offscouring of the Continent', discharged Foreign Legionnaires, 'Americanised' television violence, and so on — with a particularly fixed tradition of groaning English fears about 'Americanisation' which stretches back to the mid-nineteenth century as part of this effort to uphold the illusion of a peaceful inheritance in which violence is entirely foreign to the English national character. Indeed, it is wonderfully apt that in a key moment of this tradition, when late Victorian London christened its own unruly offspring — who were rampaging around the streets, attacking policemen in large numbers, and allegedly engaged in regular armed gang warfare — an 'Irish' name was chosen, providing the key term in the discourse: *hooligan*.

It is as a result of these inescapable confusions, and not out of any sense of malice towards the peoples of Ireland, Scotland and Wales, that the words 'British' and 'English' are freely mixed throughout this book. The book has been in preparation for a number of years, and so it is not inspired by the summer riots of 1981, although these add another chapter in the long, connected history of disorder in the streets of London and other British cities. Hooliganism may be news, but it is not new. As long as we continue to believe that it is new, however, then we will be badly handicapped in our attempts to deal intelligently with the problem.

I have many debts of gratitude to people who have helped in the making of this book. In a vital sense my interest in these matters was kindled by my parents' recollections of life in working-class Manchester between the wars — a rough old place by all accounts. I have received generous advice and hints on points of detail from Bob Ashcroft, Harry Blagg, Martin Bobker, David Brown, Barbara Castle, Mighty John Daly, Jason Ditton, Colin Fletcher, Maurice Hindle, Andrew Jacubowicz, Peter Ketley, Dorothy Lane, Phil Lee, Adrian Mitchell, Graham Partridge, Aidan Rose, Raphael Samuel,

Colin Sumner and Ian Vine. Peter Barham and Chris Barlas shared enthusiasms, and swapped agonies, on how to write usefully and creatively for our time. Stephen Collins has been an overflowing fund of inspiration and encouragement. Lorraine Hemingway endured a household threatening to be engulfed by a mountain of newspaper cuttings, photocopies and much else. I have learned from the staff and students of those colleges and universities where I have been invited to give lectures and seminars on my research, as well as conferences of social workers, probation officers, magistrates and police officers. A special word of thanks is due to the staff of various libraries who have always been courteous and helpful: Bradford Public Library, Bradford University Library, the British Library newspaper collection at Colindale, Cambridge University Library, the Institute of Criminology Library at Cambridge, Leeds Public Library, Leeds University Library, Manchester Public Library, the Police Staff College Library at Bramshill, and the Public Record Office at Kew. Without their skill and dedication, nothing would have been possible, and let us hope that the British government's passion for 'leaner and fitter' libraries — as all else — soon finds remission.

September 1982   GEOFFREY PEARSON

PART ONE

Decline and Fall of the 'British Way of Life'

'You must have seen great changes since you were a young man,' said Winston tentatively.

The old man's pale blue eyes moved from the darts board to the bar, and from the bar to the door of the Gents, as though it were in the bar-room that he expected the changes to have occurred.

'The beer was better,' he said finally. 'And cheaper! When I was a young man, mild beer — wallop we used to call it — was fourpence a pint. That was before the war, of course.'

'Which war was that?' said Winston.

George Orwell, *Nineteen Eighty-Four*

1
Present Tense: Moderates and Hooligans

To think this is England (*The Sun*, 6 July 1981)

People are bound to ask what is happening to our country . . . Having been one of the most law-abiding countries in the world — a byword for stability, order, and decency — are we changing into something else? (*The Daily Express*, 6 July 1981)

Once upon a time, so the story runs in these characteristic reponses to the summer riots of 1981, violence and disorder were unknown in Britain. The hallowed traditions of the 'British way of life' were founded upon civility, reasonableness and an unquestioning respect for law and authority. Violence was entirely foreign to the nation and its people who were renowned for fair play, *sang froid* and the stiff upper lip.

But all that is no more. Now violence and terror lurk in the once-safe streets. The family no longer holds its proper place and parents have abandoned their responsibilities. In the classroom, where once the tidy scholars applied themselves diligently in their neat rows of desks, there is a carnival of disrespect. The police and magistrates have had their hands tied by the interference of sentimentalists and do-gooders. A new generation is upon us of mindless bully boys, vandals, muggers, head-bangers, football rowdies, granny-murderers, boot boys, toughs and tearaways who laugh in the face of the law, as we stand before the rising tide of violence and disorder with a Canute-like impotence.

'Are we the same people that we were thirty, forty, fifty years ago?' Mr Enoch Powell asked himself only weeks before the riots erupted in the British cities in 1981.[1] Mr Powell, of course, has not been notably shy about declaring his belief that it is black people who are at the root of the decline and fall of the 'British way of life'. In the wake of the riots, while denouncing all sorts of 'sentiment, wishful-thinking and humbug', *The Daily Mail* also saw fit to editorialise on the black community who, it was said, 'must bear no small responsibility for the fear of the mob that has now returned after a century or more to haunt the cities of this land'.[2] Mr George Gale, on the other hand, sensed a more general deterioration in manners as the fountain-head of Britain's troubles, while bringing a much abbreviated time-scale to bear on their onset. 'Over the past twenty years or so', he announced in a *Daily Express* front-page splash, 'there has been a revulsion from authority and discipline . . . There has been a permissive revolution . . . and now we all reap the whirlwind.'[3]

'Permissive' Rot: History Lessons without Dates

It was never seriously in dispute, of course, that black and white people alike were caught up in the summer disturbances of 1981. Nor did it need riots to provoke these swan-songs for the old traditions. Throughout the 1970s, in a gathering storm of discontent, the same accusations had become a dominant and characteristic feature of the social landscape. The decline of family life, the lowering of standards in the schools, the 'permissive' worm within, the irresponsibility of working mothers and their delinquent 'latch-key' children, the excessive leniency of the law, and the unwarranted interference of the 'softy-softy, namby-pamby pussyfooting' of the 'so-called experts'[4] — these were well trodden avenues of complaint by 'law-and-order' enthusiasts and 'anti-permissive' moralists, warning of a vast historical degeneration among the British people.

In 1974, for example, we learned that 'For the first time in a century and a half, since the great Tory reformer Robert

Peel set up the Metropolitan police, areas of our cities are becoming unsafe for peaceful citizens by night, and some even by day' — from no less an authority than that great Tory reformer Sir Keith Joseph. Warning that 'the balance of our population, our human stock is threatened', Keith Joseph sensed truly momentous possibilities of decline. 'Rome itself fell,' he reminded us, 'destroyed from inside.' 'Are we to be destroyed from inside, too, a country which successfully repelled and destroyed Philip of Spain, Napoleon, the Kaiser, Hitler?'[5]

Tory politicians of the so-called New Right have undoubtedly been the most active in promoting these ways of thinking, and the 'law-and-order' question played a major part in Mrs Thatcher's victorious election campaign in 1979.[6] Rhodes Boyson, the trouble-shooting panjandrum of the new moral conservatism, has been particularly energetic in admonishing the 'mindless sociologists' and 'all that mush' which has corrupted the national character.[7] 'It has not gone unnoticed,' said Dr Boyson in 1978, 'that crime has increased parallel with the number of social workers.' 'It is equally true,' countered *The Daily Mirror* in a spirited editorial response, 'that crime has increased parallel with speeches from Dr Boyson.'[8]

Senior policemen have also queued up in numbers to deliver their judgements against the decline in public morals, and to warn of the imminent eclipse of the old standards and traditions. 'The freedom and way of life we have been accustomed to enjoy for so long will vanish', Kenneth Oxford, Chief Constable of Merseyside, prophesied in 1977; 'what we are experiencing is not a passing phenomenon but a continuing process of change in our way of life . . . our customary ways of behaving and our traditional values are being radically modified.'[9] 'The mindless violence, the personal attacks and injury,' asserted Philip Knights, President of the Association of Chief Police Officers, 'and above all the use of violence in all its forms to further political creeds, are relatively new to the streets of this country.'[10] The allegations that such developments are somehow unprecedented, together with the feeling that they involve a massive historical shift, are entirely typical. The work of the police, according to Sir

Robert Mark in 1978, now required 'not only as much physical courage and dedication as policing parts of Victorian London but a great deal more moral courage than has been required by the police at any time since Peel'.[11] Another senior police officer who more than once captured the headlines, James Anderton, Chief Constable of Greater Manchester, decrying 'the rot that has now taken a firm hold in the fabric of our society', was so moved as to describe crime as Britain's 'Top Growth Industry'.[12] So, too, if we consult the *Report of Her Majesty's Chief Inspector of Constabulary*, 1975 (or almost any other year for that matter) we find ourselves assailed within the space of only a few paragraphs with repeated references to

> vicious and ugly attacks ... becoming all too commonplace ... anxiety about violence ... this increasing resort to violence ... violent crime which is becoming an accepted part of day to day life ... the trend of increased violence in our society ... this menace to our way of life.

The report was generous enough to remind us that the personal violence over which so much ink had been spilled amounted to less than 4 per cent of known serious crime. Even so, without pause the report resumed its brooding concern over 'the apparent relaxation of standards of behaviour', 'the lowering of hitherto established values', 'the erosion of good standards, which were hitherto commonplace' and the necessity of 'reinforcing the values of what as a nation we had believed in for many years'. 'Without due care', it was feared that 'the all too common attitude of self-preservation and the growing general acceptance to do as one pleased without fear of retribution would ... lead the country to anarchy'.[13] Nor would it appear that these awful prophecies from her Majesty's Chief Inspector were calculated to depress the spirits of the royal household. For HRH Prince Philip is known to have entertained his own version of this 'law-and-order' jeremiad, warning in 1979 of 'this avalanche of lawlessness threatening to engulf our civilisation'.[14]

'Whatever achievements policemen can claim, the ability to communicate is certainly not one of them', said Sir Robert

Mark in his 1973 Dimbleby Lecture. 'We share with another more famous service a tradition of silence.'[15] If so, then we must freely admit that another time-honoured tradition of British self-restraint has very recently bit the dust. In contemporary Britain it seems almost impossible to go a single day without hearing, from some quarter or another, a senior policeman hectoring us on the deteriorated condition of public morals, while assuming the right to deliver homespun history lessons in which the past is lovingly remembered as a time of harmony. A time, that is, when the traditions of the 'British way of life' held sovereign sway, and the policeman's lot was an extremely happy one.

Locating the Golden Age

Now, what I wish to ask in this book is whether this way of thinking about Britain's decline is useful and accurate. And if it is not (and I will argue that it is *not*) then to what extent does this tradition of anguished regret for the past hinder our actions in the present and in the future? We must be careful not to place the entire blame upon the amateur historians in Britain's police force. While policemen freely peddle these cherished beliefs in the lost standards of the 'British way of life', they did not invent them. Nor when the Tory press informs us, as it does unceasingly, that 'Britain has a profound tradition of unregimented, tolerant order'[16] should we rush to indict the historical embroidery of newspaper editors. Professional historians, too, are not unknown to indulge in this kind of historical reasoning, perhaps best exemplified by T. A. Critchley's raptures about 'the native self-discipline of Anglo-Saxon England' and 'this streak of national self-discipline'.[17]

This view of Britain's history as one founded on stability and decency is deeply ingrained in the self-understanding of the British people. The present, we hardly need to be told, is extremely tense. But the past, say the accumulated traditions of our national culture, was a 'golden age' of order and security. Nowadays we need the iron fist of policing in order that we might sleep soundly in our beds. Whereas formerly we did not, and our love of tolerant freedom was spontaneous, unregimented and natural.

The extremity of these awful judgements against the moral deterioration of the British people, and the enormous vision of chaos and disorder which they conjure up, suggest the need for a cautious organisation of our thought and feeling as we approach these matters. Clearly, there is an impressive consistency in this line of thinking — both in terms of the belief in a pre-existing era of tranquility, and in the agreement that the natural moderacy of the 'British way of life' has been eclipsed in the hooligan deluge. However, when we come to more detailed considerations — such as exactly where this 'golden age' is to be located in real historical time — then we are confronted with such a disorderly jumble of datemarks and vague historical allusion as to allow for wide margins of disagreement even among dedicated 'law-and-order' enthusiasts. Indeed, at the centre of the preoccupation with declining standards and mounting disorder, there is an immense historical 'black hole'.

There are various historical reference points made available to us, by which it is said we can chart Britain's fall from grace. One of the most popular slogans suggests that we need only look back to 'Before the War' in order to reach the solid ground of tradition and stability. The Society of Conservative Lawyers, for example, confidently announced in its report on *Public Order* (1970) that such things as gang fights between youths were 'a distinctively postwar phenomenon'.[18] Patrick Jenkin, as Conservative Social Services Secretary, more recently described how he had been reliably informed that 'the increasing turbulence of modern life, with rising crime, industrial disruption, violence and terrorism, was rooted in the separation of children from their parents during the war'.[19] Sir Keith Joseph offers a flexi-time history according to which, in the same speech where he entertained the spectacular belief that Britain's streets had been plunged into insecurity 'for the first time in a century and a half', he also conjured with a more modest timescale whereby 'such words as good and evil, such stress on self-discipline and standards have been out of favour since the war'.[20] Finally, from its privileged vantage point to diagnose any deterioration in the national character, the National Front described its own understanding of pre-war social realities in a leaflet offering advice to schoolchildren on *How to Spot a Red Teacher* (1977): 'Tell the Red Teacher the poor whites during the Great Slump didn't commit muggings on defenceless old ladies.'[21] Well, we shall see.

If the Second World War is often regarded as the watershed of 'permissiveness', then those with more educated tastes — who perhaps remember the precipitating crisis of the Public Order Act of 1936 and Mosley's black shirts, or who might have read the descriptions of pre-war razor gangs in Graham Greene's *Brighton Rock* — look back beyond the war before that, to the slumbering golden years of Edwardian England which is one of the most authoritative versions of the true location of the 'British way of life'. Next in line is the Victorian era, which is commonly remembered as harbouring some kind of gold standard of untarnished moral worth. 'We need to get back towards the Victorian days of discipline' says Dr Boyson in one of his attacks on 'permissiveness', and he is certainly not alone among Tory fundamentalists in fondly remembering the glories of empire, child labour and workhouse in Queen Victoria's reign.[22]

The idea that the past harbours a golden age of tranquility also readily lends itself to the view that history might furnish us with effective methods of commonsense crime control. So, one Member of Parliament's idea 'to have girl muggers whipped' would turn back the clock to the 1820s when corporal punishment for women was abolished, whereas another Parliamentary recommendation to 'Bring back stocks for hooligans' would presumably transport us into the Dark Ages.[23] Indeed, the powerful imagery of pastoral will often suggest that the true location of the golden age lies in pre-industrial Merrie England — a traditional lament that was already well established in Queen Victoria's golden era.[24]

But although devastating historical judgements such as these can be found in abundance amidst the speculations of the 'law-and-order' movement, the urgency of Britain's contemporary predicament insists that a much more abbreviated timescale is often used to describe the rapidity of the descent into lawlessness. 'Twenty Years Ago', which conveys the sense of a generational decline, is the slogan most commonly employed. Patricia Morgan plumps for this timescale in her critique of the 'New Establishment' of social workers, psychologists, teachers and other exponents of what she calls the 'New Socio-Psychological Expertise' of child care and education. The moral collapse of the younger generation, as she describes it, is 'the logical outcome of the theory and practice of the past couple of decades'.[25] From another quarter, Baroness Faithfull took issue in 1979 with the 'simplistic belief' in the short-sharp-shock remedy which she viewed as no less foolish than 'the theories of those false prophets of permissiveness at whose door must be laid a considerable part of the blame for the rise in crime over the last two decades'.[26]

'Twenty years ago' has a ring of common sense about it. A typical letter in the correspondence columns of *The Daily Mail* in 1977 summed up the commonplace fears and aspirations which are arranged around this slogan:

> In the past two decades standards and values have so deteriorated that materialism and selfishness have become the norm . . . The general public are nostalgic for family life as depicted in the old days when love, concern and discipline were considered of greater importance . . . than wealth, permissiveness, 'doing one's own thing' regardless of the consequences to others. We don't need researchers to tell us what is wrong in this cynical 'anything goes' era. We see it all around us.[27]

This kind of commonsense reasoning, invariably linked to the perceived upsurge in crime and mischief, has become such a day-to-day feature of life in contemporary Britain that one hears complaints phrased in the idiom of 'Twenty Years Ago' amidst the gossip of bus queues, pubs and launderettes. Even so, when I stumbled across Miss Diana Dors — a 'permissive' sex-symbol of some notoriety twenty years ago — advancing its claims in a popular magazine and asking us to cast our minds towards 'my era back in the fifties', I was not immediately sure whose side she was supposed to be on. But it was business as usual. 'As an ex-sex symbol', Miss Dors confessed, 'I usually amaze those who pose the question by saying that I believe the permissive society HAS gone too far.'[28]

Nor has the Labour Party, which has traditionally kept its own counsel on 'law-and-order' matters, proved entirely immune to the surrounding clamour. Mr Merlyn Rees as Labour Home Secretary had given voice to the more usually reticent position early in 1978 when he charged Mrs Thatcher with 'an irresponsible and dangerous approach to law and order . . . whipping up people's fears in a "cynical" attempt to win votes'.[29] Later in the same year, however, appearing on television in a news item on vandalism, Mr Rees was to be found closing the commonsense consensus. 'You only have to look around,' he explained, 'and see that something has happened in the last twenty years.'[30]

It is a simple enough invitation, with no strings attached. So let us take a look around and see what is to be seen.

2

Twenty Years Ago: Teds Under the Bed

If Britain could be described in any useful way as a society at ease with itself twenty years ago, then that was certainly not how it felt at the time. Recoiling from the impact of the Teddy Boys, who were understood to have introduced an entirely foreign and unprecedented streak of violence into British life during the 1950s, the fearful preoccupation with hooliganism and 'permissiveness' was already under a full head of steam.

Given that so much of the enthusiasm for 'law and order' in Britain has been marshalled by the Conservative Party during the late 1970s, a simple impression of how different things were (or were not) twenty years ago can be gleaned from the business of Conservative Party conferences in the two periods. At its annual conference in 1978, as the Party girded itself up to meet the forthcoming General Election, there was a full-throated debate on the imminent threat to 'law and order'. Amidst calls to bring back the birch and to inaugurate 'Saturday night floggings' for soccer hooligans, Mr William Whitelaw reaffirmed his pledge to toughen up the law by introducing a new regime of short-sharp-shock Detention Centres modelled on the Army 'glass house' system of physical drill and unrelenting discipline.[1] That much, I expect, we can agree on.

But what happened twenty years earlier at Blackpool in 1958? By contrast with the unprecedented alarms of the late 1970s, 'the disturbing increase in criminal offences' was on the Tory Party agenda, and so was 'this sudden increase in crime and brutality which is so foreign to our nature and our country'. 'Is it not a fact', asked one delegate, 'that our wives and mothers, if they are left alone in the house at night, are frightened to open their doors?' There were calls to bring back flogging 'to deflate these cocksure young men' – one speaker likened the deterrent properties of the cat-o'-nine-tails with those of the H-Bomb! – while another thought that the stocks 'have much to commend them'.[2] And when it was not shouting him down as he tried to suggest that the powers of the courts were adequate, the conference heard Mr R. A. Butler pledge himself to a new building programme of short-sharp-shock Detention Centres. 'Everything should be done at the double', he explained, and 'there should be a maximum of hard work and a minimum of amusement.' Indeed, the mood of the Conservative Party Conference twenty years ago was aptly summed up by one speaker who thought: 'Over the past 25 years we in this country, through misguided sentiment, have cast aside the word "discipline", and now we are suffering from it.'[3] *Plus ça change.*

An Already Weakened People

As the Tory Party debated the 'make-believe gangsters strolling about the streets as if they are the monarchs of all', the conference hall rang with an entirely familiar pattern of complaints and accusations: 'the leniency shown in the past by the Courts of this country'; the 'lack of parental control, interest and support'; the 'sex, savagery, blood and thunder' in films and television; and the 'smooth, smug and sloppy sentimentalists who contribute very largely to the wave of crime' so that young people were 'no longer frightened of the police, they sneer at them'.[4]

Nor was it just the invigorating properties of the sea air at Blackpool that stimulated the appetite for whipping. Twenty years ago the same testy attitude was asserting itself in Parliament, prompting one MP to urge Mr Butler not to give in to 'the wild men of the Conservative Party'. The 'wild men' of Westminster were there in numbers, however, as the

House of Commons debated 'the appalling wave of crime' and the 'oppressive and startling' upsurge in violence. 'The minds of many of these young offenders appear to have been numbed by greed and indifference to violence', asserted one MP as he condemned 'the parents, indifferent to their children and utterly without social conscience'. Another, protesting that 'I am not exaggerating' against murmurs of dissent from his colleagues, believed that 'there is a danger of people taking the law into their own hands'. Although, when he had got it off his chest, he confessed that 'I am afraid I have been rather carried away'.[5]

There was nothing unusual about MPs getting carried away during debates on crime and violence, however, or for the Speaker to find it necessary to call for 'Order!' against 'shouts of sadistic enthusiasm' when whipping was on the agenda.[6] Throughout the 1950s the birchers and floggers had been ably represented by a coterie of MPs — Wing Commander Bullus, Brigadier Clarke, Brigadier Medlicott, Captain Waterhouse and the irrepressible Sir Thomas Moore — who had tormented a succession of Home Office spokesmen with their ghoulish enthusiasms, with a substantial measure of support for their aims. 'These louts who, long ago, should have been smacked on the behind by their parents' excited Sir Marcus Lipton, who was something of a Parliamentary dove on these occasions, no less than Mr Gerald Nabarro who considered that 'a proper policy ought to be to "whack the thugs" '.[7]

In the immediate aftermath of war, the Conservative Party had organised its understanding of juvenile crime around different assumptions. 'The misbehaviour of boys and girls', said its report on *Youth Astray* in 1946, 'is mainly the outcome of conditions, social, economic, and to some extent hereditary, for which they themselves cannot be blamed. The blame — for blame there is — rests largely upon society.'[8] By 1959, however, when its report on *The Responsible Society* was published, there had been a remarkable U-turn in Tory philosophy: 'We reject the notion, propagated by sincere but misguided idealists, that society shares the guilt of its criminals; that most malefactors are the victims of their environment.'[9] It was not exactly a novel sentiment, but

from now on the dominant message from within the Tory
ranks would be that the welfare state had weakened family
ties, the increase of working mothers had produced 'a growing
decline in parental responsibility', and 'affluence' had undermined the nation's moral fibre.[10]

Then, as now, the Conservative Party in the 1950s liked to
think of itself as a lonely beacon of responsibility in a moral
wilderness of couldn't-care-less 'permissiveness' and selfish
'I'm all right Jack' attitudes. However, these immediately
familiar accusations against the moral failure of the British
people touched on a much wider current of feeling in 1950s
Britain which found a crystallising focus in the problems of
the younger generation. The 'drifting youth of the welfare
state', as Arthur Bryant described them in 1954, 'become
the inevitable prey of the gang-leader or, at best, grow up
to lead, despite all the material opportunities of our age,
inert, stunted and purposeless lives'.[11] This withering criticism
of the youth of the nation was reflected by the way in which
all manner of novel terms — the 'mixed-up teenagers', the
'wild ones', the 'rebels without a cause' — entered into common usage in the 1950s, conveying the feeling that young
people were somehow more radically unintelligible to older
people than at any previous time in history. So that when
the British Medical Association decided in the late 1950s
to inaugurate a programme of discussions among its member-
ship on an appointed 'Subject of the Year', it was entirely
fitting that for its first discussion-point it should home in on
The Adolescent:

> The society in which today's adolescents find themselves is one of
> bewildering change . . . the whole face of society has changed in
> the last 20 years . . . a decrease in moral safeguards, and the advent
> of the welfare state has provided a national cushion against re-
> sponsibility and adversity.[12]

Thus, twenty years ago, and already bemoaning what
had happened in 'the last twenty years', the BMA was to be
found rehearsing the familiar diagnoses of the 'new' youth
problem — most of which appeared to have very little to
do with medical science. One child psychiatrist advised

that 'the standards of living have risen too rapidly for human nature to cope with', and as the report cast its eye over 'moral decay, uncertainty and dissatisfaction' it was characteristic of the fifties mood that the disorientations of postwar 'affluence' should receive pride of place within these medical judgements. 'Poverty is not now the cause of adolescent difficulties', we learned, 'but materialism without effort has replaced it.' And again: 'Indeed, not poverty, but unaccustomed riches seems an equally dangerous inducement to wild behaviour, even crime.'[13]

The 'easy money' said to be available to young people under conditions of full employment was the object of widespread condemnation. An earlier report, *Citizens of Tomorrow* (1955) produced by the King George's Jubilee Trust, had worked over this theme of 'too much pocket-money and too little discipline'. 'As compared with fifty, or even twenty years ago,' it was said that 'children have much more money to spend and more inducement to spend it' which led to 'that "something for nothing" philosophy which, we are told, has become much more prevalent since the advent of the welfare state'.[14] In T. R. Fyvel's *The Insecure Offenders*, which first appeared in 1961 and which represented the most systematic and unsensationalised attempt to come to terms with the youth problem, the argument pivoted upon the assumption that the impact of 'affluence' had conspired to produce a novel disorientation among the nation's youth. Employing the familiar juxtaposition of 'the remarkably law-abiding character of twentieth century English life' and 'the law-abiding England of pre-1940' as against what he repeatedly identified as 'new' — 'the new juvenile crime', 'the new rebels', 'the new generation of indifferent parents', 'a new type of violence', 'the new state of insecurity' — Fyvel thus considered that there was 'something in the way of life, in the break-up of traditional authority, in the values of the news in the headlines, which encouraged widespread youthful cynicism in general and rather violent delinquency in particular' and that this was 'a by-product of a new economic revolution which has put spending money on a scale not known before into the pockets of working-class boys and girls'. 'By the beginning of 1960', he wrote, 'it could no longer be denied that certain parts of London at night were dominated by a new spirit of insecurity': 'juvenile delinquency had *for the first time* in Britain become elevated to the status of a national problem'.[15] And so, in spite of our nostalgia for the days when Premier Harold Macmillan declared that Britain had 'never had it so good', there was nothing at all unusual in the BMA's diagnosis of the appalling state of morals in 1961:

> Looked at in his worst light the adolescent can take on an alarming aspect: he has learned no definite moral standards from his parents, is contemptuous of the law, easily bored . . . He is vulnerable to the influence of TV programmes of a deplorably low standard . . . Reading matter for teenagers was roundly condemned as 'full of sex and violence'.[16]

We can only hope, given the disparaging tone of this review of the nation's youth, that these good doctors were talking about somebody else's children. As indeed they were. The crystallising focus for these anxieties in 1950s Britain was not some generalised 'adolescent'. It was always assumed, as we will repeatedly find in these hooligan discourses, that 'the adolescent' was a boy: when the other sex figures at all it is as mothers, usually neglectful ones. What also tended to go unmentioned was that he was, specifically, a working-class boy. In fact, he was a 'Teddy Boy'. Although, it must be said that as the Teds walked out of the working-class districts of the major cities — first of all from the 'affluent' world of the Elephant and Castle in down-at-heel South London — they were unlikely candidates for the job of exemplifying the damaging effects of 'unaccustomed riches' and 'materialism without effort'. 'They were market porters, roadworkers, a lot of van boys,' said one of Fyvel's informants, 'all in jobs that didn't offer much — labourers could cover the lot.'[17]

Rock-and-Roll War Babies

The Teds took Britain by storm. 'The man who can win the allegiance of the Teddy Boys', remarked Mr Andrew

Fountaine who was later to come to prominence within the leadership of the National Front, 'can rule this country.'[18] More conventional politicians entertained more traditional remedies. 'The "de-Teddying" of Teddy Boys' was, after all, the original inspiration for R. A. Butler's short sharp shocks.[19]

The Teds took their name from the 'Edwardian' dress-style which had been originally promoted for fashion-conscious city gents who wished to cut an affluent fifties dash. When, in a remarkable act of cultural smash-and-grab, working-class youths adopted the long drape jackets as their own uniform — to which they added embellishments such as greased duck-tail haircuts, thick-soled 'brothel creeper' shoes, slim-jim ties and narrow drain-pipe trousers — no self-respecting gentleman was going to adorn himself in what had now become a vulgar 'Ted suit'. Sir Thomas Moore, seizing on the Teddy Boys as a further opportunity to sing the praises of the birch twigs, seemed to think that the name itself was a slander against the peaceful Edwardian years: 'On a point of order . . . Instead of using the word "Edwardian", would not the proper description be "young thugs", leaving it at that?'[20]

The new Edwardians — who, as I will show, had much more in common with the original Edwardian youth than is usually supposed — swiftly gained a terrible reputation for gang fights, vandalism, street robberies, rock-and-roll cinema riots, and attacks on cafe owners and late-night bus crews. Adults stared at them in not altogether dumb, but spluttering amazement. Within the gathering hysteria of the 1950s, young men wearing the 'Edwardian' style were banned from cinemas and dance halls. Law-abiding Teds were urged to throw away their zoot suits, and so repudiate the hooligan element — an initiative that entirely flopped. *The Daily Mirror* tried to organise its own weapons amnesty for flick-knives, coshes, bicycle-chains and knuckle-dusters. Special snatch-squads of women police officers infiltrated Teddy Boy gatherings dressed in bobby-sox and pony-tails. Psychiatrists were consulted for their expert diagnosis of the Teddy Boy condition, and from America it was reported that chlorpromazine — a heavy tranquilliser, and one of the new 'wonder drugs' entering into use in the mid-1950s for the control of excited schizophrenics — seemed to quieten Teddy Boys down.[21] And everyone breathed a sigh of relief . . . so the Teds were human after all.

Human, maybe, but 'British'? No. The social panic surrounding the emergence of the Teddy Boys formed part of a much wider structure of feeling in 1950s Britain that the social changes wrought on the postwar world were destroying the old 'British way of life' and the former civility of the British people, and the Teds were understood to be symptomatic of these social alterations. A principal target for these discontents was the impact of the 'Americanised' popular amusements of 'admass' which were widely deplored. Richard Hoggart's *The Uses of Literacy* (1957) was undoubtedly the most evocative survey of these postwar confusions, vividly conveying the feeling that the new 'candy floss' entertainments of the post-war era were morally inferior to the older working-class traditions, threatening a decisive break in cultural life. As he compared the 'full rich life' of the old back-street cultures which he thought were being pitted and undermined by the 'canned entertainment and packeted provision' of the new pulp culture, Hoggart made no effort to disguise his contempt for this barren cultural wasteland – the pop songs, the crooners and the heart-throbs, the hairstyles and clothing, the espresso bars and milk bars which young people frequented, together with the 'sex in shiny packets' literature and the cacophony of juke-boxes and 'nickelodeons'. All this was contrasted uninvitingly against the fondly remembered oral traditions of the working-class neighbourhoods – brass bands, free-and-easy nights at the local pub, and pigeon-fancying – as an essentially 'hollow' and 'faceless' cultural diminishment. And when Hoggart turned his attention to the 'juke box boys' who were a recognisable strain of early Teds – 'boys between fifteen and twenty, with drape-suits, picture ties, and an American slouch' – even the slouch was, characteristically, identified as 'Americanised' and hence 'postwar' and 'un-British', as the boys sipped their milkshakes and tapped their feet to the music in their milk-bar rendezvous:

> The young men waggle one shoulder or stare, as desperately as Humphrey Bogart, across the tubular chairs.

Compared with even the pub around the corner, this is all a peculiarly thin and pallid form of dissipation, a sort of spiritual dry-rot amid the odour of boiled milk. Many of the customers — their clothes, their hair-styles, their facial expressions all indicate — are living to a large extent in a myth-world compounded of a few simple elements which they take to be those of American life.[22]

It was a typical mode of response by Hoggart, contrasting the cultural solidity of the English pub and its robust pleasures with the contrived artificiality of the 'American' cafe; the fantasy world of admass set unfavourably against the down-to-earth character of working-class tradition. 'This regular, increasing, and almost unvaried diet of sensation without commitment' would 'render its consumers less capable of responding openly and responsibly to life' and 'induce an underlying sense of purposelessness'.[23]

The associations between this allegedly purposeless irresponsibility and a galloping crime rate have come to be employed regularly in postwar discourses on the decline and fall of the 'British way of life'. So, too, the feeling that life was becoming 'Americanised' has been used unsparingly to describe the process of 'permissive' rot and the collapse of traditional authority — most forcibly registered in the adoption of the term 'mugging' to disown as 'un-British' the old-fashioned crime of street robbery. After the first flutters of excitement in the immediate aftermath of war about GIs, nylon stockings, bubble-gum, television, flashy motorcars, labour-saving gadgetry and all-American razzle-dazzle, caricatures of 'Americanisation' have come to carry enormous authority within postwar deliberations on the decline of the old 'way of life'. These caricatures have offered a convenient metaphor of social change, carrying with them dire warnings of what social change might bring in its wake, with the ability to compress into a single image the ravages of modern trends such as high-speed living, urban anonymity, television violence, endangered streets, weakening affluence and shallow emotional content. The entrance of the dazzling war babies in their Ted suits, understood as harbingers of irresponsible affluence and rootless materialism, seemed to fit the bill precisely.

The Rehabilitation of the Teds

However, what is altogether remarkable is the way in which these rough working-class youths who donned Ted suits in the 1950s, and slicked back their hair in a greasy imitation of Elvis Presley, could be mistaken for the children of the 'affluent society'. The Teddy Boys first emerged, for example, from the slum neighbourhoods of working-class London — and it would be difficult to pretend that communities such as the Elephant and Castle were blessed with 'affluence', or anything approaching it. They were already exciting considerable attention in 1953, some years before the emergence of rock-and-roll which was commonly alleged to be the depraving 'Americanising' root of their violent energies. They had also made their social entrance at a time when television — so often blamed as another demoralising force — was only a minority pursuit in Britain, with no more than two million viewing licences in 1953; and when the commercial TV channel, which was most commonly alleged to be lowering standards, had not even been created. Indeed, the Teds had appeared on the streets before postwar meat-rationing had been abandoned in Britain — which might suggest that they belonged to the world of postwar austerity, rather than 'affluence'.

Many other aspects of the preoccupation with the Teddy Boys also prove to be factually unhinged. Before the emergence of the Teds there had been any number of alarms from the 1940s onwards about street violence, robbery attacks, 'Blitz kids' and 'cosh boys'.[24] Allegations of purposelessness and postwar ennui, together with declining parental responsibility, were also well in evidence before the 'affluent' fifties could be said to have worked their moral damage. The war had no sooner ended than a Mass Observation report *Puzzled People* (1947) described how 'the explosion or disintegration of orthodox beliefs has left a vacuum', and as early as 1950 the 'quest for a post-war purpose' was being anxiously scrutinised in a study of young people's lives.[25] In the following year the public were lectured from the courts on the duties of parenthood when, expressing himself 'perfectly satisfied that these crimes can be traced to neglect of parents', the Recorder of

Bradford struck the familiar harmonies of discontent: 'Parents of this time, unfortunately, do not take sufficient care in bringing up their children. They expect somebody else to be responsible' and it was a cause for great sorrow that 'Gone are the days of Queen Victoria.'[26] The Teddy Boys also coexisted with compulsory military service — which is so often wheeled out as a panacea for the troubles of youth — and national service was even condemned in the 1950s as 'a positive adverse influence on young people' because of the way in which it interrupted the transition from school to work and encouraged an 'eat, drink and be merry' philosophy.[27]

Finally, what was (and is) totally submerged in the conventional understanding of the Teddy Boys was that their style and demeanour was by no means unprecedented. Their rough-fighting, territorial edginess, for example, is better understood as a continuation of earlier forms of gang life in working-class neighbourhoods — rather than a sudden departure from tradition. So, too, the Teds had borrowed large parts of their supposedly unprecedented cultural equipment from earlier youth cultures, such as those identified in a 1949 Mass Observation report as 'Spiv' types and 'Dagos'.[28] Any number of these stylistic elements — the 'zoot suits', heavily greased 'Boston slash-back' hairstyles, and the 'Jive' and 'Jitterbug' dances — were already in evidence during the war, and even before the war. Adding it all up, it is clear that the conventional picture of the sudden and unrivalled appearance of the 'affluent' and 'Americanised' Teddy Boys — crazed by rock-and-roll, besotted by television, their pockets bulging with loose change — must be seen as a gross distortion of the actual events.

However, this was not how matters were understood at the time. The Teds were instantly recognised as symptomatic of the new 'classless' society and the 'affluent' breeze blowing in from across the Atlantic, a feeling that was massively reinforced by the wave of cinema riots that greeted the arrival of Bill Haley's *Rock Around the Clock* in Britain. But here we encounter an even more elusive difficulty. A profound historical amnesia has come to settle around the Teds whereby rock-and-roll outrages of the past, together with the magnified excitements that accompanied them, have been smuggled out of sight. The subsequent fate of the Teddy Boys – as public myth, that is – has correspondingly been one of rehabilitation and falsification.

Nowadays the mid-1950s rock craze seems to provoke nothing more than a nostalgic chuckle, and when the original Teds are remembered at all within the contemporary pre-occupation with hooliganism it is as something quaint and remarkably innocent. Whereas it was common in their own time for the Teddy Boys to be contrasted with a nostalgically remembered state of pre-existing harmony 'twenty years ago' or 'before the war', given the real horror which greeted their arrival we can perhaps only marvel at the way in which the nostalgic trick of amnesia can now work in the Teds' favour. Here they are, for example, joining in the patriotic raptures of Jubilee Year:

TEDDY GROUP 'TURN ON' SHOPPERS

Bradford Teddy Boys turned the clock back 20 years on Saturday when they gathered at an open-air concert in the city centre.

To the delight of shoppers who stopped to watch they revived some of their favourite dances of the 1950s like the solo bop and the catwalk . . . leading the dancing was the grandfather of Bradford Teds, 56-year-old William Bentley . . .

Mr Bentley reckons he is the oldest Teddy Boy in Yorkshire. 'I love rock and roll because it's great to dance to,' he said.

Nostalgia

The music of rock and roll greats like Elvis Presley, Jerry Lee Lewis and Buddy Holly brought back nostalgic memories . . .

'We've been shopping but came along specially to hear the group,' said Mr . . .

'It really brings back memories,' said his wife Christine.

Appeal Aid

. . . During the interval the group passed a hat round to collect money for the Lord Mayor's Silver Jubilee Appeal.

Lead singer, Dion, delighted by the audience response, said: 'It's great to see so many people enjoying themselves and to see so many young Teds.'[29]

Here we go again: 'Twenty Years Ago'. Fond memories of Jerry Lee Lewis who blew up a storm of indignation in the 1950s, not to mention Presley, whose subversive pelvis was banned from television in some American states where it was only permitted to film Elvis-the-Pelvis from the waist upwards. Teds passing round the hat for Jubilee Year — theirs or Hers, we might ask — a welcome for a new generation of Teddy Boys, nostalgia for the old dances that shocked a still older generation, Yorkshire's oldest Ted holding court, delighted shoppers: the process of rehabilitation, aided and abetted by total amnesia for even the recent past, seems complete.

Such a fine contrast to the wave of hysteria which greeted the rock craze in the 1950s when the press, predictably absorbed by the outlandish pleasures of the young, railed against its demoralising influence. 'Tin Pan Alley has unleashed a new monster, a sort of nightmare in rhythm', wrote a *Daily Mail* correspondent at the time of the cinema riots in 1956. 'Rock 'n Roll, often known now as rock, roll and riot is sexy music. It can make the blood race. It has something of the African tomtom and voodoo dance.'[30]

Describing the new music as 'a communicable disease' and 'the music of delinquents', *The Daily Mail* was so moved as to run a front-page editorial, 'Rock 'n Roll Babies', which apart from issuing a hollow, reassuring prophecy — 'It will pass' — stoked up the fires of respectable discontent against 'this sudden "musical" phenomenon which has led to outbreaks of rowdyism'. Here there was room to have a dig at 'trade unionists . . . too, screaming abuse and interfering with others on their way to work', alleging that excitement on picket lines and at rock films amounted to the same thing: 'These are all manifestations of the primitive herd instinct.' Also, to mount a stout defence of compulsory military service, 'to knock the rock 'n roll out of these babies, and to knock a bit of sense into them'. And then, the awful unblemished truth about this musical force that was rocking the nation:

> It is deplorable. It is tribal. And it is from America. It follows ragtime, blues, dixie, jazz, hot cha-cha and the boogie-woogie, which surely originated in the jungle. We sometimes wonder whether this is the negro's revenge.[31]

3

Since the War: Past Perfect

> That's the way we're going nowadays. Everything slick and stream-
> lined, everything made out of something else. Celluloid, rubber,
> chromium-steel everywhere . . . radios all playing the same tune, no
> vegetation left, everything cemented over . . . There's something
> that's gone out of us in these twenty years since the war.[1]

We have already met this sorry postwar blues, with its
nostalgic lament about the shallow artificiality of life in the
concrete jungle, and its jaundiced appraisal of the overwhelming changes 'in these twenty years since the war'. The complicating difficulty, however, is that this is a statement from
before the war. It is the voice of the disillusioned and disgruntled George Bowling — 'nerves all worn to bits, empty
places in our bones where the marrow ought to be' — in
Orwell's pre-war novel *Coming Up for Air*.

As he searched for the joys of his boyhood, grumpy old
George Bowling sensed deterioration all around him: in the
news headlines, in threats of imminent violence and destruction, and in the disfigurements of 'Americanisation'. 'People
then had something that we haven't got now', he thought as
he remembered the years before the Great War, 'And what
was it that people had in those days? A feeling of security,
even when they weren't secure. More exactly, it was a feeling
of continuity.'[2] And yes, there is another feeling of continuity here, involving an unusual degree of symmetry between
'pre-war' and 'postwar' perceptions of collapsing standards
and cultural decay. Nor was it only characters in novels who
were afflicted by the malaise.

Which War was That?

George Orwell was particularly fond of striking these con-
trasts between the ordered stability of the past against the
awfulness of the present, and he was also thoroughly wound
up in the myths of English civility: 'The gentleness of the
English civilisation is perhaps its most marked characteristic',
he wrote in an essay of 1940, 'Everyone takes it for granted
that the law, such as it is, will be respected, and feels a sense
of outrage when it is not.'[3] By contrast, Orwell sniffed out
deterioration in numerous spheres of public life including
what he understood to be new forms of crime, and altered
responses to crime and violence. In 'The Decline of the
English Murder' he argued that whereas in the past murder
had been a serious business involving strong personal commit-
ments and emotions, it had now become an almost casual
affair informed by 'the anonymous life of dance-halls and the
false values of the American film'. Crime fiction, too, reflected
these alterations, so that crime stories had 'greatly increased
in bloodthirstiness during the past twenty years'.[4]

Admittedly, in some of his loving characterisations of
English life Orwell almost flew off the edge — 'the beer is
bitterer, the coins are heavier, the grass is greener'[5] — but
even so, the decline of English civility under the impact of
'materialism' was not only George Orwell's passion in the
interwar years.[6] In the realm of high culture, T. S. Eliot's
writings were drenched in the same anxieties. 'The culture of
Europe has deteriorated visibly within the memory of many
who are by no means the oldest among us', wrote Eliot in his
wartime essays that reflected upon the atrophy of interwar
life. Pouring out criticism against this 'stage of civilisation at
which the family is irresponsible', 'the moral restraints so
weak', 'when parental control and responsibility passes to the
State', he thought that 'the disintegration of class has induced
the expansion of envy, which provides ample fuel for the
flame of "equal opportunity" '. And as we might anticipate
from Eliot's distaste for 'equality' there was no room for the
idea that it was possible to educate the masses: 'There is no
doubt that in our headlong rush to educate everybody, we

are lowering standards . . . destroying our ancient edifices.'[7]
Nor should we suppose that T. S. Eliot was just firing off his
big guns against R. A. Butler's wartime Education Act of
1944, for already in the 1930s there had been widespread
criticism of 'standardisation' and 'levelling down'. In 1932,
for example, Mrs Q. D. Leavis had roundly condemned the
cheapening and weakening influences of the popular press
and popular novels which produced 'merely crude states of
mind' and what she called 'the disintegration of the reading
public': 'The reading capacity of the general public, it must
be concluded, has never been so low as at the present time.'[8]

Stepping back into the present tense for a moment, we can
usefully compare Mrs Leavis's dismal judgement from the
1930s with a more recent complaint against falling reading
standards, issued by C. B. Cox and the ubiquitous Dr Boyson
in their educational *Black Paper* for 1977. There we are told
that, amidst the collapsing standards of the comprehensive
school system, successful reading standards were now only
attained in what are described as 'traditional' schools, whereas 'such standards were usual in the 1930s'.[9] But whose
word are we to take here, I wonder, in these conflicting
judgements: the backward-looking nostalgia of our postwar
jeremiahs who think they see a golden age of literacy before
the war? Or the record of the respectable opinion in the
pre-war years which was already bewailing the corruption
of morals and the decline of standards? It is a problem
that will dog us repeatedly in this history of respectable
fears.

One of the most active centres of pre-war discontent
was the 'Scrutiny' group gathered around F. R. Leavis
at Cambridge, who repeatedly and bitterly indicted the
degeneration of standards and the old 'way of life'. Cheap
literature, popular music, cinema-going, the newly acquired
habit of listening to the radio, advertising gimmicks, educational bankruptcy and 'Americanisation' were all targeted
as symptoms of decline. Because 'this vast and terrifying
disintegration', as described by Leavis and Thompson in
1933, was thought to be showing itself not only in the alleged
decline of literary and artistic values, but also in its effects

upon personal identity, family life and the destruction of community. In 1930 Leavis could write:

> The automobile (to take one instance) has, in a few years, radically affected religion, broken up the family, and revolutionised social custom. Change has been so catastrophic that the generations find it hard to adjust themselves to each other, and parents are helpless to deal with their children . . . It is a breach of continuity that threatens . . . It is a commonplace that we are being Americanised.[10]

It goes without saying, perhaps, that the feared deterioration of the nation's youth and the manufacture of supposedly 'new' forms of outrage and violence provided a gathering focus for these anxieties. Drawing attention to 'the decline in Church attendance during the last twenty years', 'the greater freedom from restraint which is characteristic of our age' and 'this rejection of conventional standards', Roy and Theodora Calvert in *The Law-Breaker* (1933) announced that 'we are passing through a crisis in morals'.[11] In an otherwise cautious account of *English Juvenile Courts* (1938) Winifred Elkin also gave vent to 'the feeling that life has no sure foundations and that the future is utterly uncertain', believing that 'it is not morally healthy for children to grow up in an atmosphere of restlessness and pleasure-seeking . . . It must change their attitude of mind and consequently their conduct.'[12] In a King George's Jubilee Trust report, *The Needs of Youth* (1939), A. E. Morgan was another who brooded over 'a growing contempt by the young person for the procedures of juvenile courts' and the 'grave reason to believe that parental control is slackening'. Juvenile lawlessness, he thought, represented 'a serious challenge, the difficulty of which is intensified by the extension of freedom which, for better or worse, has been given to youth in the last generation'.[13]

It was, then, in a context such as this that a *Times* correspondent could sum up in 1937 an entirely familiar series of complaints about mounting crime and dwindling authority:

> There has been a tendency of late to paint a rather alarming picture of the depravity of the youth of the nation . . . Headlines scream the

menace of 'boy gangsters'. Elderly magistrates deplore the abandonment of their panacea, the birch, and gain a gratifying, if brief,
notoriety by gloomy forebodings in the Press of the inevitably
disastrous results of the leniency and weakness of the present day.[14]

Hollywood Gangsters and the Professional Foul

Britain before the war already experienced itself as a society
afflicted by a deep cultural malaise, one that was described
in a language quite indistinguishable from postwar thunderings
against the 'permissive' and 'affluent' society. Moreover,
against this backcloth of generalised anxieties about moral
incohesion, there were a number of more specific allegations
against standards of public conduct which, once again, bear
a striking resemblance to the supposedly unprecedented
complaints and aggravations of the postwar era. The main
targets for this criticism were football rowdyism, the demoralising influence of the Hollywood cinema, and mounting
crime and disorder.

There had been a rumbling discontent about misbehaviour
at football matches, both on and off the field, throughout
the 1920s and 1930s which came to a head in the late thirties
with renewed accusations of declining sportsmanship and
crowd disorders. In 1936 the Football Association found it
necessary to issue a memorandum on rough play, in an
attempt to stamp out excessive violence and the 'professional
foul' which is so often identified as the hallmark of the
debased traditions of sportsmanship in postwar football.
Indeed, after a particularly heated Derby match between
Arsenal and Chelsea, *The Times* issued a curt editorial
judgement, 'Not Football':

> The most cursory reading of newspaper reports on Monday mornings
> is profoundly disquieting to all who love Association Football as a
> game, and as a game of skill. Again and again that unpleasant word
> 'incident' has a way of cropping up, reports of matches resound with
> stories of free-kicks, and crowds seem altogether too vocal and
> biased in their opinions on the conduct of the referee.[15]

Denouncing 'the cold-blooded and intentional foul' such as the Continental ankle-tap, and the deliberate provocation of players known to suffer from 'temperament', *The Times* rounded against 'the present menace to professional football'. And it was all so 'un-English': 'The shoulder charge, the fairest and least dangerous weapon in the footballer's armoury, has declined, and in its place has arisen a regiment of mean and dangerous tricks . . . What is wanted is increased firmness.'

Behaviour on the terraces was also thought to be deteriorating in the 1930s and crowd incidents — involving pitch invasions, attacks on referees and players, and occasional confrontations between spectators and the police — were exciting the same interest. In one typical incident in November 1936 when during a match at Wolverhampton Wanderers specatators had attacked visiting Chelsea players, there were more violent scenes after the game. *Reynolds's News* described how a 'big and angry crowd' of Wolves fans estimated at 2,000 people gathered outside the officials' entrance, protesting at the club's policy of selling its better players.[16] The following week police had to be called to quell disturbances at a number of grounds — including Middlesborough and Upton Park where the referee was again attacked — and *Reynolds's News* (15 November 1936) thought that 'the FA will soon have to issue another "rough play" memorandum — this time to the spectators!'

Disturbances such as these provided an intermittent focus of attention throughout the interwar years, and a number of grounds were closed because of crowd disorders. In 1921, for example, the boys section at Bradford Park Avenue was closed down for three months after the referee had been pelted with rubbish, and in the early 1920s the fierce North London rivalries between Arsenal and Spurs flared into open street battles in which some of the more zealous fans were armed with iron bars and knives.[17] Some years later, to give one final example of the kind of trouble that could break out at football games, the police found it necessary to lead a baton charge against stone-throwers during a contest between Linfield and Belfast Celtic in 1935.[18] In the absence of any sustained historical research into football in this period, it is not possible to say how frequent or how violent these occasions were, or to arrive at a balanced comparison between football disorders in the 1920s and 1930s as against those in more recent years.[19] Nevertheless, it is clear enough that the realities of pre-war football do not find agreement with postwar nostalgia.

Gambling, football pools, fun-fairs, dog tracks, amusement arcades, dance halls, popular songs, street betting and speed-tracks were all attacked at different times in the interwar years for their demoralising influence, particularly on the young. But it was the picture palaces, where weekly audiences dwarfed even the massive football attendances, which held the limelight within these respectable fears of national decline and moral deterioration. Cinema-going, as described by A. J. P. Taylor, was 'the essential social habit of the age', although he also warns that 'highly educated people saw in it only vulgarity and the end of Old England'.[20]

One potent centre of respectable discontent was Leavis's group for whom the cinema represented the worst in modern popular entertainment, involving merely 'surrender, under conditions of hypnotic receptivity, to the cheapest emotional appeals'. George Orwell was in complete agreement, contrasting the active pleasures of pub-singing and comic-turns with 'the passive, drug-like pleasures of the cinema and radio'.[21] And, once again, we can hear the echo of Hoggart's strictures against the supposedly 'postwar' aberrations of mass entertainments.

The influence of the cinema on children and young people provided a sharp focus for these anxieties, which had been aired since the arrival of the first silent movies. In a lecture on *The Problem of Juvenile Crime* (1917) Charles Russell had warned that, 'Eye-strain and undue excitement affect their health ... Their vulgarity and silliness, and the dis-torted, unreal, Americanised (in the worst sense) view of life presented must have a deteriorating effect, and lead, at the best, to the formation of false ideals.'[22] A report by the National Council of Public Morals on *The Cinema* (1917) had also scrutinised the problem, entertaining a wide variety of evidence — on such matters as the educational potential of the cinema, censorship and licensing, the molestation of children in picture palaces, and a clouded discussion of what was somewhat eerily called 'the moral dangers of darkness' — as well as some monosyllabic evidence from children themselves on whether the moving pictures gave them bad dreams. A much more specific fear was that young people would be provoked into imitative crime by the daring exploits witnessed on the screen, and the National Council of Public Morals addressed itself with particular vigour to the belief 'that the picture house is responsible for the increase in juvenile crime, and that boys are often led to imitate crimes (larceny or burglary) which they have seen in the pictures, or to steal money that they may pay for admission'. Exceptional in its moderacy, the report discounted the fear of imitative crime, arguing that 'it certainly has not been proved that the increase in juvenile crime generally has been consequent on the cinema'.[23]

Such moderacy did not, however, stem the flood of accusations against the cinema which continued to allege that the movies were encouraging new and dangerous trends of lawlessness among the young. Hugh Redwood's *God in the Slums* (1932), which described the work of the Salvation Army, would put matters this way: 'The boys of the slums are wonderful training material for good or evil. They are children in their love of pictures and music. Hollywood's worst in the movie line has recruited hundreds of them for the gangs of race-course roughs, motor bandits, and smash-and-grab thieves.'[24] In another account of youth work, Hubert Secretan rehearsed the same complaint: 'Every boy's sympathy goes out to the lithe and resourceful crook ... Occasionally a weak-minded youth may be urged by the exploits of a Chicago gangster to essay a feeble imitation.'[25]

Associated with these narrowly focused fears of imitation, there was a more broadly cast net of accusation against the 'Americanisation' of English morality, and the distorted criminogenic values inculcated by the cinema. 'A never-never land of material values expressed in terms of gorgeous living, a plethora of high-powered cars and revolvers', as A. E. Morgan described it in 1939, 'of unbridled desire, of love crudely sentimental or fleshly, of vast possessions, of ruthless acquisition, of reckless violence'. 'It is a school of false values', he wrote, 'and its scholars cannot go unscathed.'[26]

Echoing a related line of concern in 1935, an Assistant Commissioner of Prisons thought that 'over-sexed films' were 'a snare to the young'.[27]

In these criticisms of the cheap emotional appeals of the Hollywood cinema and its incitements to gangsterism, we can discern a continuing tradition which passes down into our own historical time where television has come to be understood as a major criminal influence, inviting similar accusations of 'copy-cat' crimes based on TV heroes and tough guys. We can also begin to see the broad outlines of a much longer connected history of respectable fears surrounding the demoralising influences of popular amusements. Its lineage reaches back, via the accusations against the Hollywood 'talkies' and the earliest silent movies, through and beyond the Music Halls at the turn of the century when directly similar complaints were voiced, towards the cheap theatres and penny-gaffs of early Victorian England when it was commonly alleged that the portrayal of the daring exploits of Jack Sheppard and Dick Turpin caused young people to imitate their crimes, and then back towards the eighteenth century's disapproval of popular amusements such as fairs, interludes, public shows and minor theatres. Here, if we anticipate the arguments of later chapters, we would find Henry Fielding already mulling over the fall of decadent Rome and its lesson for Old England, and warning in his *Enquiry into the Causes of the Late Increase of Robbers* (1751) of the disastrous effects of 'too frequent and expensive diversions among the lower kind of people'.[28] This monologue of fears about the moral downfall of the common people as the result of debased amusements, stretching back across more than two centuries, must be counted as one of the determining traditions within the unfolding preoccupation with the decline and fall of the 'British way of life'.

'No Crime'

The continuities between pre-war and postwar feelings of cultural deterioration are clear enough, and if we turn to questions of crime and violence in pre-war Britain then equally familiar complaints stare back at us. The excessive leniency of the law was indicted frequently enough, especially in the wake of the Children and Young Persons Act of 1933 and what appeared to be a monster 'crime wave' among the very young. The loosening of traditional morality, the decline of the family, the incitements of the movie-screen — all these were regularly cited as evidence of a breakdown of authority in a catalogue of accusations which is a carbon copy of the fears that surround the criminal question in our own time.

Running alongside these complaints, however, and often holding them in check, there was a counter-movement in the interwar years which involved a quite different moral emphasis. So that, particularly in response to rowdyism and lawlessness among the young, there was an unusual degree of sympathy towards offenders. In discussing pre-war crime, we must be faithful both to the continuities and also to the sometime surprising 'permissiveness' of the interwar years.

As an initial pointer towards this counter-movement within respectable opinion, we can take some remarks by Robert Baden-Powell, the founder of the Boy Scout movement, in an address to a conference on juvenile crime. There had been a perceived increase in youthful crime in the early 1930s that seemed to correspond to an increase in youth unemployment — and again we can reflect on the familiarity of both the problem and the complaint. But in a typically maverick comment on the matter, Baden-Powell thought that if there had been an increase in juvenile crime, then this was 'rather a promising sign'. *The Times* (25 May 1933) reported Baden-Powell's speech as follows:

> To him it was rather a promising sign, because he saw in those banditry cases, robbery with violence, and smash and grab, little 'adventures'. There was still some spirit of adventure among those juveniles and if that spirit were seized and turned in the right direction they could make them useful men.

It is the kind of remark which nowadays would get you into Dr Boyson's little black book as a 'permissive' moral hooligan.

Even so, Baden-Powell's intriguing romanticisation of what we would now call 'muggings' was not an uncommon response in these years. But it is not difficult to find conflicting judgements, as in the headline: 'TERROR GANGS TO BE WIPED OUT. Flogging advocated for Slashers and Mutilators' in a news report which described street gangs as 'this greatest social menace of the century'. Baden-Powell's characterisation of street robberies as 'little adventures' also rubs uneasily against other headlines and news stories of the period: 'DARING RAIDS BY BAG-SNATCHERS. Widow Badly Injured and Robbed'; or 'Woman injured by Violent Bag-Snatcher' when she was 'thrown to the ground and bruised' in what was 'a brutal assault upon a helpless woman'.[29] Nevertheless, even in the face of brute facts such as these, there was generally a low-key emphasis in the interwar years towards crime and punishment.

The case of street robbery is particularly interesting, because this is commonly the most sensitive area for registering public concern about crime and violence, itself reflected in the fact that robbery-with-violence was the only common offence for which an adult offender could be sentenced to whipping before the abolition of corporal punishment in 1948. There was ample evidence of sharp increases in crimes of this nature. There was a 70 per cent increase in shop raids in London between 1925 and 1929, for example, and a 90 per cent increase in bag-snatches over the same four-year period.[30] Between the First World War and the later 1920s, there was also a fourfold increase in breaking-in offences in the outer Home Counties — which almost certainly resulted from the greater mobility afforded to house-breakers by the advent of the motor car.[31] Nevertheless, there was an insubstantial public reaction to these upsurges in recorded crime, and public opinion was not effectively mobilised around these issues in any significant 'law-and-order' campaign.

It would also appear, particularly in relation to street robberies, that the law was rarely prosecuted with its full vigour. Flogging was only used as a judicial punishment in a handful of cases each year throughout the 1920s and 1930s, and the birching of young boys' bottoms was also passing out of favour.[32] There was, moreover, a considerable amount of discretion in terms of what might count as 'violence' in a street robbery, and it seems likely that street robbers were more commonly charged with 'bag-snatching' which was regarded as a less serious offence than 'robbery with violence'. It was reported in Parliament, for example, that of thirty-two reported instances of 'highway theft' over a six-month period in South Kensington in 1932, only *one* of these was treated as 'robbery with violence'.[33]

Street robbery was not the only crime to be viewed leniently in the interwar years. On another Parliamentary occasion, when it was alleged that cases of motor banditry were being grossly exaggerated in the press, reference was made to 'such trivial acts as the pulling down of shutters of an empty kiosk and stealing cigarettes and sweets' which were contrasted with what was called 'real crime'.[34] And although it is not clear what was meant by 'real' crime, it is evident that certain kinds of common theft, damage and injury were regarded as wholly commonplace in pre-war years and hardly worth a moment's thought. Pulling down the shutters of an empty shop or kiosk, we should remind ourselves, is what would today in the aftermath of Brixton and Toxteth be described as 'looting'.

Another interesting example of these altered perceptions of crime and disorder comes to us from Sir Robert Mark's memoirs where he recounts some experiences from a brief spell as a beat constable in Manchester in the late 1930s. There is nothing exceptional in what he has to say, which mirrors many other accounts of the period. He mentions 'the odd brawl and punch-up', for example, the fact that policemen only went in pairs in some districts, and that they patrolled the centre of the city in strength each weekend 'because prostitutes and drunks frequently started fights and a good time was had by all'. Already, the description of a street brawl as 'a good time' denotes an altered moral terrain.

Sir Robert also mentions the hazardous rough-and-tumble involved in making street arrests while surrounded by hostile, jeering crowds. In one such incident, described in some detail, he tells us how 'one Friday night an enormous navvy pushed the head of a constable through a shop window and started quite a battle in which uniformed and plainclothes men cheerfully joined in'. Again, it is a cheerful confrontation, even though 'it grew to quite serious proportions, stopping the traffic in Ardwick Green'. In order to facilitate a quick arrest under difficult circumstances — 'the crowd was jeering and becoming unpleasantly restive' — Robert Mark then confesses that he indulged in a little police brutality, by using his strictly non-regulation rubber truncheon to give the offender 'a hefty whack on the shin' which apparently broke his leg.

Now, what are we to make of an incident such as this? Sir Robert Mark goes on to tell us that after the prisoner's appearance in court where, with his leg encased in plaster he was fined 'the customary ten shillings', the violent navvy behaved like a perfect gent:

> Far from there being any hard feelings he greeted me cheerfully and we went off for a drink together. Nowadays, of course, it would have meant a complaint, an enquiry, papers to the Director of Public Prosecutions and a prosecution or discipline case. Not that I didn't deserve it, but times were different, thank goodness.[35]

Sir Robert Mark thus tries to squeeze out of this story a moral which points to the deteriorated relationship between the police and public. It is a common enough complaint. But what holds the attention more is the way in which he characterises these rough incidents — which, judged by other accounts of the period, would commonly involve assaults on the police, bottle-fights and sometimes determined crowd resistance to arrest — as a 'good time' and a 'cheerful' brawl. The magistrate would also appear to have been infected with the same cheerful disposition: even allowing for the ravages of inflation, a ten shillings fine is a somewhat less than draconian response to a charge of pushing a policeman's head through a shop window. Times are, indeed, different.

In what is perhaps the most usual response to these altered judgements against crime between pre-war and postwar years, of course, it is suggested that such incidents have become 'more serious' or 'more violent' as the years have gone by. However, the historical record is difficult to reconcile with this point of view. Razor gangs, race-course roughs, violent bag-snatchers, vice rackets and motor banditry were integral features of the crime picture in the interwar years, and feuds between armed mobsters were not unknown.[36] There were also moments of aggravated political violence — whether clashes between hunger marchers and the police, bitter street-fights between fascists and anti-fascists which led to the Public Order Act of 1936, or accusations and counter-accusations about 'political hooliganism' when public meetings were broken up, as they frequently were.[37] In 1921, in one of the more serious confrontations, the Recorder of Liverpool publicly censured the city's police who had batoncharged a demonstration of unemployed workers with 'most unnecessary violence'. In the Chief Constable's view the use of force was 'fully justified', believing himself surrounded by a criminally hostile population, with recent memories of the looting and disorder which had accompanied the police strike of 1919 in Liverpool.[38]

There was a continuing thread of disturbance, reaching a new crescendo in 1931 when more than thirty towns witnessed clashes between the police and unemployed demonstrators protesting at dole cuts. In October 1931 the police led baton charges in Cardiff, Glasgow, Manchester, Salford and elsewhere. In some places army reserves were called out to protect public property, and in Manchester high-pressure water-hoses were used against demonstrators. At Glasgow, where there was a full-scale riot when police broke up a meeting of 50,000 people at Glasgow Green, shops were ransacked and the police were bombarded with missiles by tenement dwellers. While the police were thus tied down, in the Garngad district there was 'an organised attempt at looting'.[39]

There is nothing in the history of the 1920s and 1930s to justify the cosy nostalgia that is now cloaked around the pre-war years. In the more notorious slum districts, there appears to have been little or no respect for the law. These areas provided havens for gambling schools, and the police did not dare to venture there except in strength — when attempts to break up street-gambling, or to douse the high spirits of Bonfire Night could lead to violent eruptions.[40]

Without even trespassing into any of these more perilous aspects of pre-war street life, the Mass Observation study *The Pub and the People* (1943) filled in some of the detail of the rowdy bonhomie of the working-class weekend, and the 'high point of mass drunkenness' during the exodus from the northern towns to Blackpool. The following excerpt is written in a Mass Observationer's shorthand, which accounts for the bumpy grammar:

> Along promenade the air is full of beersmell, that overcomes sea-smell. It arises from people breathing. A swirling, moving mass of mostly drunken people, singing, playing mouthorgans, groups dancing about. Chaps fall over and their friends pick them up cheerfully and unconcernedly. At one spot a young man falls flat on his face, his friend picks him up and puts him over his shoulder, and lurches away with him. Immediately a fight starts among four young men: the crowd simply opens up to give them elbow room as it flows by; some stop to look on. One of the fighters is knocked out cold and the others carry him to the back of a stall and dump him there. Back streets are not so densely crowded, but even more drunks. In a litter of broken glass and bottles a woman sits by herself being noisily sick.[41]

Other details of this allegedly gentle pre-war street life are filled in by the writings of youth club workers — Butterworth's *Clubland* (1932), Hatton's *London's Bad Boys* (1931) and Secretan's *London Below Bridges* (1931) — which are teeming with rowdy incident, outbreaks of hooliganism, shoplifting sprees, youngsters terrorising old ladies, foul language, youth club riots and vandalism. Hatton was so impressed by his bad boys that he gave them colourful 1930s 'punk rock' pseudonyms — Alf Artful, Billy Dustup and Reggie Smashem — which are no more suggestive of obedience and docility than other pre-war descriptions of brawls, affrays, legless drunks, or street robbers armed with sand-bags and cut-throat razors. 'You will continually be living on the edge of a volcano', wrote Hatton offering advice to budding youth workers, 'for no one can know when an outburst of general indiscipline will occur.'[42] James Butterworth followed the hooligan careers of similar boys — 'Sam Smiler' and 'Thomas Tiddler' — along with the apprenticeship of 'Tiddler Junior', because the British hooligan was thought to be getting younger in his time, as in ours:

> Usually he begins the evening by pitching a stone or a ball through a window. Within an hour, and for varied reasons, he will have been chased around several streets, or leaped on every passing vehicle, and may decide to see London 'for nuffin' by jumping on every bus or tram whilst the conductor is upstairs . . . the vocabulary and physical feats of Tiddler junior are remarkable. He knows more about sex perversions and crude stories at age thirteen than most people are likely to know at age thirty . . . Somehow or other he will have visited every cinema in the locality or succeeded in getting pitched out of every Band of Hope. Unable to resist the appeal of loose railings, he must send the boards outside shops crashing to the ground. Half stuck or well stuck posters on hoardings must be defaced or altered, or if low enough receive a savage kick. He will always appear to be running away from someone . . . Scared old ladies positively gasp . . . Later he will be found climbing on to premises which clearly enough foretell the fate of trespassers.[43]

To offer one final example of these pre-war accounts of the untameable energies of young people, here is Hatton's description of a visit to a Day Continuation School for young workers. The class, it will be noticed, was regulated by the traditional order and discipline existing before the 'permissive' deluge. It was on the subject of 'Education and Citizenship':

> Four lads were sitting at the window taking pot-shots with ink-wells at passers-by in the street below, a little group of four were sitting in a corner quietly playing cards, several were pushing chairs and desks about for fun, and two or three lads in the front row were pretending to listen to the teacher. As I entered the room he was declaiming to them — 'So we, as citizens, have to ask ourselves, What is Liberty?'[44]

Pre-war Permissives

In this uninterrupted narrative of rowdyism and mischief running through the writings of these Christian youth workers in the 1920s and 1930s, it is not only the behaviour itself that is difficult to reconcile with the nostalgia which has come to settle around postwar perceptions of pre-war social realities. The moral tone is also not what we are led to expect. Whereas we are encouraged to remember the pre-war years as the home of traditional discipline and common sense, we can hardly fail to notice the sympathy which reaches out to Hatton's bad boys or to Butterworth's hyperactive little terror — a sympathy, what is more, that nowadays would often be slapped down as a sentimental, modern, postwar 'permissive' fad.

Sometimes this sympathy could involve quite extraordinary leniency. In 1937 Basil Henriques, a youth worker, magistrate and pillar of respectability, found it reasonable to excuse shop-lifting from multiple stores, for example, because they offered 'that most disgraceful temptation . . . the most attractive gadgets and toys in open trays well within the reach of children'. Henriques also condoned the practice of fiddling coin machines, thieving from lorries and joy-riding: 'Again it seems hardly fair to blame children for stealing from the back of lorries, which is such a very common offence, the result, generally, of perfectly innocent joy-riding.' But what seemed to fall rather short of perfect innocence was a case of 'attempting to obtain money by threats of violence' where two youths had sent a menacing note to the old lady next door — 'Unless you provide £500 in old notes . . . you will be shot by revolver' — thereby reducing her to hysterics. There are all sorts of reasons why one should not readily excuse such cruel behaviour, but Basil Henriques considered the crime to be nothing more than a boyish prank. 'Thus what appears to be a serious charge may prove in the end,' he wrote, 'to be a very harmless, rather exciting good game.'[45]

Another vivid example of this kind of reasoning was offered in a book on *The Troublesome Boy* (1936) by Dr H. S. Bryan, a medical officer in the child guidance service and an Assistant County Commissioner in the Boy Scouts, where he brought a little psychoanalytical inspiration to Scouting together with the romanticism of the movement's founder. After one visit to a juvenile court where some gang members had been committed to Approved School after 'carrying out depredations against shopkeepers over quite a wide area', Dr Bryan 'could not help feeling a little depressed at the thought of so much high spirit, imagination, ingenuity and daring shut up behind high walls'. Generally speaking, he thought that the enterprise of young villains received a shoddy deal in the courts:

> He gets no marks at all for ingenuity — in the Court it is called 'low cunning' — no sort of credit for his daring — it is merely referred to as 'audacity' — his high qualities of leadership are dismissed with 'That lad was the ring-leader, Your Worship'; and if he has faced the music with a courageous bearing he is 'brazenly defiant'. All that is remembered of him is that he took what didn't belong to him, and steps are taken to protect the community against those very qualities which should have been elicited in its service.[46]

It is not necessary to reach agreement with Dr Bryan's moral scheme in order to see that it involves quite a different moral emphasis from that projected on to the 1930s by post-war nostalgia. We invariably find a quite explicit moral alignment, in fact, on the side of young people in the writings of these pre-war youth workers. Hatton, for example, summed up the delinquency of Reggie Smashem and Billy Dustup as 'nothing more serious than the symptoms of healthy, vigorous, adventurous adolescence': 'I propose to make a practical examination of this question of the "hooligan", for I am seriously concerned that he is not getting a fair deal.' Pointing to the lack of decent recreational facilities in the slums, Butterworth also believed that 'it is pointless to denounce street evils, gang hooliganism or to mourn the absence of team spirit in poorer areas . . . Platitudinarians should live for one week where society has compelled millions to live. They will then cease to hold their hands in horror at giggling girls and boisterous youths around lamp posts, or condemn the pastimes of the young in back alleys.' Secretan arrived at the same conclusion: 'It is scarcely to be wondered at that youthful craving for variety and excitement sometimes leads gangs of boys to try and put a little colour into their leisure hours in ways which lead to conflict with authority or to degradation of character. The line between mischief and crime is not easily drawn.'[47]

The judgements are typical and uniform. A fair deal for

youth is what is advocated, informed by a recognition of the
ease with which boisterous youthful energy can make itself
objectionable and even dangerous to others, linked to the
necessity of not allowing its troublesome character to dull
the awareness of the natural and even positive qualities of
youthful misconduct.

The motives behind these uniform statements of allegiance
to youth were undoubtedly mixed and complex. The conditions of mass unemployment certainly helped to support
the feeling of leniency, in that crime was thought to be an
inevitable consequence of poverty, so that there was an active
sympathy for the young unemployed whose miserable condition was further highlighted in a perceived increase of sui-
cides among the young.[48] The experiences of the First World
War, often registered in a feeling of horrific waste, also left a
deep impression on the mental landscape of the interwar
years and helped to form the low-key response towards crime
and hooliganism. An active sense of guilt for the generation
that had been sacrificed encouraged the belief that there was
a debt to be repaid to the rising generation.[49] Finally, the
'progressive' educational movement was making great strides
in the 1920s and 1930s, with a sphere of influence that
reached beyond experiments such as Dartington Hall,
A. S. Neill's Summerhill or Home Lane's Commonwealth.
Describing conventional education as a 'conveyor belt' and
noting 'the dullness of the eldest pupils compared with the
brightness and self-sufficiency of the infants', Denys Thompson of the Scrutiny group thought in 1932 that while education was 'very busy mass-producing interchangeable little
components for the industrial machine' the concern of
education 'should be to turn out "misfits", not spare parts'.[50]
Aggressive criticisms of assembly-line education such as this
from the 1930s should cause us to stop and think for a
moment. Indeed, it is here above all that the contemporary
'law-and-order' enthusiasts who slap down 'permissiveness' as
a postwar invention are badly in need of a history lesson. It
was, after all, as long ago as 1899 that John Dewey enunciated
the principle of his 'Copernican revolution' in education
whereby, just as 'the astronomical centre shifted from the
earth to the sun', so 'In this case the child becomes the sun

about which the appliances of education revolve; he is the centre about which they are organised.'[51]

'Progressive' educational sentiments also provided important elements in Baden-Powell's Boy Scout philosophy, and he never tired of criticising what he saw as the dulling conformity and uninspired education provided by the State. In *Aids to Scoutmastership* (1919) Baden-Powell likened his movement to Montessori's system of education applied to older youths, recommending this as 'the line that eventually education will take when it comes to be set upon a right footing'. The boy or girl was not 'a blank piece of paper on which the teacher should write', and it was in this liberal spirit that he condemned drill: 'Military drill fashions him to an approved standard as part of the machine; whereas the aim of Scouting is to develop his personal character and initiative.'[52]

There was much more of this kind of thinking in Baden-Powell's writings where he sometimes committed himself to outrageously libertarian positions on questions of education and authority, although these were perfectly in line with the emerging contours of 'progressive' educational philosophy. 'A plant doesn't need to be taught how to grow; and neither does a child have to be taught, in the old-fashioned meaning of teaching', Herbert Casson had written in a series of articles for *Teacher's World* in 1918. 'A plant needs air, sunshine, moisture, and certain chemicals — given these it does its own growing', he explained as he amplified his educational stance. 'So a child needs things to look at, to touch, taste, smell and hear. Given these, the child will do its own growing, as the plant does.'[53] Baden-Powell warmly approved of Casson's ideas, and he quoted large chunks of them in his writings. It must also be said that Herbert Casson's admiration for youth could outbid even Baden-Powell's undying romanticism:

> A boy's world has its own events and standards and code and gossip and public opinion . . . The code of the teacher, for instance, is in favour of silence and safety and decorum. The code of the boys is diametrically opposed. It is in favour of noise and risk and excitement.

Fun, fighting and feeding! These are the indispensable elements of the boy's world ... According to public opinion in Boydom, to sit for four hours a day at a desk indoors is a wretched waste of time and daylight. Did anyone ever know a boy — a normal healthy boy, who begged his father to buy him a desk? ... Certainly not. A boy is not a desk-animal. He is not a sitting-down animal. Neither is he a pacifist nor a believer in 'safety first', nor a book-worm, nor a philosopher.

He is a *boy* — God bless him — full to the brim of fun and fight and hunger and daring and mischief and noise and observation and excitement. If he is not, he is abnormal.[54]

For page upon page, across three issue of *Teacher's World*, Herbert Casson went on like this, at the same unrelenting pace. And he demands to be quoted at length. Because these were not casual, throw-away remarks, but a sustained celebration of youthfulness which has now become virtually unthinkable within the thickening twilight of liberal education:

So, if the aim of education is to de-nature boys — to penalise and destroy all that is typically boyish — there is nothing to be said against the present methods of the average school.

Let the battle go on between the code of the teachers and the code of the boys. The boys will win in the future as they have in the past. A few will surrender and win scholarships, but the vast majority will persist in rebellion and grow up to be the ablest and noblest men in the nation ... Is it not possible to treat boys as boys? ...

Is not the boy *right*, after all, in maintaining his own code of justice and achievement and adventure?

... Is he not really an amazing little *worker*, doing things on his own, for lack of intelligent leadership?

Would it not be vastly more to the point if the teachers were, for a time, to become the students, and to study the marvellous boy-life which they are at present trying to repress?

Why push against the stream, when the stream, after all, is running in the right direction?

Is it not time for us to adapt our futile methods and to bring them into harmony with the facts? Why should we persist in saying dolefully, 'boys will be boys', instead of rejoicing in the marvellous energy and courage and initiative of boyhood? And what task could be nobler and more congenial to a true teacher than to guide the wild forces of boy nature cheerily along into the paths of social service?[55]

This kind of exhilaration has gone out of writings on the youth question, and some people will think that it is no bad thing. But it is not necessary to share Herbert Casson's breathless enthusiasms, or to reach point-by-point agreement with his educational philosophy, to recognise the quite different moral emphasis that shows through repeatedly in the writings of pre-war youth workers and educationalists: an emphasis which saw youthful energy and also youthful misconduct as the spark of life, rather than the death-knell of the old traditions. Something to be nurtured, rather than stamped upon.

'There was a postwar cult', wrote Mrs Le Mesurier in 1931, 'which took it for granted that as the devil has all the good tunes, so youth had all the good qualities', and faced with the giddy enthusiasm of people such as S. F. Hatton, Basil Henriques, James Butterworth, Herbert Casson, H. S. Bryan and Robert Baden-Powell we can perhaps see what she was driving at. Even so, her own assessment of the needs of young people confirmed the general impression of a positive emphasis in the interwar years. 'The problems of youthful crime are nearly all problems of education,' she thought, 'for although some human problems seem problems of despair, all the problems of youth are problems of hope.'[56]

And it was indeed hope, education and reformation that dominated the sphere of juvenile justice in these years, most solidly embodied in the Children and Young Persons Act of 1933 which consolidated these developments in the treatment of young offenders. With lamentable predictability, however, there was a wailing from certain quarters against 'our "namby-pamby" methods' and 'our drawing-room courts',[57] and what was taken to be the excessive leniency of the 1933 Act was accused of unleashing a tidal wave of crime among the young. Levels of recorded crime certainly did shoot up in the years following the implementation of the 1933 Act, and the crime rate for boys under 14 years of age found guilty of indictable offences almost doubled in only three years.[58] However, the recognition which is generally held was that the increase in the criminal statistics was because police and public alike were more willing to bring charges against young offenders because of the reshaping of the court system towards help and reformation, rather than punishment. Indeed, this was the very reason that the Departmental Committee on the Treatment of Young Offenders had recommended, in 1927, the reform of the system: 'When it is realised that these courts are specially equipped to help rather than punish the young offender, we hope that the reluctance to bring such children before them will disappear.'[59]

On more than one occasion, *The Times* endorsed this view, reminding its readers that 'the statistics really reflect the growth of confidence in the system as reformed' and that it was 'not that children have suddenly become more wicked, but that the legal machinery has become more efficient'.[60] This emerged as the consensus view on the juvenile 'crime wave' of the 1930s, and *The Times* was also speaking for a wide consensus when it suggested in a lead article that, 'It is a good and wise rule that, as far as possible, delinquent children ought to be left at home.'[61] This was reflected in the decisions of the courts, where slightly more than half of juveniles charges with indictable offences received a probation sentence in the 1930s. By contrast, since the Second World War this proportion of young offenders receiving a sentence that involves supervision in the community has dropped steadily. Since the implementation of the much-maligned Children and Young Persons Act of 1969, moreover, while the proportion of young offenders receiving custodial sentences has soared, the proportion dealt with by supervision orders has continued to decline. So much so, that it has fallen from the 50 per cent standard of the 1930s, to less than 15 per cent in the late 1970s — which is no better, and in some areas far worse, than the standard already achieved before the First World War when the Probation Act of 1907 had hardly consolidated itself.[62]

It is therefore necessary to depart quite sharply from conventional postwar wisdom about the pre-war years — a wisdom that rests on the twin myths of firm punishment in the courts, going hand-in-hand with little or no crime and an untroubled youth — and to state a rather different version of events. It is not only in the actualities of pre-war crime, nor in the fears surrounding crime, that we find simple contradictions of postwar nostalgia. With the progressive wing of opinion in the ascendancy, the operations of the criminal justice system — which have appreciably toughened since the 1930s, in spite of postwar wailings about the weakness of the law — also give a jolt to the customary understanding of the pre-war years.

Nevertheless, what is most notable is the remarkable stability of the complaints and accusations that were arranged around the criminal question, providing firm lines of continuity between pre-war and postwar Britain. Then, as now, fears of national decline and cultural adulteration were much in evidence, and it was a cause for great concern that the nation's youth were slipping away from the standards of their forebears. Here is James Butterworth, for example, writing fifty years ago and reciting an uncannily familiar catalogue of 'postwar' trends against which the boys' club leader of the 1930s must labour:

> The passing of parental authority, defiance of pre-war conventions, the absence of restraint, the wildness of extremes, the confusion of unrelated liberties, the wholesale drift away from churches, are but a few characteristics of after-war conditions.[63]

Again we must ask ourselves, 'Which war was that?' Because this is where we came in. The world may change, but somehow this vocabulary of complaints against declining standards and morals is immunised against change. And the 'golden age' is there once more: glimmering in the distance, just out of sight, back over the next hill, twenty years ago, 'before the war'.

PART TWO

The Original Hooligans

Colonel Onslow: 'Those boys are not exactly the very lowest
Hooligan class?'
Mrs Bagot: 'Some of them . . . are pure Hooligans.'
Colonel Onslow: 'I should have thought from that list you
have handed in that they are hardly the pure Hooligans?'
Mrs Bagot: 'We have some good specimens of Hooligans.'

*Report of the Inter-Departmental Committee on Physical
Deterioration*, Minutes of Evidence, 1904

The best class of boy — that is, the hooligan.

Lieutenant-General Sir Robert S. S. Baden-Powell, speech to
the National Defence Association, Piccadilly Hotel, London,
6 May 1910.

PART TWO

The Original Hooligans

4

The Traditional 'Way of Life'

Within the remembered traditions of the 'British way of life', the late Victorian and Edwardian years — from the Gay Nineties until the Great War — hold a privileged position as a time of unrivalled tranquility. The cosy fug of the Music Halls, the barrel-organ streets, the unhurried pace of a horse-drawn civilisation — before the motor car, before the cinema, before the sweeping changes of the twentieth century and their attendant disorientations — here, we are repeatedly encouraged to believe, is the original home of 'Old England' and a life ordered by tradition and familiarity.

The horrible details of the 1914—18 war undoubtedly serve to heighten the poignancy of this feeling, and the creative energy of the war poets evokes its own sense of loss for a stable life snatched away, amidst 'the shrill, demented choir of wailing shells'.[1] So many young men, too, this sorrowful voice from the past reminds us, torn away in the flower of their youth. The 'lost generation', they are sometimes called, lost forever in the Flanders mud.

The sentiment finds many forms of expression, both popular and apparently scholarly. The popular feeling is beautifully summed up in a recently published collection of faded Edwardian photographs, entitled *The Golden Years, 1903—1913*. On the book's cover there is an appealing family portrait of a shy little girl in a pretty white dress, sitting on an elderly gentleman's lap, with an appropriate caption: 'A pictorial survey of the most interesting decade in English history, when the generation gap meant no more than the gap between grandfather and grand-daughter.'[2]

Taken in isolation, it is a view that might be easily dismissed as trivial sentimentality. But it finds agreement with more sober, weighty judgements on the period provided by various studies of the official criminal statistics. V. A. C. Gatrell and T. B. Hadden, for example, have argued that there was 'a real decline in criminal activity, and quite a spectacular one' in the late decades of the nineteenth century, and T. R. Gurr and his colleagues agree that crime and public disorder in London (as reflected in the official crime figures) reached a low ebb at the turn of the century. In another review of the criminal statistics, F. H. McClintock and N. H. Avison also direct us towards the relative stability in recorded crime levels between 1900 and 1914 which, they suggest, 'might be described as the stable but carefree Edwardian era'.[3]

Youth and Nation: 'Affluence' Amidst Poverty

It would only be possible to describe these years in such glowing terms, however, if we were to place our curiosity under strict curfew, refusing to allow it to look beyond the frozen images of faded snap-shots or the scratchy surface realities of the official crime statistics. It is not a description that would have satisfied Mr C. G. Heathcote, for example, the Stipendiary Magistrate for Brighton, when asked for his opinions on the question of juvenile crime in 1898:

> The tendencies of modern life incline more and more to ignore, or disparage social distinctions, which formerly did much to encourage respect for others and habits of obedience and discipline ... And if it be true, as is so frequently asserted, that the manners of children are deteriorating, that the child of today is coarser, more vulgar, less refined, than his parents were, then, it must be admitted, whatever be the proficiency attained in arithmetic, and however much the intelligence may be sharpened, that the education presented to the children of the poor falls lamentably short of its ideal, in a most important particular.
>
> In selecting a TEACHER, *moral* influence is less easily tested than intellectual attainment. Of the two, it is the *more important*.[4]

Mr Heathcote's remarks are preserved in a report on *Juvenile Offenders* compiled by the Howard Association which had scouted the opinions of the magistracy and police. The general impression running through its pages was a riot of impunity, irresponsible parents, working mothers and lax discipline in schools, with magistrates and police believing themselves to be impotent before a rising tide of mischief and violence — particularly 'the recent serious increase of ruffianism among city youths'. Any number of voices piped up to recommend 'the "short and sharp" punishment of whipping', and there was general agreement that Parliament's refusal to extend the powers of birching — which were largely restricted to use against boys under 14 years of age — was a sign of morbid sentimentality. It was, as *The Times* observed in the following year, a sorry fact that there was 'a vague dread of a wholesome birching' and that nowadays 'the father of a scapegrace' no longer saw fit to 'save his son from the taint of gaol by loyally and soundly whipping him'.[5] Youthful offenders were also believed to be getting younger, and according to one magistrate parental authority was at such a low ebb that 'it is melancholy to find that some parents are not ashamed to confess that children of seven or eight years old are entirely beyond their control', while another thought that 'in nine cases out of ten, *children are entirely masters of the position*'.[6]

The sense of moral crisis and social discontinuity reflected here was deeply characteristic of late Victorian and Edwardian society, and from the late 1890s until the First World War there was a flood of such accusations against the youth. 'A somewhat unlovely characteristic of the present day', Mrs Helen Bosanquet wrote in 1906, was that 'there is among the children a prevailing and increasing want of respect towards their elders, more especially, perhaps, towards their parents'. A few years later, Mary Barnett reiterated the position: 'One of the most marked characteristics of the age is a growing spirit of independence in the children and a corresponding slackening of control in the parents.'[7]

These typical judgements against dwindling authority formed part of a wider fabric of anxiety in this era, and there were some quite delirious fears in circulation about a supposed deterioration – both physical and moral – among the British people which was believed to be producing new and unprecedented forms of violence and depravity. The wretched condition of so many recruits for the Boer War had brought this matter very forcibly into public attention, leading to the extraordinary fact-finding mission of the Inter-Departmental Committee on Physical Deterioration in 1904. And although the committee believed that the problem had been overstated, this did little to allay the anxieties.[8] Baden-Powell summed up the feeling in the first edition of *Scouting for Boys* in 1908. We have already encountered Baden-Powell in his romantic–progressive mode of address, but before the First World War he was more usually to be found singing a different tune:

> Recent reports on the deterioration of our race ought to act as a warning to be taken in time before it is too late. One cause which contributed to the downfall of the Roman Empire was the fact that the soldiers fell away from the standards of their forefathers in bodily strength.[9]

Here he is again, sounding off to the Royal United Services Institute in 1911, in a typical Edwardian Tory response to the Liberal government's programme of welfare reforms:

> Over-civilisation threatens England with deterioration. Free feeding and old-age pensions, strike pay, cheap beer and indiscriminate charity do not make for the hardening of the nation or the building up of a self-reliant, energetic manhood. They tend, on the contrary, to produce an army of dependents and wasters.[10]

The creation of Baden-Powell's Boy Scouts is invariably remembered in heroic terms, as a celebration of patriotic spirit and fresh-air fun. But in fashioning his movement, Baden-Powell skilfully wove together any number of the political questions that preoccupied his contemporaries, and the movement's spectacular growth drew on deep funds of social anxiety — anxieties which invariably settled around the excessive liberty allowed to young people and the attendant demoralisation which was, in turn, linked to a newly perceived upsurge in crime and violence among the young. 'The class of lads and young men who spring up in every city', wrote Sir John Gorst in *The Children of the Nation* (1901), 'have emancipated themselves from all home influence and restraints.'[11] Writing on the boys' club movement in 1904, W. J. Braithwaite thought that 'it is dangerous for the club and the boys that many of them should have tasted too much of freedom'.[12] In evidence before the Committee on Physical Deterioration, Dr T. F. Young from Liverpool described how, particularly at the point when they started work, young people 'throw off all parental authority . . . get to congregating about the street corners at night . . . become what we call "corner boys", and get drunken habits'. 'Our young people have no idea of discipline or subordination', said Dr Young, 'They would not subordinate themselves to anybody', and before the same committee E. T. Campagnac and C. E. B. Russell recounted a similar state of affairs in Manchester.[13]

The accusations were flat and uniform, although what is truly remarkable is that the youth of the nation were believed not only to be free of all discipline, but also excessively affluent. 'Rejoicing in their newly found freedom from school discipline and with more surplus cash than they will ever again possess', one of the contributors to Whitehouse's *Problems of Boy Life* (1912) believed that youths were 'tempted to spend as little time at home as possible . . . the street, rather than the sleeping place, is the home of the average youth'.[14] Reginald Bray, who was associated with the settlement movement in Camberwell, even seemed to doubt whether the youths needed to sleep, describing in 1904 how they would stay out on the streets 'until it is dark, and often in summer until dawn begins to break . . . the street and not the house ought probably to be regarded as the home'. 'Speaking generally,' Bray wrote in *Boy Labour and Apprenticeship* (1911), 'the city-bred youth is growing up in a state of unrestrained liberty', and describing how 'the habits of school and home are rapidly sloughed off in the new life of irresponsible freedom' he agreed that 'the large amount of money he has to spend on himself is by no means an unmixed benefit'.[15]

These statements reflected generalised anxieties about the

youth, but particularly aggravated accusations of irresponsibility, freedom and affluence were brought against young people employed in various kinds of street work: as van boys, messenger boys, boys to hold horses' heads, and street traders. Pointing to the easy pickings and careless pleasures of newspaper sellers, flower sellers, barrel-organ boys and other youthful street traders, a government report of 1910 provided what was perhaps the most extravagant version of these common Edwardian fears:

> Much of this money, so easily made, is spent with equal despatch ... on sweets and cigarettes, and in attending music halls ... The situation becomes even worse when the money is used for gambling ... or where it enables the gamins of our large towns to live a bandit life away from their homes, free of all control.[16]

Nippers and Dead-End Jobs, Suffragettes and Strikes

It is probably as well to pause here a moment, in order to take a few social bearings against which to judge these accusations. We need to remind ourselves, and quite forcibly, that these typical complaints come from the period of history in which Charles Booth and Seebohm Rowntree conducted their pioneering studies of urban life which revealed such awful poverty among the common people.[17] The bandit freedoms of young street traders would be indulged in the grubby common lodging houses of the slum areas, in the company of more elderly bandits such as tramps, habitual drunkards, casual labourers, drifters and infirm beggars.[18] The disparity between the frequent allegations of luxury and freedom, as against the wretched conditions of the lower rungs of the working class, is truly astonishing. In such a context, therefore, it comes as less of a surprise to find Sidney Webb actually advocating a *cut* in the wages of working youths — in evidence before the 1909 Royal Commission on the Poor Laws, of all places — so that 'the youth, who now has even too much pocket-money, and gets, therefore, too soon independent of home, and too easily led into evil courses' could be brought down a peg or two. 'The undisciplined youth, precocious in evil, earning at seventeen or eighteen more wages than suffice to keep him' could be brought under more effective control, Webb believed, 'his leisure absorbed under discipline', by a system of compulsory physical training and technical instruction for all youths under 18 years of age.[19]

The similarities between such a scheme of reclamation and discipline and those widely mooted proposals of the 1980s to reclaim the youth through compulsory job-training or 'community service' should not pass unnoticed. Nor should the similarities in the broader dimensions of the problem of youth employment escape our attention. The Edwardians were much perturbed by what was known as the problem of 'boy labour' and the structural unemployment which was built into the labour market for youths.[20] Young people would start work at any point between the ages of 10 and 14 years, for although the school-leaving age stood at fourteen there were many irregularities in the enforcement of the regulations.[21] On leaving school there was an enormous demand for boy labour in many spheres of work. In factories and workshops, advances in machine technology had deskilled numerous working-class jobs, thus making it possible for employers to replace skilled men with successive relays of unskilled boys, and at lower wages. The uneven development of the technologies of production and communication had also produced a sharp, and apparently increasing demand in the job market for boys to do all sorts of simple work in the sphere of communications and transport: van boys, errand boys, messenger boys, boys to answer telephones, boys to hold horses' heads and other kinds of trivial but essential work. Finally, respectable England required various other, if less essential, fetch-and-carry amenities: hotel pages, uniformed door-openers, billiard-cue chalkers, boy golf caddies, and a myriad of other forelock-tugging dogsbodies and serfs.

'Considering how troublesome errand-boys are,' wrote Helen Bosanquet in 1898, 'it is wonderful how many of them are wanted. They are like postcards, so easy to send and so cheap, that everyone likes to have one handy.'[22] It was a typically snotty remark from this doyenne of the Charity

Organisation Society which, nevertheless, managed to sum up the gulf between social classes at the turn of the century. Mrs Bosanquet might also have mentioned, without stretching the point too far, the wonderful convenience of being able to give these troublesome boys the sack at a moment's notice. Because respectable England, being what it was, did not want to be waited upon by gangling adolescents with spots, nor to have itself paged by unmodulated voices that were just breaking, and youths in such positions invariably got the push when they grew out of the uniform, or lost their boyish looks.

'Boy labour' in all spheres was a transient period of employment, and even in the more essential areas of work boys would lose their jobs — whether as 'nippers' or 'handy lads' in factories, or as van boys and messenger boys — when they reached early maturity and lost their enthusiasm for boyish wages. Consequently, the jobs available to youths came to be known as 'dead-end' jobs or as 'blind-alley' employment in this period of history. It was greatly feared, in fact, that the structure of employment was such that it supplied the rising generation with little discipline and even less skill, and that it threatened to produce an endless tide of loafers, unemployables and ne'er-do-wells who had been thrown on to the scrap heap in their late teens or early twenties.

The employment opportunities for working-class girls — whether in factory work or in domestic service — would not appear to have excited either the same sympathy or alarm. But when it looked at the boys, Edwardian England was invariably moved. 'Without a trade, without a craft, without any values — scrap iron that does not count, rubbish fit only for the waste heap' is how Canon Henry Scott Holland summed up the problem: 'We the public have used him up: he is no more to us now than a squeezed orange.'[23] Or, to strike another chord of apprehension, as expressed in the Report of the Prison Commissioners for 1907–8: 'He drifts, and the tidy scholar soon becomes a ragged and defiant corner loafer.'[24] Whichever way it was phrased, Edwardian Britain considered that in the problem of 'boy labour' it faced a crisis of some magnitude in the social reproduction of steady work disciplines and skills.

These feelings of dwindling authority and social discontinuity which focused on the young were informed by the wider political insecurities of this anything-but-carefree era which was plagued by engulfing fears of national decline and incohesion. In global terms, the industrial advance of the United States and Germany insisted on a reappraisal of Britain's position in the world economy, while the muddled fortunes of the Boer War came to underline the fragility of the British Empire in military terms. The early years of the century witnessed widespread invasion scares, and extra-parliamentary pressure groups were actively campaigning for the introduction of compulsory military service which had never existed in Britain. On the domestic front, there was what one historian has described as 'the sense of impending clash' with widespread labour unrest.[25] There were bitter struggles in the courts on the right to strike and the power of trade unions, which led to the creation of the Labour Party, with fearful signs of a new and radical anger among the working class through and beyond the strike-bound year of 1911 when even schoolchildren came out on strike in some districts, 'for shorter hours and no stick'.[26] The movement for women's emancipation was also spreading its wings, sending ripples of anxiety through British society which were not unassociated with the common allegations of mounting parental irresponsibility and the decline of family life. In 1909 there was a constitutional crisis of considerable magnitude over the right of Parliamentary veto in the House of Lords which shook England to its respectable depths. Taken as a piece, these describe the not altogether calming preoccupations of this 'golden' Edwardian era. The question of Ulster was there, too, with the shadow of the Irish rebellion hanging over the constitutional unity of the British Isles. Yes, this was 'our' England, and no other.[27]

Amidst all this shaking and trembling, respectable opinion was also waking up to the fact that new forms of life and organisation had emerged among the working class — both in a political, cultural and material sense. Working-class life had changed, quite measurably, in the last decades of the nineteenth century. While one third of the people lived near or below a stringently drawn poverty line, there had been nevertheless tangible improvements in the living conditions of the bulk of the people after the squalid upheavals of the earlier phase of industrialisation and urbanisation. For better-paid workers and their families, housing conditions were much improved and the diet was better. Meat consumption had increased by something like a third between 1870 and 1890, and working-class people had begun to eat fruit, which had previously been a luxury. New developments in the production of clothing and footwear, involving the manufacture of cheap commodities for a mass market, meant that people were better clothed and also that they had a purchase on 'style' — including, as we shall see, 'youth styles'. Hire purchase was another development of the 1890s, and relatively cheaper consumer durables such as the sewing machine came within the reach of more prosperous working-class families. There might even be a piano in the working-class parlour hinting at 'affluence', and the bicycle boom of the 1890s enlarged the mobility of many people — as did the new transport system of the tram. A whole range of material and cultural innovations in the late nineteenth century had begun to transform urban life. The football stadiums, the Bank Holiday, the Co-ops which boomed from the 1880s, the New Unionism and the socialist revival, the music hall, the seaside excursion, even the fish-and-chip shop, should all be added to this already impressive list of cultural and material innovations in this period. 'In a word,' writes Eric Hobsbawm in his summary of these developments, 'between 1870 and 1900 the pattern of British working class life which the writers, dramatists and TV producers of the 1950s thought of as "traditional" came into being.' But he also adds a warning that, 'It was not "traditional" then, but new.'[28]

We can push Hobsbawm's point a little further. Because what is truly remarkable, given the nostalgic lament which has accompanied the subsequent displacement of this 'traditional way of life', is that in their own historical time these emerging cultural institutions were greeted not only as something 'new', but as signs of an alarming development among the British people which threatened to destroy the 'British way of life'.

'Football Madness' and the 'Cyclist Terror'

Almost every aspect of popular culture came under fearful scrutiny at the turn of the century. The music halls, professional football, the 'penny dreadful' comics and the 'penny bloods' which were said to be inducements to crime and immorality, the rowdy presence of working-class people at seaside resorts on Bank Holiday excursions, the evening promenade of young people that was ridiculed by their elders as the 'monkey parade', the depravity and violence associated with the pub — they all came under attack at different times. Even the poor old bicycle was dragged into the act, amidst a blizzard of respectable fears.

The Music Halls, as might be readily anticipated, attracted the familiar accusation that they lowered moral standards and encouraged imitative crime. Asking 'how far a Music Hall programme may be held to encourage lawlessness', one observer considered that the types of song in currency 'could never have been written if the loafer, the liar, the drunkard, the thief, and the sensualist had been regarded as subjects unfit to be glorified in song'.[29] Another critic who took up the moral cudgels against the 'spicy' jokes and suggestive songs described how 'this kind of garbage is part and parcel of the *repertoire* of nearly every music hall in the kingdom ... it puts decency and clean-living at a discount, and it glorifies immorality all round'.[30] In his *Manchester Boys* (1905) Charles Russell also recounted how 'horrible murders and terrible tragedies were enacted before the footlights', leading to 'so many instances of violence on the part of young men, in the back streets of the city'.[31]

Soon, the early moving-pictures would be condemned in the same terms as 'a direct incentive to crime, demonstrating, for instance, how a theft could be perpetrated'.[32] 'Before these children's greedy eyes with heartless indiscrimination horrors unimaginable are ... presented night by night ... terrific massacres, horrible catastrophes, motor-car smashes, public hangings, lynchings' is how the lurid impact of the cinematograph was seen in 1913. Many children, it was said, 'actually begin their downward course of crime by reason of

the burglary and pickpocket scenes they have witnessed':
'All who care for the moral well-being and education of the
child will set their faces like flint against this new form of
excitement.'[33] In the same year, when a judge confronted
with a boy burglar at the London Sessions was to be found
pontificating against the cinema as 'a grave danger to the
community' which was 'responsible for the downfall of many
young people', the prosecutor jokingly remarked that 'it was
perhaps an example of retributive justice that one of the
houses broken into belonged to a cinematograph proprietor'.[34] But, given the doom and gloom already surrounding
the earliest silent movies, maybe he wasn't joking at all.

As for football, it also came under the hammer for the
usual reasons. The Football League had been founded as
recently as 1888, with its base firmly in the North and
Midlands. The behaviour of the crowds — vulgar, noisy and
violent — immediately excited considerable apprehension,
and the excesses of the transfer market and professionalism
were thought to be ruining the native traditions of 'fair play'
and sportsmanship.

Football had been a traditionally rowdy and sometimes
violent game, but as a regulated spectator sport it provided
novel opportunities for conflicts between the players, referees
and fans, and there is a well documented history of pitch
invasions, attacks on referees and players, and fighting between rival fans throughout the latter part of the nineteenth
century and into the new century.[35] A few scattered examples
can give some indication of these disorders. In 1893, spectators burst on to the field during a game between Nottingham
Forest and West Bromwich Albion, and a fight ensued between
players and fans with the Albionites attempting to defend the
referee, although it was observed 'that none of the home
players could be seen assisting in trying to stop disorder or to
protect the Referee'.[36] Earlier, in 1888, another referee
had complained bitterly about his ill-treatment by a Bolton
crowd and 'the dirty-nosed little rascals, who spoil every football match they go to'.[37] In the same year a Northern
sporting rag reported how 'a continuous hail of empty bottles'
had showered the pitch during a recent game, and here there
were further complaints against the ragged discipline of the

players themselves. On their way to a match against Great
Lever, it was said that four members of the Accrington team
became so 'liquored up' when they stopped to take refresh-
ment at Blackburn that they missed their train. While not
wishing to 'suggest that Blackburn ale is too potent for
Accrington heads', the football correspondent thought that
this kind of thing happened too frequently.[38]

With the advent of the new Leagues, and with larger
attendances at football games, efforts were made to regulate
the conduct of players and crowds, and the clubs were encouraged to protect referees more effectively. Even so, this
did not stop the trouble. In a blistering attack on 'The
Football Madness' in 1898, Ernest Ensor was particularly
shocked by the epidemic of excitement among the fans: 'A
constant attendant at great football matches must have seen
more than once a large crowd *vertere pollicem* in a manner
which made him thankful that murder is illegal.' Rounding
against the people of the North of England, 'whose warped
sporting instincts are so difficult to understand, even when
they are quite familiar', Ensor condemned the commercialisa-
tion of sport, the sensationalism of football journalism, and
the adoption of what he understood to be French and
American coaching tactics, as a wholesale corruption of
sporting values. 'As regards morality,' he thought, 'the old
English feeling for "sport" and "fair play" has receded to
thinly-populated or remote districts where athletes cannot
be exploited for money', prophesying that 'soon the only
football played, as used to be the case, for the love of the
game, will be seen among University men'. At the end of his
torment, Ensor was to be found down on his knees in prayer
'that the inherent virtues of cricket may continue to preserve it' from the hooting and yelling mobs of the football
stadiums.[39]

Many of these fearful criticisms of the working class
centred on the feeling that they were getting above their
station in life, or that they were encroaching upon previously
reserved territories of the middle class. For some years there
had been a gathering discontent around the boisterous arrival
of working-class people at holiday resorts, where the Bank
Holidays were regularly associated with heavy drinking,

shrieking girls and the occasional free fight.[40] The plebs were getting everywhere, and in a survey of 'Cheap Literature' Mrs Bosanquet even found reason to frown upon the working-class lads who were now sauntering into the public libraries:

> Harmless enough, of course, had it not been work hours, and, after all, they were better there than on the street corners. But one thing I did regret, and that was that, in learning to read, they had not also learned how to use books properly. To press them open with the palm of the hand, and a gesture as of French polishing, and to moisten the thumb and finger for every page turned over — surely the Board School should have taught them that this is unnecessary.[41]

However, undoubtedly the most extraordinary aspect of this grumbling against the tendency of the working class to assert its noisome presence in places where it clearly had no right to go, was to be found in the magnified excitements which surrounded the bicycle craze of the 1890s. Cycling was at the centre of a number of social panics. It was feared that the push-bike was a health hazard, for example causing 'bicycle face', 'bicycle hand' and 'bicycle foot', as well as the dreaded *kyphosis bicyclistratum,* or 'cyclist hump', which resulted if the handle-bars were set too low.[42] Evidence placed before the Physical Deterioration Committee even suggested that cycling was a threat to the nation's manliness, inducing varicocele of the testicles 'from the pressure of the saddle'.[43]

More grievous allegations were brought against the bicycling 'scorchers' who went too fast or, to strike another note of discontent, who went too far and barged into middle-class leisure haunts. There were editorial fumings in *The Times* (15 August 1898) about 'the East-End or suburban "scorcher", dashing along quiet country roads and through peaceful villages with loud shouts and sulphurous language, and reckless of life and limb', and *The Lancet* (6 August 1898) saw fit to have a medical entry on 'The Fool on the Cycle'. Accounts of youths whizzing about madly on their bikes, causing pandemonium among the traffic, frightening horses, and knocking over pedestrians were as commonplace as the headlines which repeatedly sensationalised 'The Cyclist

Terror', 'The Risks of the Cycle', 'The Perils of the Wheel', 'Moloch of the Wheel', 'The Dangers of City Cycling' and 'Cyclomania'.[44]

There were many complaints by cyclists of harassment by the police and, in the midst of a social panic such as this, woe betide anyone who fell foul of the law while in charge of a bike. *The Daily Graphic* (30 March 1898) described the fate of one young man, Thomas Duff, who had been unlucky enough to be charged with 'riding a tricycle to the common danger' and to encounter a magistrate who took an extremely dim view of the matter. Thomas Duff, who had been going about his business as a messenger boy when it was said that he 'nearly ran in to two gentlemen', put up a stout defence in court. He 'produced his bell and rang it, stating that that was what he did at the time', but the magistrate told him 'that he must not think that everyone had to scamper out of the way upon hearing the sound of his bell'. Under its headline 'Mercantile Tricycles Denounced', the *Graphic* described how, in default of paying a 10 shillings fine plus costs, this cycling desperado was sentenced to seven days' imprisonment — and what is more, poor Thomas Duff had been estimated by the police to have been rattling along at somewhere between 8 and 10 miles per hour.[45]

There were, however, more tangible reasons for concern in that bicycle deaths and injuries were frequently reported in the press, with moments of aggravated alarm about 'hit-and-run' cyclists. This provoked some heated confrontations in coroners' courts when cycling cases were brought before them. In one hit-and-run case, one of the jurors had the effrontery to challenge the coroner's authority, stating that he was a cyclist himself and that pedestrians were often at fault because they took insufficient care. 'The manly part for the cyclist,' retorted the coroner, 'whether he is to blame or not, is to face the consequences of his acts.' In another coroner's court, called to enquire into the death of a 70-year-old man after an alleged hit-and-run accident, there was further uproar when the jury defied the evidence of medical experts and returned a verdict of 'heart disease from natural causes'. 'You discard the doctor's evidence?' asked the astonished coroner. 'Yes,' replied one of the jurors, 'and the cyclist story too.' This kind of squabbling in the courts was most unseemly, and *The Daily Mail* launched an angry editorial broadside: 'There were cyclists on the jury, we read, and this fact has a grim sound . . . Steps should be taken to put these people down.'[46]

The woman cyclist was another object of fearful contemplation, and there were snide allusions to the improper 'rational costumes' women were adopting to facilitate travel by bike, as well as their recklessness in traffic.[47] There was always more than a hint, of course, that the real source of anxiety was that the bicycle might be enlarging the freedom of women in undesirable directions, because both in terms of class and sex the bicycle was a great leveller. Indeed, among these villains of the wheel, the woman cyclist was possibly even more of a portent than the cyclist juror.

The bicycle was obviously shaking the old order to the roots, and with its customary irreverence the socialist *Clarion* (30 July 1898) — which had a large stake in the matter, because of the enormously popular Clarion Cycling Clubs — wondered 'how it is no one has written a cycling melodrama, with a hero and a heroine and a villain on wheels'. No doubt the rapid growth of the Clarion Clubs, spreading the socialist cause by bike, was another of the spectres haunting Old England in its alarmist response to the pedal cycle:

> Down to the haunts of the parson and squire
> Putting opponents to rout;
> Bestriding his steed with a pneumatic tyre.
> Through village and hamlet thro' mud and thro' mire
> Rideth the Clarion Scout
> Nailing down lies and disposing of fables
> Improving the landscape by sticking up labels.[48]

The bicycle was a powerful symbol of social change in this era, summing up so easily the fears brewing around popular freedoms and popular amusements, and it seemed to touch a brittle nerve of the process of democratisation. *The Times* (15 August 1898) had given the broadest indication of the shock-waves produced by the push-bike when it delivered its editorial judgement on 'The Bicycle as a Social Force', which bristled with otherwise unaccountable fears and allusions to deeper moving forces within society. The bicycle was accused of enlarging the scope for theft, and we were encouraged to linger over some of the more squalid details of profiteering and corruption which had accompanied the boom in the cycling industry. Pondering over the cycle's military potential, whether or not it might 'mitigate the decline of the rural population', fearing that it would tempt people away from the churches, but rejoicing that it would lure others away from 'demonstrations in Hyde Park or low-class places of amusement', *The Times* thus moved its discussion skilfully between different planes of anxiety. Indeed, behind the fears and accusations which surrounded the villainous working-class 'scorcher', his emancipated female accomplice, and the unruly cyclist juror we can perhaps sense the vaguely incoherent feeling that the democratic bicycle — which was now only upsetting the respectable pleasures of a quiet Bank Holiday weekend in the countryside — was representative of a force that might be calculated to upset a few other things as well.

A Frightening New Race of People

The alarm bells that were ringing around popular amusements and freedoms as the new century arrived moved in concert with a much darker current of anxiety about national decline and incohesion, involving some quite spectacular fantasies of racial degeneration. Theories of 'urban degeneration' which suggested that the conditions of city life were manufacturing a deteriorated race had been aired since the 1880s, lending themselves to a number of schemes of reclamation.[49] General Booth's Salvationist doctrine was a notable example, recommending mass emigration from the city slums to virgin colonial territories.[50] There were also many more limited ventures such as Pearson's Fresh Air Fund, established in 1896 by Arthur Pearson, the founder of *The Daily Express*, to provide country holidays for city children, and this was itself among the inspirations for the fresh air philosophies of Baden-Powell's Boy Scouts launched in 1908.[51]

Some rather fanciful Darwinian speculation had helped to inform these developments, as when Karl Pearson had brooded over the damaging evolutionary processes at work in *National Life and Character: A Forecast* (1894) where he had identified the growth of towns, the reliance on standing armies which would induce mechanical habits, the decline of individualism, family feeling and national pride as the emerging contours of the future. As to 'its effect upon national character', Pearson thought that 'whether we are changing in the direction of a higher or lower morality is . . . the point that is most really at issue'. But although he could not be said to have reached any hard-and-fast conclusions to this question, so fearful were the prospects of this supposed evolutionary degeneration that Karl Pearson took refuge (and a certain amount of comfort) in the fact that its results were far away: 'Happily, what the distant future of the world may be is a matter that does not much concern us, and about which we may rejoice to know nothing.'[52]

A few years later, however, the distant future showed every indication of having already arrived when these nagging anxieties grabbed the headlines around the large numbers of recruits who had been found unfit for service in the Boer War, and in spite of the half-hearted reassurances of the Physical Deterioration Committee of 1904 fears of racial deterioration were rampant. 'Race suicide is possible', exclaimed an anonymous commentator on 'Sport and Decadence' in 1909, while another author writing under the cloak of anonymity warned in 1912 of 'a canker at the heart of the people which will surely destroy it', believing that 'the first stage of decay has already been reached when the stolid, God-fearing puritan of two-and-a-half centuries ago has given place to the shallow, hysterical cockney of today'.[53]

Apocalypse was in the air, and in strict accordance with the traditions of this connected history of fears of British decline, the ghosts of Rome were summoned to make their judgement. Writing on 'The Fall of the Roman Empire and Its Lessons for Us' one author had already struck the easy notes of comparison in 1898 — the decline of the arts of soldiery and manliness, the financial oppression of the middle classes, subsidised food prices, bread and circuses (that is, football) and the recruitment of the barbarian 'lower races' into the imperial armies were all listed as forces 'which may tend to enervate and degrade us, to destroy our love of truth, to poison the fountains of family life'.[54] Baden-Powell was particularly fond of this extravagant, but nevertheless deeply felt historical posture, and he saw the shadow of Rome hanging over the huge crowds attending the football stadiums which he likened to the 'unmanly' attitude of the young Romans who loafed around the circus entertainments — 'they paid men to play their games for them, so that they could look on without the fag of playing, just as we are doing in football now' — as he charged into battle against this betrayal of the British traditions of 'fair play' and sportsmanship:

> Thousands of boys and young men, pale, narrow-chested, hunched up, miserable specimens, smoking endless cigarettes, numbers of them betting, all of them learning to be hysterical as they groan or cheer in panic unison with their neighbours — the worst sound of all being the hysterical scream of laughter that greets any little trip or fall of a player. One wonders whether this can be the same nation which had gained for itself the reputation of being a stolid, pipe-sucking manhood, unmoved by panic or excitement, and reliable in the tightest of places.[55]

The pattern for these accusations had been set by the young Liberal Charles Masterman in *The Heart of the Empire* (1902) where he had thundered out his warning of inevitable decline as the result of the 'perpetual lowering in the vitality of the Imperial Race in the great cities of the Kingdom through over-crowding in room and in area':

> A certain temper of fickle excitability has revealed to observers during the past few months that a new race, hitherto unreckoned and of incalculable action, is entering the sphere of practical importance — the 'City type' of the coming years; the 'street-bred' people of the twentieth century; the 'new generation knocking at our doors' ... The result is the production of a characteristic physical type of town dweller: stunted, narrow-chested, easily wearied; yet voluble, excitable, with little ballast, stamina or endurance.[56]

What was never entirely clear was whether it was merely a

physical deterioration that was eating away at the 'Imperial Race', or if a moral decay was not also in evidence. The blurred sense of catastrophe usually insisted that it was both. Jack London, as an American journalist visiting Britain, picked up the mood in *The People of the Abyss* (1902). Under the conditions of city life he believed it 'incontrovertible that the children grow up into rotten adults, without virility or stamina, a weak-kneed, narrow-chested, listless breed'. But within this 'huge man-killing machine' of the city he also sensed a temperamental alteration: 'A new race has sprung up, a street people ... The traditional silent and reserved Englishman has passed away. The pavement folk are noisy, voluble, high-strung, excitable.'[57]

Reginald Bray, a friend of Masterman's, would remark on the same development:

> A deliberate slowness in action was once the characteristic of the Englishman. He would look around a situation before he leapt into it ... This quality has of late years been less in evidence ... Few careful observers have failed to notice the change.

As Bray organised the arguments of his powerful Christian treatise on *The Town Child* (1907) around deep shades of pastoral contrast between the serenity of natural phenomena and what he regarded as the unnatural and shallow inconsistency of the irreverent city, he thought that 'the most remarkable effect of an urban environment is to be sought in the disappearance of the habit of self-control':

> The crowd of the town in a moment flashes into a delirious mob ... The invention of the new term 'Mafficking' is alone sufficient to indicate the extent of the transformation ... a wild spirit of unrest ... Nerves are ever on the strain ... on the most trifling occasion, exploding like a pistol at the mere touch of the hair-trigger. In the face of the vast population, penned in within the walls of a city, such possibilities of unpremeditated violence constitute a standing menace to the general welfare.[58]

The riotous jingo crowds which had accompanied the Ladysmith and Mafeking celebrations during the Boer War had indeed provided one of the most visible manifestations of these perceived alterations among the British people, and observing that 'to "Maffick" is not really congenial to the British character' *The Times* (30 October 1900) had mused upon whether 'our national character was changing for the worse'.[59]

However, there were even more terrible signs of this supposedly new streak of violent irritability to be found among the youth of working-class neighbourhoods, which could not even be justified on the grounds of over-enthusiastic jingo patriotism. It showed itself at the turn of the century in a rash of gang fights, stabbings and street robberies, and in some parts of London there were excited rumours of youthful gangs armed with guns. The phenomenon had first been noticed in the last years of Victoria's reign, among the new generation coming through who would be the new Edwardians and who would inherit the new century. Indeed, the golden age had invented another new word to name its fears: it was called 'Hooliganism'.

5

Victorian Boys, We Are Here !

The word 'hooligan' made an abrupt entrance into common English usage, as a term to describe gangs of rowdy youths, during the hot summer of 1898. 'Hooligans' and 'Hooliganism' were thrust into the headlines in the wake of a turbulent August Bank Holiday celebration in London which had resulted in unusually large numbers of people being brought before the courts for disorderly behaviour, drunkenness, assaults on police, street robberies and fighting. One of the more alarming aspects of these Bank Holiday disturbances was that they highlighted fierce traditions of resistance to the police in working-class neighbourhoods, so that not uncommonly policemen attempting to make street arrests would be set upon by large crowds — sometimes numbering two or three hundred people — shouting 'Rescue! Rescue!' and 'Boot him!'[1]

At first it was not entirely clear where the word 'Hooligan' had sprung from — and it remains unclear to this day — or exactly what it meant, other than some kind of novel reference to street violence and ruffianism. It seems most likely, however, that it was a word like 'Teddy Boy' or 'Mod' or 'Skinhead' which, coming out of the popular culture of working-class London, had been adopted by youths in some localities in order to describe themselves and what they took for their common identity. A Music Hall song from 1890s, introduced by the Irish comedians O'Connor and Brady, had probably first popularised the word:

> Oh, the Hooligans! Oh, the Hooligans!
>   Always on the riot,
>   Cannot keep them quiet,
> Oh, the Hooligans! Oh, the Hooligans!
>   They are the boys
>   To make a noise
>   In our backyard.[2]

How it came to be adopted by, and applied to, youthful street gangs is something of a mystery.[3] But whatever its humble origins, when the new word was picked up by the newspapers in August 1898 it was quickly transformed into a term of more general notoriety, so that 'Hooligan' and 'Hooliganism' became the controlling words to describe troublesome youths who had previously been known more loosely as 'street arabs', 'ruffians' or 'roughs'. And once they were christened, as we might expect, the 'Hooligans' were understood as an entirely unprecedented and 'un-British' phenomenon: indeed, we must allow that it was most ingenious of late Victorian England to disown the British Hooligan by giving him an 'Irish' name.

In other ways, too, the phenomenon was located within a scale of alien values and temperaments, thus stamping it as foreign and 'un-English'. When *The Times* (17 August 1898) first turned its attention to the August disorders, describing them as 'something like organised terrorism in the streets', it struck the key-note in an editorial on 'The Weather and the Streets':

> It is curious that simultaneously with reports of excessive heat should come the record of an unusual number of crimes of lawless violence . . . Does the great heat fire the blood of the London rough or street arab, with an effect analogous to that of a southern climate upon the hot-blooded Italian or Provencal? . . . Or is the connexion between heat and lawlessness not so much one of cause and effect as coincident circumstances — heat generating thirst, and thirst a too frequent consumption of fiery liquor unsuitable for a tropical climate?

A couple of years later, asking 'What are we to do with the "Hooligan"? Who or what is responsible for his growth?' *The Times* (30 October 1900) would harp on the same theme, announcing that 'Every week some incident shows that certain parts of London are more perilous for the peaceable wayfarer than the remote districts of Calabria, Sicily, or Greece, once the classic haunts of brigands'. In the heat of the immediate events of 1898, however, while denouncing the excessive leniency of the law, *The Times* (17 August 1898) had boomed out an even more momentous possibility that 'un-English' violence might have to be curbed by un-English methods:

> In Continental cities, or in the free Republic of America, they have very little scruple about calling out troops and shooting down organised disturbances of the peace ... But if we do not adopt Continental methods of dealing with street lawlessness ... if we do not wish our police to be formidable as an armed force, we must not grudge an increase in their numbers.

Headline News

If the 'Hooligans' were regarded as an un-English phenomenon, they were also understood as an entirely unprecedented development and respectable England felt itself to have been suddenly engulfed in a new rush of crime. A pattern of trouble quickly came to be associated with the street gangs. The Hooligans fought pitched battles among themselves — Chelsea Boys against Fulham Boys, or Chapel Street against Margaret Street — and they were said to take great pride in their famous victories over rival neighbourhoods. The Hooligans were also said to hunt in cowardly packs, however, and news reports regularly featured them smashing up coffee-stalls and public houses, assaulting staff in pubs and cheap eating-houses, robbing and assaulting old ladies, attacking foreigners such as Italian ice-cream vendors or 'Froggy' cafe owners, and setting upon policemen in the streets with savage howls of 'Boot 'em!' Because, if the supposedly traditional habit of respect for the law was not much in evidence here, then frequent headlines such as '"Boot 'em" at Waterloo', 'They Play Football with a Man' and 'Kick a Man like a Football' serve to remind us that the English 'fair play' tradition of fighting with the fists — and not with the feet — had also gone into eclipse. In South London, for example, it was said that the gangs wore 'boots toe-plated with iron, and calculated to kill easily'.[4]

Not everyone was agreed, however, that the Hooligans represented a novel development, nor about the scale of the outrages. When a question was asked in Parliament in August 1898, the Home Secretary's department was 'not satisfied that there was any such insecurity as was alleged'. Mr Patrick McIntyre, a South London publican and former New Scotland Yard detective who wrote a regular crime column for the *South London Chronicle*, was another who cast doubt on the Hooligan panic, accusing newspapers of being in their 'silly season' and of taking the matter up merely 'as a suitable and sensational means of filling their columns at the present moment'. Thomas Holmes, the distinguished London Police Court Missioner, agreed and described the affair as 'press-manufactured Hooliganism'.[5] Nor was there much evidence of concern in the correspondence columns of *The Times* — that bush-telegraph of respectable opinion — which were absorbed with more pressing matters such as the scarcity of swallows in England that summer. There were even back-biting accusations among some sections of the press that their competitors were indulging in 'silly season' sensationalism.[6]

Further controversy was prompted by a manifesto issued from the self-styled South London Ratepayers' Association which called for a 'display of fearless strength' by local people, advising that 'a discriminating application of the "cat-o'-nine-tails" will soon sweep away this reign of terror'.[7] There were any number of flogging editorials in response to the Hooligan outrages — in *The Daily Mail*, for example, the *News of the World* and even the medical journal *The Lancet* — and the Ratepayers' Association manifesto was widely reported in the press as evidence of public support for flogging. But *The Sun* thought that 'the meeting was a bogus one, if it was held at all', further alleging that this clandestine organisation (which said that it had met in secrecy because it feared Hooligan reprisals) was a put-up job by someone in the pay of *The Daily Telegraph*.[8] Amidst such confusion as

A REMEDY FOR RUFFIANS

Hooligan. 'What are you up to, Guv'nor!'
Policeman. 'I'm going to introduce you to the 'harmless, necessary Cat'!'

this, however, the press was more commonly inclined to shout down the leniency of magistrates, or 'this appalling apathy on the part of the police', because if in some quarters the press were accused of bulling up the Hooligan affair, elsewhere the police were said to be playing it down.[9]

More radical sections of the press placed further doubts against the feeling that there had been a sudden eruption of street violence. Describing London as 'a city of illusions, subject every now and then to a series of harsh awakenings', *The Echo* (11 August 1898) believed that while some of the stories were undoubtedly exaggerated they nevertheless served a purpose: 'We steadily shut our eyes to the submerged lawlessness of less fortunate districts until a series of Whitechapel outrages, or Hooligan exploits, make us not only aware of what is going on, but actually afraid of our lives.' In a similar line of argument, *Reynolds's Newspaper* (14 August 1898) viewed the Hooligan panic as an indictment of the hypocrisy of a civilisation that took 'so painful an interest about moral handkerchiefs and hymn books for the barbarians of the wild Soudan' while turning a blind eye towards 'the far wilder barbarians they may find within a few paces from their own street-doors'. For the socialist press, in any event, the burning issue in working-class London during the hot summer of 1898 was not the Hooligans, but the water shortage which was reaching crisis proportions. With a fine eye for a 'newsworthy' item, the *News of the World* (28 August 1898) blamed youths for wasting water by larking about with street taps, but the socialist press saw a more permanent difficulty in the negligence of the private water companies. Indeed, urging people not to pay their rates to the East End Water Company, *Reynolds's Newspaper* (28 August 1898) conjured with the circumstances under which, in the struggle against what it called 'Horrible London', even the horrible Hooligans might lend a hand:

> If they would only attack the present cabinet, we should feel inclined to be a little more lenient . . . if Chamberlain, or Chaplin, or Balfour, or Goschen were knocked down in the Old Kent Road by a Hooligan gang, we should soon hear of some scheme to improve London life.

The Clarion, with its devilish sense of fun, would no doubt have agreed. Although it hardly seemed to notice the Hooligan affair, and its only immediate response was a front-page poem 'Hot Weather and Crime' which can only have been intended as a slap in the face for *The Times* leader on 'The Weather and the Streets':

HOT WEATHER AND CRIME

I scarcely can fink
That 'ot weather and drink
Is sole causes of murders and priggins,
And I'll tell you my views
(Which the same mayn't be news)
Wot I frequent relates to Bill 'Iggins

I'm one of the group
Of pore cowves in the soup
I knows wot the treadmill and clink is;
I ain't quite t-t,
For I'm boozed frequentlee
So I knows wot the evils of drink is

Us chaps drink a lot
When the weather is 'ot —
That statement I will not deny it;
But it ought to be told
That we drinks when it's cold
And whene'er we can steal it or buy it

We lives and we dies
In foul dens and styes
Without any fun or hexcitement
Like sparrers in cages —
'Ard work and low wages —
Till we figgers vithin a hindictment.[10]

The message was clear enough: if it took crime and violence to attract the attention of the mighty to the lives of the poor, then so be it. It was not that ruffianism was thought to be funny, but the radical and socialist press wished to place a different emphasis on the criminal question which took full account of the social and material circumstances of working-class life.[11] What they could find room to laugh at, however, was the way in which respectable England could ignore the

realities of slum life for so many years, while showering
the Empire with the benefits of Christianity and imperial
wars, and then get itself into a respectable lather in such
a short time about a few broken heads among rough lads.

A Tour of the Quiet Streets

Before looking in more detail at who the 'Hooligans' were,
and in order to place the controversies that surrounded them
in perspective, it will be helpful to make an imaginative effort
to reconstruct the kind of social world in which the original
'Hooligans' moved. On so many occasions, the way in which
'Hooliganism' was greeted implied a sudden, alien interruption
of a peaceful and well-ordered way of life. But what did this
way of life look like at street level? And what were the habits
of the Hooligans' gentle neighbours and families and friends?
A brief tour of inspection of London's streets at the time
that the Hooligans were publicly christened will help us to
see something of what these quiet streets were made of.

In some localities trouble had undoubtedly been expected
at the time of the Bank Holiday, and it was reported in Lambeth police court that plainclothes men had been specially
stationed 'for the purpose of dealing with cases of street
ruffianism'.[12] The newspapers were particularly impressed
by the appearance in Marylebone court of 88 people in a
single day, 70 of whom were charged with disorderliness
of some sort, although *The Times* (16 August 1898) observed
that 'the majority of cases were of a very ordinary kind'. The
troubled signs of this 'ordinary' street life were very much
in evidence, however, and press reports were packed with
accounts of assaults and robberies, 'dipping' gangs at race
meetings, gang fights and stabbings, vandalism, punch-ups
and 'free fights'. The 'free fight' must have been sometimes
quite an occasion: a Bank Holiday bust-up in the Old Kent
Road, for example, consumed the energies of 200 people.[13]

In the foreground of the Bank Holiday outrages were the
'Hooligan' gangs themselves. In one disturbance that received
wide publicity, a policeman had stumbled across a gang of
about twenty youths, said to be known as the 'Chelsea Boys'

who 'armed with sticks and stones were fighting a contingent
of similar young ruffians from Battersea' at Cheyne Walk by
the river.[14] A 17-year-old paper-stainer, James Irons, was
brought before the magistrate — described by the police
as a ring-leader and by his mother as 'a good boy' — where
it was said that he had 'used disgusting language, and discharged a number of stones larger than walnuts from a
powerful catapult'. Charged with disorderly conduct and
with discharging stones from a catapult to the common
danger, he was found to have four previous convictions
against him for gambling, disorderly behaviour and stone-
throwing. Regretting 'that he had no power to send him to
prison without the option of a fine', the magistrate imposed
a fine of 40 shillings (probably amounting to more than a
month's wages) or twenty-one days' hard labour.

Another typical Bank Holiday incident of the kind that
brought such infamy to the Hooligans involved four young
men, described as 'larrikins' aged between 17 and 20 years,
who were charged with damaging an ice-cream feeder belonging to an Italian ice-cream vendor, and assaults on police
and a park-keeper.[15] There had been an argument and the
youths had overturned the ice-cream barrow, and after a
chase there was a scuffle with the police. Identified by police
witnesses as the 'Somers Town Boys', the two youths charged
with assault received six weeks' hard labour and a month's
hard labour. According to one witness, as they ran away
across a park they were heard to shout, 'Look out for the
Hooligan gang.'

After these incidents the look-outs were certainly posted
in the press, and the word 'Hooligan' began to be used widely,
if at first somewhat indiscriminately. More to the point, if
'Hooliganism' was an entirely novel outburst as was usually
supposed, then a tropical growth of gang life must have
sprouted overnight. From August onwards the newspapers
were over-flowing with the exploits of the various gangs in
London: the 'Lion Boys' from the Lion and Lamb in Clerkenwell; the so-called 'Clerkenwell "Pistol Gang" '; the 'Girdle
Gang' which took its name from Thomas, alias 'Tuxy', Girdle;
the 'Somers Town Gang' who were said to be the pests of
Euston Road and Gower Street; the 'Pinus Gang' who in-

fested Leather Lane and Clerkenwell; the 'Drury Lane Boys'; the notorious 'Waterloo Road Gang'; the 'Pickett Gang'; 'McNab's'; the 'Rest Gang'; the 'Fulham Boys'; the 'Chelsea Boys'; the 'Velvet Cap Gang'; the 'Plaid-Cap Brigade' from Poplar; the gangs who romped around King Street and Great Church Lane in Hammersmith and who were said to be 'not "Hooligans" but worse'; and many others, including a band of youngsters who had adopted the dare-devil title of the 'Dick Turpin Gang'.[16]

At first the press were inclined to brand anything as the newly named 'Hooliganism'. When the Girdle Gang appeared in court for an assault on a man whom, it was said, they had kicked 'like a football', *The Daily Graphic* described them as 'a gang of the Hooligan type'. Mr Girdle's solicitor, on the other hand, complained that 'the "Girdle Gang" did not really exist, except in the imagination of a "needy para-graphist" '.[17] But although 'Tuxy' Girdle may not have been a youthful Hooligan, it did emerge that he had been running whores and he received a substantial sentence of penal servitude for the assault on the man whom the gang had suspected of being a police spy.

The new word quickly settled down, however, as a regular pattern began to emerge in the trouble associated with the London Hooligans. They cluttered up the streets in noisy gatherings, swearing at passers-by, spitting on them, and sometimes assaulting and robbing them. *The Daily Graphic* (15 August 1898) reported the antics of the 'Velvet Cap Gang' from Battersea: 'Some dozen boys, all armed with sticks and belts, wearing velvet caps, and known as the "Velvet Cap Gang", walking along . . . pushing people off the pavement, knocking at shop doors, and using filthy language.' And then, a few days later there was a similar story from another part of London: 'A gang of roughs, who were parading the roadway, shouting obscene language, playing mouth organs, and pushing respectable people down. The young ruffians were all armed with thick leather belts, on which there were heavy brass buckles' (*The Daily Graphic*, 25 August 1898).

There were innumerable accounts of a similar character, describing 'larking' in the streets. The frequent reports of people being hustled, or pushed off the pavement, probably derived from the practice among working-class youths known as 'holding the street'. This violent ritual of territorial supremacy, as described by Walter Besant in 1901, sounds remarkably like the modern practice at football grounds of 'holding the End': 'The boys gather together and hold the street; if anyone ventures to pass through it they rush upon him, knock him down, and kick him savagely about the head; they rob him as well . . . the boys regard holding the street with pride.'[18]

Fights and disturbances in pubs were also commonly reported. One 18-year-old youth appeared in court after throwing glasses at a publican's head, while in another pub case that ended in court a landlord had refused to serve Bank Holiday revellers whereupon they 'knocked him down, and kicked him in the eye and about the body'.[19] Back in the open street things were no better. We hear of 'an elderly woman . . . set upon by a gang of young ruffians who knocked her down and stole a bag of provisions she was carrying', and in another case a 17-year-old youth was charged with assaulting an elderly woman on Bank Holiday night: 'Both her eyes were blackened and there was an abrasion on her nose.'[20]

These kinds of incidents could be repeated time and time again, and nor were black eyes and bruises the only injuries sustained. Arriving home late one Sunday night on a railway excursion from Herne Bay, a bottle-fight broke out among the holiday-makers as a result of which a man was killed. But what must astonish us, I think, more than the details of violence is that the only charges brought as a result of this death were against three men who were charged with assault and punished with a 20 shillings' fine, with the additional requirement that they should pay the doctor's bill on the dead man.[21]

In another case, headlined as 'The Alleged Hooligan Tragedy', a man died after a street-fight and it was reported that on arrival at hospital he had made a statement to the effect that, 'I got my injuries in the Borough through being kicked to death by Hooligans.' Eye-witnesses denied this, however, saying that he had been engaged in a 'fair' stand-up fight, but that when other people joined in he had fallen and struck his head on a tramline.[22] There were other cases of deaths in the streets which could not be cleared up, except as 'accidents', and reluctance to give evidence must be counted as an important aspect of popular hostility towards the law.

It was assaults on the police, however, together with fierce resistance to street arrests, that provided the most vivid illumination of popular feeling. In one almost comic instance, a man described as a 'wooden-legged ruffian' who was well known for drunk-and-disorderly offences had kicked a policeman with his wooden leg. In a violent struggle, the policeman found it necessary to unscrew the man's wooden leg as he wrestled him to the ground, striking him across the head with his truncheon. A crowd then assembled and threw pepper at the police, causing such a commotion that it was only possible to get the one-legged prisoner to the police station with the assistance of twelve constables.[23]

In a more typical case, when attempting a street arrest 'a hostile mob raised the cry of "Boot them" against the police'; in another, police attempting to separate a man and woman who were quarrelling were 'set upon by a crowd of 200 persons, who called out "Boot them", and they were assaulted and kicked'. On yet another occasion at Alexandra Park Race Day in 1898, which was said to be 'infested with a crowd of scoundrels and ruffians of the worst race-course stamp', when police arrested a pick-pocket 'the constables were surrounded by a crowd, who kicked them and brutally ill-treated them, and released the prisoner'.[24] There were repeated instances, in fact, of assaults on policemen who then found it necessary to draw their truncheons and fight their way out of a crowd. In a 'desperate struggle in a drunken crowd' a police officer had been stabbed to death in Wilmer Gardens, Hoxton, said to be 'a low neighbourhood infested by a very dangerous class'.[25] While at the height of the Bank Holiday disturbances there was what was described as a 'Midnight Riot' in the vicinity of Euston Road when a policeman attempted to deal with a disorderly woman who 'began to shriek, and . . . screamed that she was being choked'. Surrounded by a hostile crowd who began to hiss and hoot, the policeman blew his whistle for assistance. 'Unfortunately for the constable', we were told, 'this only had the effect of bringing reinforcements to the mob.' A roar went up of 'Rescue! Rescue!' and among those who joined in were the notorious Somers Town Boys.[26]

'Hooliganism' was invariably portrayed as a totally alien presence, but here we see Hooligans acting in concert with their neighbours, reflecting the fact that in many working-class neighbourhoods hostility towards the police was a remarkably cohesive force. Typically sparked off by what might have been seen as an unfair arrest or an arbitrary use of police power, resistance to arrest on this scale was such an entirely common feature of working-class life before the Great War that it constitutes the most articulate demolition of the myths of deep-rooted popular respect for law and authority in England. A report by Robert Blatchford of a visit to a Music Hall in the 'Gay Nineties' offered a vivid portrait of how these feelings expressed themselves in everyday life. Blatchford did not reckon much to the artistic qualities of the old-fashioned melodrama presented on the stage, but he thought the audience 'were human enough for anything'. Amidst the banter of the assembly of dockers, costers, labourers and mechanics, with their wives and sweethearts and babies — the lads at the back whistling improvised mood music to the events on stage, some pelting those in the pits below with orange pips, and all howling with laughter at their own jokes — he considered that 'very significant were the marks of popular interest and favour':

> When the police arrested the hero in the streets and a rescue was attempted by the denizens of the Boro', the audience became quite excited, many of them stood up, and all fell into the spirit of the scene — sympathy being manifestly against the law; and when the stage was darkened and the fortunes of the combat could not be distinguished, open resentment was displayed by the gods, one of whom yelled out to the gasman to 'turn up them bloomin' glims an' let's see the bloomin' scrappin".[27]

Attacks on the police touched on complex structures of loyalty and tradition which cut across simple-minded notions

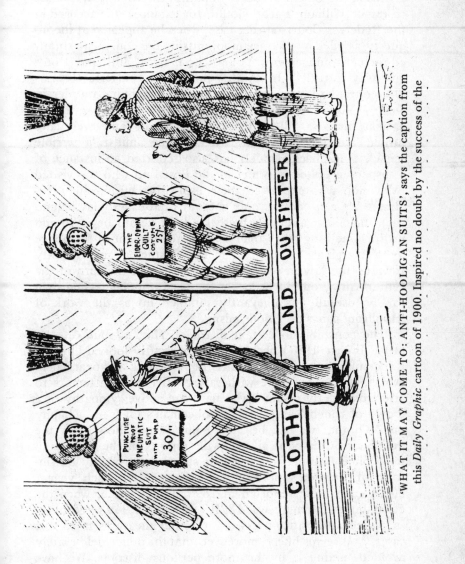

'WHAT IT MAY COME TO: ANTI-HOOLIGAN SUITS', says the caption from this *Daily Graphic* cartoon of 1900. Inspired no doubt by the success of the

from on high about obedience and civility. Even murderers
could be the object of local sympathy. An attempt was made
to rescue William 'Fatty' Gould, for example, the accused in
the Redcross Court murder case, when he appeared at the in-
quest: 'assailed by a savage mob' outside the court who shouted their encouragement, 'You will be all right, Bill!' and 'Don't
give way Fatty!'[28] In another murder case, after a 19-year-
old youth had been found guilty of a stabbing murder in
Oakley Street, a woman who had given crucial evidence
against him was ill-treated by neighbours and eventually
turned out of her Oakley Street home amidst 'a terrible
scene'.[29] Raphael Samuels has also reported an instance of
a suspected police informer in the East End who was visited
by a mob who expressed their displeasure by burning efffi-
gies.[30] We can perhaps only guess at what exactly lay behind
such incidents, although these kinds of details begin to add
up to something more than a fringe resentment of the police
by a marginal 'criminal element'. Suspicion and hostility
towards the law in working-class London at the turn of the
century drew on much deeper funds of popular feeling than
can be usefully or relevantly summed up as the work of
'Hooligan' gangs or 'Hooliganism'.

   'The constable in certain districts', *The Pall Mall Gazette*
(19 February 1901) observed, 'is apparently looked upon as
the common enemy whom it is right to kick and beat when-
ever that can be done with safety.' 'When he attempts to
arrest disorderly persons who have the active sympathy of a
crowd of roughs', it added, 'a policeman's lot is not a happy
one.' Of that we can be sure. Some idea of how badly the
police were treated is given by the reports of the Metropolitan Police Commissioner which show that roughly one-in-
four of London's policemen were assaulted each year —
3,444 cases were reported in 1899, for example, when the
constabulary strength was 13,213 men and 1,949 sergeants —
as police authorities pressed for firmer measures in assault
cases.[31] It seems likely, moreover, that the police deliberately
avoided mixing it in the more perilous districts. We have
already heard complaints against the apathy of the police,
and publicans who complained about violence were said to
have 'got the name among the police of being "fussy" '.[32] It

would have been a disappointed reader, however, who turned to *The Daily Mail's* titillating headline 'HE ATE A POLICE-MAN' at the high pitch of the Bank Holiday alarm in 1898 for more news of the monstrous Hooligans, because the story thankfully described the exploits of a truculent crocodile.[33]

Against this background of a bustling, potentially violent and effectively unpoliced street life, we can point to a wide variety of other kinds of rowdyism and misbehaviour at this time in history. There are stories of gangs of roughs waylaying cyclists and pelting them with stones, and in one case a South London cowboy was brought before Lambeth court for lassoing cyclists — 'a kind of horseplay that must be stamped out at once' said the magistrate, with good reason.[34] The police were also being urged to take action against the practice of 'throwing coloured lights' from coaches that were returning from holiday excursions, and there was a growing concern about a wave of incidents in which obstacles — sometimes quite large ones — were placed on railway lines by people described as 'wreckers'.[35] Throughout the late 1890s the police had been bothered by complaints about young boys throwing stones or spitting from the London bridges on to boats and their passengers below. In 1896 while sculling at Putney, an oarsman had been sunk by a stone-throwing youth, and in the following year there was a complaint that a yacht's skylight had been broken at Lambeth Bridge and then 'a shower of horse dung greeted us at Chelsea'. 'I find the spitting this year worse than ever', complained a gentle-man in 1900. And although the names given of some of the boys arrested for these offences — David Stones and Arthur Gobbing, for example — suggest the possibility of a hoax, police reports repeatedly referred to 'this dangerous practice' and that 'the danger to the public seems sufficiently marked to warrant some special steps'. Indeed, from 1896 plain-clothes men had been deployed to patrol the bridges.[36]

We read in the newspapers of other cases of vandalism. Gas-lamps that are broken, and night-watchmen assaulted when they complain. A case comes to hand of two children, a boy of 8 years and a 10-year-old girl, who broke into their local school and 'then completely wrecked the school furn-ishings', and this was not the only instance of vandalism and arson in schools.[37] In one Southwark neighbourhood attempts had been made to prevent children from using the drying area on the roof of a block of model dwellings as a playground. Doors and bolts had been fixed, but in a three-month period it was said that '14 dozen locks' had been broken, the children had burned down the door, and even iron gates had not stopped them from gaining access to the roof and throwing stones on people below.[38] There are graffiti, too, and commenting on the improvements in children's drawings since the advent of the Board Schools, the *Westminster Budget* (12 August 1898) described for us how these 'wall sketches' commonly depicted 'the little disagreements which are natural to healthy children'. Here is an example of this Board School artistry: 'This [pointing to a drawing of a girl] is fanny Ives and she is going to have a smack in the Jaw for hitting Nellie Western.'

Smacks in the jaw between little girls are one thing, perhaps, but there were more formidable indications that all was not well with the gentle sex. A brawl among three women, for example, resulted in one of them 'scoring her face with a door key' because the other woman 'tore her hair and beat her with a poker'. Elsewhere, three girls aged 15 and 16 years were brought to court for robbing a woman of 9s 2½d after they had hustled her. Described by the police as a well-known gang of 'expert pick-pockets', the news headlines identified them as 'Girl Hooligans'.[39] There were other mentions of 'Hooligan Girls' and 'Female Hooligans' and their 'hooligan-esque' behaviour. Young women, for example, who were 'arm-in-arm right across the pavement, and kept pushing people off', or another court report which described how 'a respectably-dressed young girl was set upon by four factory girls and unmercifully beaten'. She said that she had 'accidentally brushed against one of the four girls who were standing on the pavement', whereupon 'all four caught hold of her, and beat her in a most savage manner, using fearful language' and left her on the ground bleeding profusely from the nose and mouth.[40]

Sometimes in these accounts of the hurly-burly of the streets, we must feel that we are edging into an unfamiliar world, but here the characters need no introduction and eighty years later their motives are immediately familiar and life-like. We can easily picture the respectably dressed girl, swinging her skirts as she approached, and as she not-quite-accidentally brushed the 'common' girls to one side. We do not need to be told that the factory girls were probably doing their best to make sure that it was impossible for her to pass without brushing against them, and that this would be construed as an insult. Nor to be reminded of their smouldering resentments against this girl of their own age who was so 'lady-like' and 'nose-in-the-air' so that they might feel that she needed to be brought down a peg or two. None of this excuses their behaviour, of course, but this is an unusually human account of an all-too-human encounter in the streets which reminds us of a certain constancy of human motive, and of conflicts built around the human meanings that are attached to the social realities of class, physical appearance and territory. And nothing in these accounts, whether familiar or otherwise, is compatible with the myths peddled by the merchants of nostalgia.

With the sexes thus reunited in the obscure origins of the word 'Hooligan', let us pay a final visit in our tour of these troubled streets and pop in to see Mrs Jenkins and her family of Bean Street, South London, on the occasion of that fateful Bank Holiday. Happily, we find them at home 'sitting on their front door in the cool of the evening, enjoying a song and a glass in a quiet way'.[41] Can this, at last, be a glimpse of that untroubled way of life in the cobbled, horse-drawn streets of Old England?

But no. Quiet, untroubled summer evenings do not usually command the headlines, and trouble arrives quickly enough in the shape of 18-year-old Maria Powers and her young man. Maria (whose name is pronounced 'Mah-Rye-Yah', as in 'Black Maria') is the daughter of a Bean Street neighbour, and suddenly without provocation it is said that she starts an uproar of a fight in which Mrs Jenkins is stabbed. In fact, Mrs Jenkins is left in such a poorly condition that she is unable to present her version of events when the matter is brought before the police court.

Next, Maria Powers is called to give evidence. She is described as 'a decent-looking workgirl, employed at a mineral-

water factory', and hers is a rather different tale of woe.
There is no point denying that there was a 'free fight' in Bean
Street between the Powers' and Jenkins' families, with men
rolling on the ground. Nor that Mrs Jenkins emerged from
the confusion with a knife wound. Maria's only crime, however, was that she was 'peaceably promenading Bean Street'
with her young man, when without provocation the Jenkins
family started 'singing at' her. Here is the offensive chorus of
the song that started the fight:

> Oh, Annie Maria!
> Stick your nose up higher
> You're getting flash and cutting a dash,
> And Bean Street won't hold you much longer![42]

The magistrate listened to all this with a benevolent interest,
although he confessed that it sounded like six-of-one and
half-a-dozen-of-the-other, and that it would be unwise to
take any action without clarifying evidence. And so the miscreants trooped back home to Bean Street, perhaps to ban-
dage the wounds of their neighbourly dispute. As things
stood, no 'crime' had been committed and their moment of
human folly would pass unremembered in the official calendars of criminal acts. Nor are there likely to be any surviving
family snapshots of the Bean Street Bank Holiday stabbing
affray. What self-respecting photographer would have risked
his new-fangled box camera within a stone's throw of a 'free
fight'? Criminal statistics, which reflect only the informal
justice which was held compatible with these all-too-human
streets, and faded photographs of carefully posed moments
of tranquillity, tell us one thing about this 'stable and carefree
era'. The annals of the police courts, and headlines in the
newspapers, tell a rather different story.

Dressed to Kill: the Fashionable Hooligan

One thing that quickly became apparent in the aftermath of
the Bank Holiday affair was that the Hooligans all looked
alike. But it was not in the way that the poor had always

At twelve—his literary   At seventeen—a full-fledged Hooligan
       education

looked alike — it was not, that is, because they were shabby,
shoeless and grubby as moles — but because the gangs wished
to look alike, and had adopted a uniform dress-style. 'Look
at them well,' said *The Daily Graphic* (16 November 1900)
when the dust had settled a little and the danger could be
looked in the face, 'They are the genuine article — real Hooligans':

> The boys affect a kind of uniform. No hat, collar, or tie is to be
> seen. All of them have a peculiar muffler twisted around the neck,

a cap set rakishly forward, well over the eyes, and trousers very tight at the knee and very loose at the foot. The most characteristic part of their uniform is the substantial leather belt heavily mounted with metal. It is not ornamental, but then it is not intended for ornament.

There can be no doubt that the buckle-end of a belt could be a formidable weapon, but in fact the belts were often pricked out in fancy patterns or embellished with metal studs in much the same way that modern motor-bike boys adorn their jackets with stud designs. Newspaper cartoons depicting the London Hooligans added another small detail of fashion: the bell-bottom trousers were shown with a tasty buttoned vent in the side. Local gangs also improvised local variations in style — velvet caps in Battersea or plaid caps in Poplar, for example, as a badge of identity — and there were certainly trend-setters among the Hooligans. One way-out youngster appeared in court following the Bank Holiday disturbances with his hair dressed in what sounds remarkably like the 'Mohican cut' which had a brief moment of popularity among more outlandish Teds in the 1950s and which has reappeared with the Punks. 'The appearance of the witness caused some amusement in court,' observed *The Daily Graphic* (6 August 1898). 'His hair had been clipped as closely as possible to the scalp, with the exception of a small patch on the crown of the head, which was pulled down over the forehead to form a fringe.' It was probably no more than a daring exaggeration of the 'donkey-fringe' style which was the standard Hooligan haircut. But here was a youth so far ahead of his time that if he had turned up on the streets of London sixty or seventy years later, he would still have been recognised as a sure sign of an alarmingly unrivalled degeneration among the young.

What is perhaps even more remarkable, given postwar wisdom about the unparalleled nature of postwar youth cultures, is that the youth style that came to be associated with the London Hooligans was a nationwide phenomenon. In Manchester, the gangs were known as 'Scuttlers' — a word which went back to the 1880s — and their gang fights and rowdyism as 'Scuttling' or 'Scuttles'. Local gangs such as the infamous 'Forty Row' from Ancoats, the 'Bengal Tiger' from Bengal

ALES

THE HERO OF THE HOUR: A HOOLIGAN'S RETURN FROM PRISON

Street, the 'Bungall Boys' from Fairfield Street, 'Alum Street' or 'Hope Street' from Salford would do battle for neighbourhood supremacy, sometimes retiring to parks or open crofts for these engagements. One fight reported from Newton Heath in 1890 involved a pitched battle in Holland Street of between 500 and 600 youths, and shopkeepers were obliged to barricade themselves behind shutters to prevent damage and looting when a 'Scuttle' was announced. The Scuttlers also jealously guarded the territorial seclusion of their local beer-house — known as the 'blood-house' or 'blood-tub' — and they were such a force in Lancashire that the public authorities made various petitions to the Home Secretary for sterner repressive measures to put them down.[43] Charles Russell described the Scuttler's appearance:

> You knew him by his dress. A loose white scarf would adorn his throat; his hair was plastered down upon his forehead; he wore a peaked cap rather over one eye; his trousers were of fustian, and cut — like a sailor's — with 'bell bottoms'. This fashion of the trousers was the most distinctive feature of his attire and make-up.[44]

In 1890 Alex Devine, Police Court Missioner to Lads in Salford, had described how the 'professional scuttler' was attired in a 'puncher's cap', 'narrow-go-wides' trousers, and narrow-toed brass-tipped clogs. Devine was particularly taken by the ornamental designs on the Scuttlers' belts, produced with metal pins: 'These designs include figures of serpents, a heart pierced with an arrow (this appears to be a favourite design), Prince of Wales' feathers, clogs, animals, stars, etc., and often either the name of the wearer of the belt or that of some woman.'[45]

Early in the new century the Manchester and Salford Scuttlers were succeeded by a new generation calling themselves 'Ikes' or 'Ikey Lads', a name which may have had something to do with distinctive dress-styles made by Jewish tailor shops. Robert Roberts recalls that the Scuttler's girl friend also had her own style of dress — 'clogs and shawl and a skirt with vertical stripes'[46] — although I know of no other references to female attire, and as usual within these hooligan preoccupations attention was rootedly fixed on the boys.

In Birmingham, corner boys and street gangs were known as 'Peaky Blinders', or less commonly as 'Sloggers', and they too had adopted the standard uniform of bell-bottom trousers, neck scarf, heavy belt, peaked cap and short cropped hair

'Done half-a-moon'

with a 'donkey fringe'.[47] There was even a character in *Comic Cuts* in the 1890s, a youthful prowler named 'Area Sneaker' — and what a pseudonym that is to conjure with from this supposedly untroubled late Victorian era — who reflected the fashion. Young Area Sneaker was the faithful companion of 'Chokee Bill', himself a prototypical comic-strip crook with swag-bag and cosh, and in their weekly scrapes with the law — personified for *Comic Cuts* readers in the ineffectual shape of 'Fairyfoot the Fat Cop' — he was quite recognisably dressed in a budding Hooligan's attire: bell-bottoms, flowing neck-scarf, cap set at a jaunty angle, and boots two sizes too big.[48]

The Scuttlers, Peaky Blinders and Area Sneaker himself all pre-dated the christening of the Hooligans, and in other towns there were similar gangs — the 'Grey Mare Boys' from Bradford or the 'High Rip' gangs of Liverpool — and London also had an earlier tradition of gangs such as the 'Tiger Bay', the 'Monkeys' Parade' gang at Bow, or the 'Bowry Boys' of Poplar who were already in evidence in the late 1880s. It is possible that some elements of the Hooligan dress-style were derived from the clothes favoured by costermongers in mid-nineteenth-century London. Henry Mayhew described how the costers preferred tasty cable-cord trousers, 'made to fit tightly at the knee and swell gradually until they reached the boot, which they nearly cover'. The bell-bottom trousers, together with the King's Man neck-scarf, a small cloth cap and well-kept boots were the main features of the coster style. The boots, Mayhew tells us, were an object of special pride, often 'tastily ornamented . . . with a heart or thistle, surrounded by a wreath of roses, worked below the instep'.[49] We should remember from Mayhew's account that the boots also came in handy for kicking policemen and other traditional foes of the costers. Arthur Morrison's subsequent descriptions in *A Child of the Jago* (1896) of the clothes in fashion among the cosh-carrying denizens of the slums again resembled Mayhew's costers. However, his version of the Jago people buying their 'kicksies', 'benjies' and 'daisies' — that is, their trousers, coats and boots ('daisy roots') — from a local 'ikey' tailor may simply have been borrowed from Mayhew. In any case, Morrison's narrative of violent neighbourhood rivalries, robberies and attacks on policemen — 'for kicking practice' as he put it — did not need to be either borrowed or invented in late nineteenth-century London.[50]

The 'Hooligan' fashion also bore a resemblance to that of their Australian cousins, the 'Larrikins', who wore a uniform of high-heeled boots, bell-bottom trousers, neck scarves, heavy belts and snazzy hats. Before the word 'Hooligan' had fully established itself in England, young ruffians were often described as youths of the 'Larrikin type' or as 'London

Comic Cuts characters in 1897, from left to right: 'Fairyfoot the Fat Cop', determined to look the wrong way; young 'Area Sneaker' in Hooligan attire; his bulky companion 'Chokee Bill'; and a representative of the outraged respectable public.

Larrikins'.[51] The Larrikins, who can be traced back to 1870 in Australia, were also organised into local gangs or 'pushes', and even allowing for exaggeration and over-involvement (we need not readily accept, for example, that they gorged themselves on raw meat or rigged elections by terrorising voters, as was sometimes alleged) their behaviour was unbeatably appalling. Assaults on policemen, Chinese and defenceless women, window-smashing, gang fights, breaking up holiday resorts, and gobbing on the steps of churches and also the worshippers assembled there, were among their least terrible adventures. A verse from the *Sydney Bulletin* in 1882 summed up a familiar controversy about how to interpret a phenomenon such as Larrikinism:

> The larrikin is all a myth,
>   An ideal scourge, forsooth;
> And all that we are troubled with,
>   'Exuberance of Youth!'
>
> Thus David, oracle sublime,
>   Propounds a wondrous truth;
> This is the hoodlum's simple crime,
>   'Exuberance of Youth!'
>
> That blacken'd eye, that broken beak,
>   That swiftly loosened tooth,
> These little trifles but bespeak,
>   'Exuberance of Youth!'
>
> That language foul which shocks the ear
>   Of some fair modest Ruth —
> What of it? Don't you know it's mere
>   'Exuberance of Youth!'[52]

We must leave the question of the origins of the 'Hooligan' style where it rests, however, as simply one murky aspect of an otherwise murky affair. It is difficult enough, in any case, to unravel how contemporary youth styles such as 'Skinheads' or 'Teddy Boys' originated and were disseminated, and we can recognise the Hooligan uniform for what it was: a simple adaptation of the clothing available to young working-class people in order to create an easily reproducible style. The Scuttlers in their clogs and fustian would no doubt look somewhat dowdy alongside modern youth in their crease-proof, sta-prest trousers, their swinging blue jeans, or their body-hugging drip-dry shirts. But the rudimentary nature of the 'Hooligan' style was not in any essential way different from the later youth fashions in the 'affluent' postwar era where the kids would put together their 'unprecedented' styles out of various permutations of available scraps such as tight trousers, baggy trousers, long hair, short hair, no hair, jeans, braces, T-shirts, string ties, broad ties, no ties, heavy boots, narrow winkle-picker shoes, long jackets, short jackets, etc. With the Punks, of course, this jumble-sale of fashion would arrive at a self-consciously surreal conclusion in that the scraps were now held together, literally and very visibly, with safety-pins. As for the Hooligans, newspaper cartoonists' sketches of their dress permutation depicted a more sharply defined style than anything that can be discerned by modern eyes from surviving photographs of the period — although that should not surprise us, because it is also a characteristic feature of the emphasis given to the cut of clothes within 'high' fashion sketches. The essential point, moreover, is that the 'Hooligan' style was recognisable to their contemporaries (and presumably to themselves) as a distinctive mode of attire, thus helping to form the feeling which was struggling to give itself expression in other areas, that too much freedom and affluence had been given to the working class at the turn of the century. The evening promenade, ridiculed as the 'monkey walk', when young people gathered together in their finery hoping to 'click' with a member of the opposite sex was another sure sign of the unchaperoned freedoms of the new street people who would inherit the new century. Not only could slum youth sometimes afford to pay their fines when they appeared in the police courts — a shocking enough fact to their respectable contemporaries that was often re-marked upon — but they could even pick and choose what clothes they would wear when they came to court. Where would it all end?

Was the Hooligan Armed?

Amidst the excitement of what *The Daily Mail* (17 August 1898) aptly termed 'Hooliganiana', accusations and counter-accusations flew thick and fast about whether the sudden alarm was justified. However, of all the confusions that confront us the rumours alleging that the Hooligan gangs were armed with guns are particularly difficult to unravel, or to state in any balanced way.

Without doubt, the late Victorian and Edwardian gangs did not restrict themselves to fist fights or kicking contests. A private collection of weapons confiscated from Manchester Scuttlers included 'old cutlasses, pokers, pieces of strap having iron bolts affixed to the end, the tops of stone "pop" bottles fastened at the end of a piece of string and used for whirling round the head, specially made pieces of iron . . . knives, and loaded sticks'.[53] Describing how the boys of Cable Street would 'constitute themselves, without asking the permission of the War Office, into a small regiment', Besant provided another inventory of this street-fighting armoury:

> They arm themselves with clubs, with iron bars, with leather belts to which buckles belong, with knotted handkerchiefs containing stones — a lethal weapon — with sling and stones, with knives even, with revolvers of the 'toy' kind, and they go forth to fight the lads of Brook Street. It is a real fight.[54]

Of the last point, I think we can be sure, although Walter Besant was obviously less confident that they were armed with 'real' guns. In the penny oracles of the press, however, there were bolder accusations as when *The Daily Graphic* (16 November 1900) confidently asserted that 'the pistol is the ideal weapon of the Hooligan . . .his love for it can be traced directly to the influence of the "penny dreadfuls" '. Or when the London *Echo* (7 February 1898) warned of 'the young street ruffian or prowler, with his heavy belt, treacherous knife and dangerous pistol'.

There can be no doubt that in the early years of the twentieth century the use of revolvers was widespread among adult mobsters in London's criminal underworld, and that feuds between rival outfits were not uncommonly settled by gun battles in the open streets.[55] What does seem more difficult to believe, however, is that the practice of carrying firearms was habitual among Hooligans. The streets may not have been nearly so safe as nostalgia for 'Old England' suggests, but it is likely that if working-class youths had been firing off guns throughout London, then we would have heard a little bit more about the matter.

Even so, the question of the 'pistol gangs' was not entirely a mare's nest. Cases of wounding by pistol shots occasionally came before the courts and in at least one instance a child was killed, although apparently by accident, which nevertheless brought great notoriety to the so-called 'Clerkenwell Pistol Gang'. The background to this affair involved rivalries between the gangs of Chapel Street and Margaret Street. 'The lads', it was said, 'were in the habit of attending a cheap place of amusement at Sadler's Wells, and quarrels arose about girls who accompanied them.' In an ensuing fight around Christmas time 1896 the police had swooped and arrested twenty-eight youths some of whom were found to be in possession of pistols, which was taken to link them to a young girl's death — although this was some months later. Another 15-year-old youth, arrested for an entirely separate offence — pushing people off the pavement — was also subsequently charged, and the upshot was that five youths (including one 15-year-old girl) received prison sentences ranging from three weeks to six months.[56] It was an extremely murky business, but on any reckoning the details do not seem to add up to systematic armed gang warfare. Nor do other reported pistol cases: such as a 13-year-old boy who shot an 18-year-old in the leg on a canal tow-path, or a boy of 14 who was charged with shooting his 2-year-old brother.[57]

The allegations suggesting regular armed combat among Hooligans usually mentioned pistols or 'toy pistols'. A case that caused some alarm in 1908, however, revealed that revolvers could also fall into the hands of youths. What proved particularly shocking in this instance was that the licensing of firearms was so haphazard that a 16-year-old Whitechapel youth, who had already stood trial on a charge of wounding his 16-year-old girlfriend with a revolver, could obtain a licence at a later date without even having to show proof of his age. The girl had not been seriously hurt in the shooting, suffering only a superficial wound, and police reports said that she was 'fortunately wearing a large quantity of underclothing which, no doubt, prevented a more serious wound' — which, unless the young lady's underwear was armour-plated, must cast serious doubt on the power of the weapon employed. Having secured his new gun licence, however, the youth, who was said by the police to be 'nightly associated with a gang of Hooligans who undoubtedly used revolvers', had then waltzed into such a commonplace retail outlet as a barber's shop and purchased a five-chamber revolver.[58]

For some years attempts had been made to prohibit the sale of firearms and a Pistols Bill had been presented to Parliament in 1893. Describing it as 'grandmotherly legislation', Charles Hopwood figured largely in opposition to the Bill, believing it to be an encroachment on the rights of the free-born Englishman. 'Why should not Englishmen arm themselves?' he asked. 'It was natural, and they should not interfere with such a right. Why did they not interfere with catapults? — these did more injury than other weapons.'[59] There was nothing in the Parliamentary debate, in fact, to suggest that the pistol cases were particularly serious and the Bill was easily thrown out — although it must be admitted that the gentlemen of Westminster have more than once shown a remarkable capacity for getting things wrong.

The continuing refusal of the Home Secretary's Department to support the prohibition of pistols provoked controversy for some years. *The Clarion* (24 December 1898) seemed to think that the Home Secretary's intransigence was some kind of Malthusian plot:

> For our little girls and boys
> With pistols and such 'toys'
> May shoot each other indiscriminately
> 'It will lessen the population,
> 'Tis a blessing to the nation,
> In disguise', he seeme to utter sedately.

In another discussion of 'Those Pistol Cases' *The Daily Graphic* (15 February 1898) had taken a more traditional line, recommending more traditional remedies: 'If birching and short sentences will not stop it, then more birching and longer sentences will have to be tried.'

The case which had prompted these remarks involved a 13-year-old schoolboy, John Bird from Camden, who had shot an 18-year-old greengrocer's son in the arm. Engaged in a quarrel, in which some bullying might have been going on, the younger boy had produced a pistol and shouted: 'You won't touch me when I have this. I'll put daylight into you.' The victim had then chased the boy and caught him, before realising that he had been shot in the arm, which once more suggests that it cannot have been a terribly powerful weapon. But *The Daily Graphic* drew the gravest conclusions, suggesting that whereas earlier shooting cases had been accidents, they had become increasingly frequent and serious:

> The latest pistol cases have almost all been cases of boys, hardly in their teens, deliberately using pistols as weapons of aggression ... Those "gangs" of young ruffians who terrorise certain districts of the metropolis seem, in fact, to be provided with firearms, and to think little more of discharging them than they would of throwing stones.

Wherever we might finally strike the balance, it seems clear that whereas nostalgia for the once-safe streets and the once-quiet youth is phoney, we can be equally sure that those who sensationalised the 'pistol gangs' sometimes got carried away with themselves. We must remember, even so, that this was the golden age's own assessment of its own golden youth, and the repeated alarms about pistol gangs gives a further indication of the depth of the fears surrounding working-class youth at this time. Because while from the safety of our historical vantage point we may doubt whether this kind of incident was anything more than an isolated occurrence, and while the details leave room to quibble about the gravity of the wounding cases, to commentators at the turn of the century here was a sure sign that something dangerously new was afoot, which had come all-too-terribly alive in the person of the 'Hooligan'.

Perhaps one final vignette can move us closer to a balanced view of the Hooligan's weaponry. After Parliament had eventually passed a Pistols Act in 1903, the police were persuaded in 1907 to bring a charge against the London firm

of Gamages at Holborn who were advertising pistols for sale
through the post. The weapon was an air-pistol with a barrel
extending to 7½ inches, and this was probably the kind of
'toy' most commonly available to youths. The police were
advised that it was a potentially fatal weapon, but when the
case was brought before Mr Bros at Clerkenwell, he ruled
that although the pistol was a 'weapon' it was not a 'firearm',
and so did not fall within the prohibitions of the Act. The
police pursued this question of 'pop-gun or firearm', as
it came to be known, through a High Court which referred
the matter back to the magistrate. Whereupon Mr Gamage
himself appeared and stated that he was fully prepared to
be shot in the hand from close range, in the full view of the
court, in order to defend his honour and his business interests.
The magistrate was having none of this, however, believing
that it would lower the dignity of the law, although the
prosecuting counsel had a better idea and asked Mr Gamage
if he was equally prepared to be shot in the face. Mr Gamage
declined the offer, and given his proximity to the matter, his
is perhaps the most adequately balanced appraisal of 'Those
Pistol Cases' that can be reached.[60] Mr Gamage was fined
20 shillings on two summonses, plus one guinea costs. Boys,
however, should be birched.

The Hooligan Prepares for War

> For it's Tommy this, an' Tommy that, an' 'Tommy wait outside';
> But it's 'Special train for Atkins' when the trooper's on the tide . . .
> For it's Tommy this, an' Tommy that, an' 'Chuck him out, the brute!'
> But it's 'Saviour of his country' when the guns begin to shoot.[61]

Armed or otherwise, the Hooligan was in the headlines. In
November 1898 it was said that effigies representing 'Hooliganism' were burned on Guy Fawkes Night,[62] although the
new folk devil was destined for even more global notoriety.
Early in the new century, for example, the Hooligan's name
was snapped up as far away as Tsarist Russia where it was
used to describe crimes as diverse as murder, arson and rape,
as well as a wide scatter of mischief such as obscenity, win-

dow-breaking and stone-throwing, defacing buildings, singing indecent songs, blocking public thoroughfares, brawling and stealing carriage wheels. Sometimes mistaken for the name of a tribe of redskins, the word 'Hooliganism' established itself in Russia with such authority and incomprehensible rapidity that one observer thought in 1912 that it was 'as if it had long been expected, as if necessary for the filling of an empty space'.[63]

Back home, the observation would have been no less apt. In the years leading up to the First World War the Hooligan embarked on a remarkable career, appearing in name if not in person before numerous governmental and semi-official bodies of enquiry. He loomed large in the apocalyptic discourse surrounding the fears of racial decline and physical inefficiency. He figured centrally in the Edwardian era's deliberations on the 'boy labour' question. He would crop up repeatedly in the anxious preoccupation with the demoralising influence of popular amusements, the collapse of 'fair play' sportsmanship, and the allegations of excessive 'freedom' and 'affluence' that were levelled against the young. The name of the Hooligan, in fact, provided a crystallising focus for any number of overlapping anxieties associated with imperial decline, military incapacity, the erosion of social discipline and moral authority, the eclipse of family life, and what was feared to be the death rattle of 'Old England'.

Most emphatic, however, was the feeling that some new initiative was required in the education and early work training of youths, to rescue them from the undisciplined authority of the streets. The authority of the Board Schools (otherwise known as the 'Bored Schools') was widely regarded as suspect and frail. 'It is a common experience', said Urwick, 'to find a boy a Jekyll in the classroom, and a Hyde in the street.'[64] Even so, as Arnold Freeman argued in *Boy Life and Labour* (1914) if it were not for the admittedly frail system of compulsory schooling, 'we should be manufacturing a race of hooligans who would make our existing civilisation an impossibility'.[65]

When the Hooligans first put in an appearance, the floggers and die-hards had been much in evidence, but they were

eased aside with the growing recognition that Hooliganism
was a pointer towards a general dislocation among the youth
— and not just a 'hard core' — and that the problem was
therefore immune to a narrow penal response. The task,
then, was to supplement the existing system of elementary
education and an extraordinary range of schemes were
proposed (although not necessarily implemented) for gym-
nasia and football pitches, Continuation Schools and night
classes, schemes of physical training and drill, fresh air
funds and camping holidays, and all manner of initiatives
within the boy's club movement from Bible classes to boxing
clubs. On occasion the underlying philosophy was extremely
crude, recommending that 'if you provided them with footballs and made them kick footballs, they would not be so
inclined to kick policemen in the street'.[66] More usually,
however, it was the public school ethos that was embraced,
linking sporting activities to the development of *esprit de
corps* and instruction in the art of 'playing the game'.[67]
Above all, advised Viscount Haldane the War Secretary in
1911, the scope of national education must be enlarged to
include moral instruction and physical training 'if you want
to eliminate the hooligan'.[68]

In the space of a few years the word 'hooligan' had outstripped its humble local origins and its specific reference
to London gang life (it had also begun to lose its capital 'H')
and had come to be understood and feared as a much more
general affliction among the nation's youth. The feeling, if
not the reality, that hooliganism was a universal problem
could be gauged by Baden-Powell's anguished calculations
in *Scouting for Boys*:

> We have at the present time in Great Britain 2 million boys, of
> whom a quarter to a half a million are under good influence out-
> side their school walls ... The remainder are drifting towards
> 'hooliganism' or bad citizenship for want of hands to guide them
> ... just for the want of a guiding hand or two ... Cannot we find
> these guiding hands amongst us?[69]

As the new word gained in popularity, military allusions
also came thick and fast. Within weeks, the *Westminster
Gazette* (15 September 1898) had taken it up in order to

ridicule the enemy forces in the Sudan campaign. 'The KHALIFA with his 50,000 Dervishes was a powerful foe,' it was admitted, 'but . . . the KHALIFA was, after all, only a sort of Soudanese Hooligan.' Lord May cast a different slant on the word early in the new century when he called for a 'Hooligan Conference', later to go under the more dignified title of the Twentieth Century League. 'As for Hooliganism,' he explained, 'it consists really in a mis-application of energy. High spirits that would be of use on board a man-of-war or on the march find vent in "bashing" the casual pedestrian or demolishing coffee stalls.'[70]

But perhaps the most remarkable adaptation of this versatile word was to be found in Robert Buchanan's fierce attack on Rudyard Kipling's poetry, which he denounced in 1899 as 'The Voice of the Hooligan'. In Kipling's verse, especially *The Barrack-Room Ballads*, Buchanan argued that the British army was portrayed as 'a wild carnival of drunken, bragging, boasting Hooligans in red coats and seamen's jackets, shrieking to the sound of the banjo and applauding the English flag'. 'The Tommie Atkins they introduce', he insisted, 'is a drunken, swearing, coarse-minded Hooligan, for whom, nevertheless, our sympathy is eagerly entreated.' It was not that Buchanan doubted the accuracy of Kipling's descriptions of army outrages: soldiers rampaging drunkenly in the streets, for example, fighting with the buckle-ends of their belts. His objection was that these poetic celebrations of the coarse side of army life were an offence against English traditions of Christian civilisation, forming part of a larger 'back wave' which was manifesting itself in various ways: 'the Hooligan in Politics, in Literature, and Journalism', 'the Hooligan spirit of patriotism', and all the other barbaric symptoms of 'the restless and un-instructed Hooliganism of the time' above which 'the flag of a Hooligan Imperialism is raised'.[71]

The irony of Buchanan's attack on 'Hooligan Imperialism' was that one important way in which the Hooligan figured within the troubled preoccupations of his contemporaries was precisely as a fighting-fit recruit for the imperial armies. What was never entirely clear was whether Hooliganism represented the end-point of the evolutionary deterioration of the 'Imperial Race', or just the kind of rough boys needed as a warrior class to defend the Empire. The Hooligan, in fact, was not at all unlike Rudyard Kipling's celebrated 'Fuzzy-Wuzzy' who broke the British square: 'a pore benighted 'eathen but a first-class fightin' man'.[72]

The confusion was there from the beginning. *The Spectator* (27 August 1898) had provided the clearest statement of the degenerative thesis, identifying the 'London Larrikins' as a throwback or 'reverted type' which was said to be 'one of the very central ideas of evolutionary doctrine' produced by 'every kind of artificial civilisation'. E. J. Urwick, on the other hand, found it difficult to reconcile talk about 'the decline of physical energy' with 'a class of boys bursting with animal energy'.[73] And he was not alone. Thomas Holmes thought that slum youth were faced with a simple choice, 'whether to become dull-eyed, weak-chested, slow-witted degenerates, or hooligans. Of the two, I prefer the latter.' 'What can big lads of this description do in such surroundings?' he asked. 'Either to stay in their insufferable homes, or to kick up their heels in the streets . . . Curl up and die, or go out and kick somebody. The pity is that they always kick the wrong person.'[74] Charles Russell also found much to admire in his Manchester Scuttlers, seeing in their violent gang fights a 'sense of comradeship' which he could not altogether disapprove of: 'The "Scuttler" was not wholly bad; he would rather be a blackguard than a dullard. His real desires, as I have said, were natural and healthy . . . Here at least was force, and something can be made of that.'[75]

There was no doubt a certain amount of wishful thinking in these common beliefs that gang fights represented some kind of scaled-down patriotism, but Britain's military pre-occupations were never too far out of sight when Hooliganism was on the agenda, involving reversals such as these on the Hooligan's worth and character. Baden-Powell, the man who galvanised the hopes and fears of Edwardian England into a truly spectacular social movement, was also given to some equally spectacular celebrations of Hooliganism. 'Scouting attracts the hooligans,' he told the National Defence Association in 1910, 'who are really the fellows of character if you can turn them in the right way; and no doubt these fellows will be of some use to us in the future instead of being absolute waste material, fit only to be buried.'[76]

There was considerable irony in the fact that it was Baden-Powell, the maverick hero of Mafeking, who should come to rescue England from its Hooligans, if only because the feverish excitement of the jingo crowds and the 'Mafficking' that accompanied the South African campaign was thought to be no less of an affront to the English *sang froid* than 'Hooliganism' itself. There may even have been a certain temperamental affinity between Baden-Powell's Scouting philosophy and the restless energies of Hooliganism, and he was even so outrageous as to recommend the Hooligans to the National Defence Association as 'the best class of boy':

> We say to a boy, 'Come and be good.' Well, the best class of boy — that is, the Hooligan — says, 'I'm blowed if I'm going to be good!' We say, 'Come and be a red Indian, and dress like a Scout', and he will come along like anything.

Predictably, his remarks invited the characteristic reversal of the problem, when a member of the National Defence Association asked:

> You referred to hooligans. Do the Boy Scouts touch a class that really want stirring up more than the hooligans — that is, I think what you call the lower middle class? ... If your movement does that, or will do it, that will be helping very much. It is a class that wants stirring up very much indeed.[77]

In common with so much of this history of respectable fears, we find ourselves once more in the realm of feeling rather than fact, for although Baden-Powell never tired of claiming that Scouting could reach the Hooligans, on the available evidence it would seem that the movement's major recruiting base was among middle-class and lower middle-class youths, rather than among slum youth.[78] Nor did Baden-Powell's optimism about reclaiming 'unclubbable' Hooligans receive universal support within the boys' club movement. The Reverend Peter Green warned in *How to Deal with Lads* (1911) of how 'the club is rushed by a swarm of rough lads whom you don't know and over whom it is impossible to exercise any control'.[79] Urwick also poured cold water on the idea, believing that boys' clubs could only cure Hooligans if there were 'a separate club for every one or two, but not otherwise ... Any gang of hooligans will quickly break up any club.'[80] It would also appear that in some areas the rougher element ganged up against Boy Scout troops in the early years of the movement, throwing stones at them and mocking their uniform of floppy hats and silly short pants.[81] In any case, what did the Hooligan want with a uniform? He already had his own.

We must entertain doubts about Baden-Powell's enthusiasm for Hooligans, and the extent to which it represented Edwardian wish-fulfilment rather than real accomplishment. But there can be no doubt that the Boy Scouts made an extraordinary impact on the era. When *Scouting for Boys* first appeared in a series of fortnightly instalments in 1908, the fly-leaf of the final issue was already claiming that 'at the present moment something between 500,000 and 700,000 young men are interested in this scheme, which will come into full swing about April'. The figures were wildly optimistic, although the real events were dramatic enough in themselves. Within not much more than a year, the Boy Scouts had already outstripped the older Boys' Brigade and Church Lads' Brigade movements, claiming more than 100,000 members by 1910. By the outbreak of war, with the Boy Scouts riding along on the crest of a wave, the figure stood at 150,000. When the war ended it had reached 200,000 and by the early 1920s there were a quarter of a million Boy Scouts.[82]

The wildfire growth of the Boy Scouts serves to remind us of the enormity of the Edwardian era's preoccupation with its youth, and the groundswell of not only national enthusiasm but also deep funds of social anxiety. Dissuaded by his friend and mentor Arthur Pearson from his original intention to call the movement the 'Imperial Scouts', Baden-Powell performed a remarkable juggling act in the early editions of *Scouting for Boys* where he struck every nerve of the Edwardian anxiety — as fresh air philosophies, nature study and camp fire yarns jostled for space alongside a tub-thumping

imperialism, anti-socialist harangues and shuddering prophecies of racial doom. On the militarist question, there can be
no doubt that the Boy Scouts made a significant contribution
to the growth of the war mentality, although the early movement was nearly torn apart by the question of militarism
which eventually led to break-away groups such as the Woodcraft Folk.[83]

Even so, Baden-Powell's own response to the military
associations of the Boy Scouts was extremely uneven. It is
hardly surprising that in the aftermath of the First World
War, when there was a rising current of anti-militarism, the
Boy Scout Association felt it necessary to issue a disclaimer
in 1920: 'Our Scouting has nothing to do with SOLDIERING;
it is merely the practice of backwoodsmanship ... We do
not preach war and bloodshed to the lads, and we do not
favour military drill for them.'[84] Following the war, a
great deal of redrafting of the official creed took place, and
Scouting for Boys was repeatedly updated so that not only
was militarism explicitly disowned, but the earlier racial
imperialism was swapped for international brotherhood and
goodwill.

Before the Great War, however, Baden-Powell's public
attitude towards the military significance of the Boy Scouts
had been hedged about with all sorts of reservations, and he
had always actively disfavoured drill which he thought
produced merely mechanical obedience. True enough, in
the original imprint of *Scouting for Boys* he had sounded
off with all the usual gusto about 'How the Empire Must
be Held':

> The surest way to keep peace is to be prepared for war. Don't be
> cowards ... You know at school how if a swaggering ass comes
> along and threatens to bully you, he only does so because he thinks
> you will give in to him ... And it is just the same with nations.

There was much more in the same vein. For example: 'There
is a very great danger, because we have many enemies abroad,
and they are growing daily stronger and stronger.' Or: 'Manliness can only be taught by men, and not by those who are
half men, half old women.' Or: 'Your forefathers worked

hard, fought hard, and died hard to make this Empire for you. Don't let them look down from heaven, and see you loafing about with your hands in your pockets, doing nothing to keep it up.' And finally: 'Don't merely talk, like some gas-bags do, about shedding the last drop of your blood for your country – the difficulty with them, when the time comes, is getting them to shed the FIRST drop of their blood.'[85]

However, after this early burst of full-frontal militarism, Baden-Powell became decidedly shy about the matter. Perhaps there was some amount of crafty deception here, as he explained to the National Defence Association: 'By not insisting on military drill we catch a lot of boys who would otherwise have no idea of coming into the education that we are trying to give.' The meeting's chairman, Sir George Taubman-Goldie, KCMG, quickly cottoned on to the idea:

> I think Sir Robert is very wise in keeping out the appearance of militarism; but the Boy Scouts must, little by little, familiarise the parents of this country with the idea of national defence. Many a mother, proud of seeing her boy coming back with badges . . . will become a convert. I say mothers, because it is the mothers we have to look to.[86]

'Softly, softly, catchee monkey' was one of Baden-Powell's mottos for his Boy Scouts, and no doubt the same stealthy philosophy was in evidence here. In the following year, addressing the Royal United Services Institute, he was to be found covering his tracks across the same ground: 'They accept us now; they used to suspect us of being a trap to catch boys for the Army . . . Anti-military parents will allow their sons to join the Boy Scouts, but prohibit them from joining a Cadet Corps . . . So we will fill a gap.'[87]

We find ourselves in one of the gathering grounds of Edwardian opinion, moving towards a resolution of its deeply felt anxieties. We must remember that there was no compulsory army conscription in Britain – compulsion in schools was bad enough, and standing armies had long been anathema to the 'freeborn Englishman' – and it was not until the years following the Second World War that compulsory national service would come into existence in peace-time Britain. But there were powerful pressure groups at work such as the militarist National Service League who were not slow to advance their cause by arguing that compulsory military training would act as a tonic against 'the physical and moral degeneracy attendant upon industrial civilisation'.[88] Militarism also infected some sections of the socialist movement, as in the later jingo-outpourings of Robert Blatchford of *The Clarion*. 'A mob of pale-faced, weedy ragamuffins,' wrote Blatchford in *My Life in the Army* (1910), 'with town stoops and town slouches had become clean, well-groomed, alert, upstanding young soldiers, with bronzed faces, muscular arms, and bright eyes . . . We were new men . . . I am strongly in favour of compulsory universal military training.'[89] No doubt Sergeant Blatchford and Lieutenant-General Baden-Powell would have found much to argue about — not least the question of full-time socialist agitators — but here was agreement of sorts, although as we have seen Baden-Powell was more inclined to smuggle in militarism behind fresh air philosophies, nature study and the smoke of jolly camp fires. 'We put patriotism and self-sacrifice into them, and there is no doubt that after they have learnt a certain amount of that,' he explained as he outlined his strategy to the National Defence Association, 'they will feel bound to take up the defence in one form or another, should it be necessary, when the time comes.'[90]

'When the time comes . . . ' It was a phrase that Baden-Powell let slip more than once in his speeches and writings in the thickening twilight before war. And when the time did come, there was great rejoicing in the land that Britain had recovered its sense of purpose and destiny.[91] There was also a renewed enthusiasm for the birching of boys' bottoms in the courts.[92] But as the news leaked back from the trenches of the horror and futile brutality of the Great War, the mood changed to one of sorrow and mistrust, and even an old trooper like Baden-Powell could not hide his feelings. 'The convulsion of war has opened our eyes to many strange things', he wrote in 1919, 'Few of us had realised till war had exposed it how thin is the veneer of civilisation over the underlying animal proclivities . . . the failure of religion to direct, and education to balance, the actions of men.'[93]

When Britain came to mourn her dead — three-quarters of a million killed, nearly two million wounded — the 'lost generation' of the First World War would usually be remembered as the flower of the youth, the cream, the Oxford lieutenants, the gifted warrior poets, the junior officers, the early volunteers. But no doubt some of the original Hooligans — 'instead of being absolute waste material, fit only to be buried' as Baden-Powell had somewhat indelicately described the goal of reclamation — were buried alongside them, remembered only in the writings and memoirs of youth workers which act as their tombstones. 'Very soon after the campaign of unspeakable suffering had commenced,' James Butterworth wrote in 1932, 'those who had laboured long in building up a club saw the once-hooligan juniors, who had become stalwart seniors, whipped away as by magic . . . All the struggles of years appeared wasted.' 'If the wholesale destruction of Youth be considered a saner method for world betterment than training the Boy,' he added as the bitterness showed through, 'then the club movement will not press its claim.'[94]

AN UNEQUAL MATCH

PART THREE
The Stable Traditions

Is not every juvenile delinquent the evidence of a family in which the family bond is weakened and loosened? Is not every dishonest apprentice an evidence of the same? Is not every trustless servant an evidence of the same; every ruined female, every ruined youth, the infinite numbers of unruly and criminal people who now swarm on the surface of this great kingdom, and inundate the streets of this great city, and fill these huge calendars of crime which our Judges and our Juries can hardly find time to dispose of?

Edward Irving, *The Last Days*, 1829

The morals of the children are tenfold worse than formerly.

Lord Ashley, House of Commons, 28 February 1843

Educate! Educate! is the cry of the day, or England's flag may be struck, and her sun set forever in a sea of blood.

Micaiah Hill, *Juvenile Delinquency*, 1853

The dangerous classes seem to be getting the better of society ... Under the influence of philanthropic sentiments and a hopeful policy, we have deprived the law of its terrors and justice of its arms.

The Times, 2 January 1863

6

A New Variety of Crime

If the original Hooligans do not confirm the lovingly remembered traditions of order and stability in late Victorian and Edwardian England, then what of the generations that went before them? To their contemporaries, with a few notable exceptions, the Hooligans' violence was a sure sign of a novel deterioration in the national character, symptomatic of the lowered morality of the new 'city type' or urban degenerate. 'The break-up or impairment of the old ideas of discipline or order, and the life of great cities create occasions for some varieties of crime', is how *The Times* summed up the feeling in 1899. 'Instead of civilisation exterminating them, it seems, though perhaps only temporarily, to encourage some of them ... The pickpocket is dying out, the Hooligan replaces him.'[1]

Different timescales were invoked in order to delineate this sensed deterioration. Grandiose evolutionary theorising on the fate of the 'Imperial Race' presumably implied centuries of wastage and human alteration. But it was also in keeping with the felt rapidity of the descent into a new barbarism that the advance of lawlessness should be phrased within a much more compressed historical scenario. William Tallack, who as Secretary of the Howard Association had experience of criminal affairs reaching back towards the mid-nineteenth century, was among those who took this line. For him, violent crime had advanced because of the excessive leniency of the law: 'the crime of cruel laxity' as he put it. Frowning upon influential American experiments in penal reform and 'the modern and far too numerous school of *pseudo* "humanitarians" ', Tallack recounted in his *Penological and Preventive Principles* (1896) how 'during the last years of the Nineteenth

Century there has arisen in Great Britain, also, a specially cruel class of "humanitarians" so called'. 'Partly as a result of excessive leniency,' he went on in a familiar line of argument, 'there has been developed a pestiferous class of young ruffians who have caused great suffering to the respectable . . . to whom they have become a terror.' And all this had come about 'during the last quarter of the Nineteenth Century'.[2] In other words: 'Twenty Years Ago', before the sentimentalists and do-gooders, when traditional discipline meant that violent ruffianism was unknown. And where have we heard that before?

Another Golden Age . . .

What would we find if we were to accept William Tallack's invitation to retreat a little further into history in search of the lost traditions? If we take his timescale literally and approach the late 1870s and 1880s, and merely flick through the pages of *Punch* magazine − a sure guide to the pulse of respectable discontent in Victorian England − we have an uncanny experience of *déjà vu*, assailed by complaints of assaults by 'roughs' on London's underground railway system; riotous holiday excursions; 'brutal assaults on elderly females' by frightful characters such as 'Burly Jack', 'Bloodstained Bill' and 'Smashjaw Ned'; the streets already disfigured by fights involving 'the too free use of that popular institution the British boot'.[3] We also come across nervous jokes that fashionable Belgravia was to be renamed 'Burglaria' because of the frequency of house-breaking, and numerous stabs against the ineffectual reassurance of 'the defective police', the 'seldom-at-Home-Secretary' and his 'not-at-Home-Department'. The sentimentalists are there, too, as Mr Punch lampooned the sumptuous diet afforded to convicts and the dancing lessons provided for the 'Roughs' in Her Majesty's Prisons.[4]

The early 1880s also witnessed some quite extraordinary scenes of disorder when an organisation calling itself the 'Skeleton Army' mobilised these same roughs against the Salvation Army, attacking their meetings and bombarding the

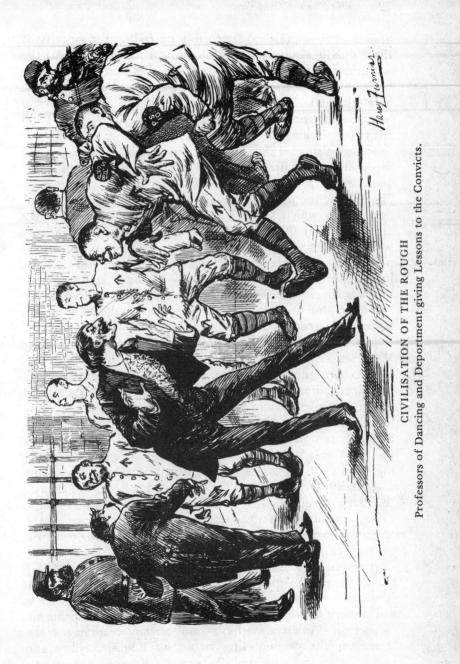

CIVILISATION OF THE ROUGH

Professors of Dancing and Deportment giving Lessons to the Convicts.

houses of sympathisers. Ostensibly defending the sanctity of the Sabbath against the joyful musical interruptions of the Salvationists, it was reported from one area that rioting Skeletonites were dressed in 'coloured rags and tinsel, masks, helmets, and other pantomime clothing', and in several localities police chiefs found it necessary to ban Salvation Army processions for fear of riots.[5]

It was also in 1883, amidst considerable alarm about the increasing use of firearms by burglars, that the London police were armed for the first time in their history. Government papers sanctioning the issue of arms referred to 'the constant dangers' to which London was exposed, which 'were never greater than at this present time'. Some sections of the press were apprehensive about the 'un-Englishness' of an armed police, but within a year 821 police constables had received instruction in the use of firearms — although some of their senior officers believed that their men were 'nervous and excitable', 'men of excitable temperament' who were 'not to be trusted to use revolvers with discretion'.[6]

It is not exactly an auspicious beginning to our search for Victorian civility, and if we journey up North things are no better. According to Mr Punch 'kicking out teeth' was a regular pastime among the good citizens of Oldham, and Salford — which would give birth to the Scuttlers at some later point in the 1880s — was already on the boil. 'Rowdy Salford', complained a local rag in 1876, was too much in the headlines: 'Brutal Assault in Salford: Maliciously Wounding with a Knife'; 'A Kicking Case in Broughton'; 'Knocking a Man's Eye Out in Salford'; 'Assault with a Poker in Salford'; 'Breaking a Woman's Jaw in Salford'; 'Another Assault on the Police in Salford'. Or, to strike another familiar note, the 'penny-farthing' bicycle was already the object of significant alarm in the late 1870s.[7]

It would seem that the rot had set well in. So, perhaps we should enter into the heart of the respectable Victorian tradition, and travel in the company of Matthew Arnold. He is not a very reassuring guide. Bemoaning the corrupting influence of 'Americanisation',[8] and already reading the last rites over the decomposing virtues of English civility and order, Arnold's influential *Culture and Anarchy* (1869) was

DANGERS OF THE METROPOLIS.

TRAVELLING BY OMNIBUS—THE CADS.

TRAVELLING BY UNDERGROUND RAIL—THE ROUGHS.

regularly punctuated with fearful glimpses of 'a multitude
of miserable, sunken, and ignorant human beings' in the city
slums. 'My friends of the Liberal or progressive party, as they
call themselves,' wrote Arnold, 'are kind enough to reassure
us that a few transient outbreaks of rowdyism signify nothing.'
But he saw things differently:

> The outbreaks of rowdyism tend to become less and less of trifles,
> to become more frequent rather than less frequent ... And thus
> that profound sense of settled order and security, without which a
> society like ours cannot live and grow at all, sometimes seems to be
> beginning to threaten us with taking its departure.[9]

Arnold's fearful preoccupation with the violence of his time drew on a number of sources, for it was not only the 'rough' of the East End slums who was 'asserting his personal liberty a little, going where he likes, assembling where he likes, bawling as he likes, hustling as he likes'.[10] Agitation over the Irish question had assumed the proportions of a major political threat in the 1860s, bread riots were not unknown in London in this period, and in the shadow of the second Reform Bill of 1867 there had been occasions of political violence over voting reforms. The notorious 'Hyde Park railings affair', when an angry political assembly of more than 100,000 people invaded the park by smashing down the gates and fences, had left a particularly deep impression on Arnold's already troubled mind. Because the awful prospect of extending the Englishman's permissive habit of 'Doing as One Likes' to what he called the 'playful giant' of the working class was one of the most worrying signs of incohesion. The promise of enlarged democratic rights had encouraged the 'playful giant' to be less submissive than formerly, Arnold thought, and he was beginning to assert with increasing regularity 'his right to march where he likes, meet where he likes, enter where he likes, hoot as he likes, threaten as he likes, smash as he likes':

> For a long time, as I have said, the strong feudal habits of subordination and deference continued to tell upon the working class. The modern spirit has now almost entirely dissolved those habits, and the anarchical tendency of our worship of freedom in and for itself . . . is becoming very manifest . . . All this, I say, tends to anarchy.[11]

Matthew Arnold thus proposed in the late 1860s that crime and disorder should be understood as a consequence of the already evident 'permissive' disintegration of the stable traditions, and although he was not narrowly obsessed with street violence and rowdyism, nevertheless these were an integral feature of his vision of decay — something which was deeply characteristic of this era.

The early 1860s had witnessed the culmination of the great modernising transformation of the criminal justice system in

Britain: away from the reliance on hanging, whipping and transportation that had dominated the 'Bloody Code' inherited from the eighteenth century, towards an essentially novel emphasis on the reformation of character through the discipline of the penitentiary.[12] Transportation had been virtually abandoned in 1853 and then abolished in 1857, although with a great show of reluctance, the government's hand having been forced by the refusal of the Australian colonies to accept any more convicts.[13] With the abandonment of transportation, prison sentences and penal servitude had correspondingly assumed their pivotal role within the criminal justice system, and the 1850s also saw the beginnings of reformatory institutions for young offenders. After the first round of hanging reforms some forty years earlier, capital statutes were greatly reduced in number by the legislative changes of the early 1860s as a result of which the only common crime punishable by the death penalty became murder. Flogging for adult male offenders was abolished in 1861, and after a large amount of public controversy, public hangings were terminated in 1868.[14] As a piece, although the overall process had taken almost a century to unfold and the measures were sometimes half-hearted in terms of their practical realisation, these changes signalled the arrival of a distinctively modern penal system which rested on the reformative and deterrent influence of the prison as its major instrument.

At the moment of its inception, however, the reformed system of criminal justice was greeted with howling disapproval. The introduction of the 'ticket-of-leave' system of parole for convicts who could no longer be transported provoked waves of anxiety from 1853 onwards that dangerous criminals were being released to prowl the streets of the metropolis with no evidence of the character reformation promised by the new prison disciplines.[15] Respectable England was haunted by the feeling that 'the safety of society would soon be at an end'[16] and that the 'dangerous classes' were gaining the upper hand because of the weakened authority of the law. It was immediately much regretted that the death penalty could not be applied to burglars and footpads, and the prison system was the object of particularly fierce criticism. *Punch* regularly indicated the 'mildness of magistrates' and the 'luxurious' convenience of a 'snug cell in prison' which 'unless the Government interfere to make the living less luxurious . . . will be popularly looked upon as one of the most comfortable ways of spending life'.[17] 'The present gaols are really beautiful penal toys', wrote a complaining correspondent to *The Times* in 1863, 'the perfection of lodging-houses-for-single-men architecture . . . in a better situation Pentonville would sell well as "chambers" for Bank clerks and MPs of limited income'.[18]

The moral vocabulary of these accusations against sentimentality, leniency and crinolined philanthropy that unfolded in the wake of the great legislative transformations of this era is one which we would find entirely familiar in our own historical time, and which has rolled down to us virtually unchanged across more than a century of resistance to penal reform. It is also worth noting another entirely familiar set of complaints centred on the demoralising effects of indiscriminate charity and fears of a growing mass of pauperised scroungers. Matthew Arnold echoed the belief in 1869 that the social system was groaning under the weight of 'those vast, miserable, unmanageable masses of sunken people — one pauper at the present moment, for every nineteen of us'.[19] It was in the same year that *Culture and Anarchy* first appeared that the Charity Organisation Society was founded, to busy itself with the task of classifying and purifying the demoralised lower orders, and to sift out the 'deserving' from the 'undeserving' poor.[20] Although, if we wish to test the depth of these mid-Victorian fears and also to judge the constancy of the vocabularies of reaction, then we must edge back a few years to an episode that would bring back flogging as a judicial punishment almost as soon as it had been abolished.

Putting the Hug On

Panic swept through respectable London in the winter of 1862 about what *The Times* (10 June 1863) would eventually describe as a 'new variety of crime'. 'This modern peril of the streets', it was observed, 'created something like a reign of terror' in which 'whole sections of a peaceable city community were on the verge of arming themselves against sudden attack'.

Here is one example of what the new crime amounted to: 'Suddenly set upon by two men, one of whom seized him by the throat and threw him upon the ground, whilst the other thrust a quantity of mud in his mouth' (*The Daily News*, 15 December 1862). Here is another case, which took place in the Caledonia Road: 'An elderly woman . . . seized by the shawl, and dashed upon the pavement. There was a good deal of ill-treatment, which ended with robbery' (*The Times*, 28 November 1862). This second assault was committed by two girls, said to be under the age of twelve. Again speaking about 'this new rush of crime', *The Times* wondered whether 'they had learnt the new crime at play, and practised "putting the hug on" as boys used to rehearse the best tricks of Jack Sheppard'.

The new crime was called 'garotting', a form of violent robbery that involved choking the victim. A correspondent for *Cornhill Magazine*, who claimed that in order to gain an inside understanding of 'The Science of Garotting' he had visited an experienced convict in his cell and offered himself up as a guinea-pig victim, described the main elements of this 'most inclement ruffianism that ever disgraced a nineteenth century'. Garotting gangs were said to work in threes — a 'front stall' and a 'back-stall' who acted as look-outs — and a 'nasty man' who moved in from the rear:

> The third ruffian, coming swiftly up, flings his right arm around the victim, striking him smartly on the forehead. Instinctively he throws his head back, and in that movement loses every chance of escape. His throat is fully offered to his assailant, who instantly embraces it with his left arm, the bone just above the wrist being pressed against the 'apple' of the throat. At the same moment the garotter, dropping his right hand, seizes the other's left wrist; and thus supplied with a powerful lever, draws his back upon his breast and there holds him. The 'nasty man's' part is done. His burden is helpless from the first moment, and speedily becomes insensible; all *he* has now to do is to be a little merciful.[21]

It was common to allege that the technique of 'putting the

hug on' had been used by guards in the convict hulks in order to subdue troublesome prisoners, and that this was where the original garotting gangs had learned the art. Be that as it may, the story certainly helped to shape and support the belief that discharged 'ticket-of-leave' men were responsible for the outrages. But 12-year-old girls would certainly not have possessed the physical strength for such a form of attack, and although the rubric of 'garotting' was used universally to encompass these crimes, most of the cases reported in the newspapers seemed to describe fairly straightforward street robberies — sometimes using a variety of coshes, knuckle-dusters, 'Indian claw' devices and other forms of life-preserver — or what we would now call 'muggings'.

It is obviously a very old crime, although this was not obvious in 1862. Moreover, it was understood to be a crime which was entirely foreign to the national character, and in one of its earliest references to the affair *The Times* (7 November 1862) registered the compulsive feeling that the new crime was 'un-British': 'When the outrages first commenced, it was doubted whether the crime was not of foreign importation . . . but the ruffians who have been arrested are of pure English breed.'

Even so, like a dog at the bone, *The Times* was driven to search out the foreign disposition of the garotters, accusing them of abandoning the traditional civility of the traditional English highway robbery: 'Without the old challenge and parley in use among highwaymen, your garotter knocks a man's head against the kerbstone as the best way of getting at his pocket.' And so, drawing together the threads of this obsessive preoccupation with the civility of 'Old England' which had been ripped apart by a new strain of hot-blooded and un-English violence, the Old Thunderer arrived at a truly horrific conclusion: 'Our streets are actually not as safe as they were in the days of our grandfathers. We have slipped back to a state of affairs which would be intolerable even in Naples.'

Other sections of the press reflected the same feeling, as when *The Spectator* entertained the view that 'roads like the Bayswater Road are as unsafe as Naples', or *The Observer* lamented how 'the "gentlemanly" highway-man' had 'degenerated into a coarse, brutal ruffian'.[22] Charles Dickens had something similar on his mind when, in an embittered flogging essay of 1860, he accused 'The Ruffian' of making London's streets as perilous as a 'solitary mountain-spur of the Abruzzi'.[23]

During an earlier panic about garotting robberies and stabbing incidents in 1856, *The Times* had enjoyed the good fortune actually to discover some real foreigners to blame for the outrages, pointing the accusing finger at 'men who have been discharged from the foreign legions'. The use of the knife, identified as an un-English custom, was the most worrying sign. 'Happily,' we were told, 'this specific change in the character of London crime' could be dealt with 'in a very summary manner indeed'. 'The half-hundred Italian ruffians who are now rollicking about Whitechapel and Stepney with their stilettoes and bowie-knives', together with their legionnaire friends, could be 'got rid of at once' through deportation.[24] During the garotting panic of 1862, however, there was no such luck and it was therefore necessary to scramble about for alien pejoratives in order to disown this home-brewed violence. Not only were the garotters thought to be visiting hot-blooded Neapolitan outrage upon English soil, but on other occasions they were said to be 'like the sanguinary fanatics of the French Revolution' as well as resembling the 'Indian "thuggee" '.[25]

If the impression created by these furious responses was that garotting (as in other instances of street violence that we have already encountered in other historical periods) represented a novel departure in the national character, then elsewhere the garotting panic itself was taken as a sign of temperamental instability. *Reynolds's Newspaper* viewed 'all the fuss and bother' as 'a mere club-house panic', for example, while *The Daily News* repeatedly warned of the way in which 'a social panic naturally produces a great deal of wild excited talk', believing that 'the enormous crop of exaggerated and fictitious stories' was 'furnishing food for farce writers and arrangers of pantomimes':

Owing to our peculiar constitutions and our peculiar taste for peculiar jokes, garotting is far from being an unpopular crime. The very children play at garotting in the streets, and comic songs . . . are already appearing in music-shop windows. Who can wonder after this that we are problems to our foreign neighbours?[26]

Mr Punch and the Crinoline Robberies

The most obvious sign of this peculiarity of the English was the behaviour of Mr Punch who went completely overboard on the garotting outrages. In the space of only a few weeks in the winter of 1862 *Punch* carried more than a dozen cartoons and a score of witty articles, fake court reports and novelty songs — including a seasonable Christmas Carol. One of the better songs, 'Sweet Sentiment's Pet', showed enormous flair for improvising irresistibly improbable rhymes:

> Come let us be merry and drink while we may,
> More Punch, Tom, and see that it's hotter,
> And hope going home we shan't meet on the way
> Sweet Sentiment's Pet, the Garotter . . .
>
> A gentleman's walking, perchance with a crutch
> He'll suddenly stagger and totter;
> Don't think that the gentleman's taken too much
> He's unluckily met a Garotter . . .
>
> There are but three ways to get out of his beat
> Turn coachman, or tiler, or yachter,
> For no one who walks on Her Majesty's street
> Is safe from the scoundrel Garotter

The final verse, a sort of policy recommendation, advocated the remedy that Parliament would so readily agree to in the ensuing months; one that was 'cheapest and quickest and best':

> Just take a good cord, and divide her in nine
> Let a skilled boson's mate rig and knot her
> Then lay the sound lesson of 'line upon line'
> Into Sentiment's Pet, the Garotter

> *(Punch*, 6 December 1862)

Mr Punch's attitude to the whole affair was thoroughly ill-tempered. Gruesome flogging cartoons and fantasies of violent

GOING OUT TO TEA IN THE SUBURBS
A Pretty State of Things for 1862.

reprisal dominated the response, and when the magazine crashed down against the garotting packs and the sentimentalists (and it was not always clear who was supposed to be the real villain) both humour and artistic quality were sometimes surrendered as hostages to the gout. For example, 'The Song of the Anti-Garotter':

> Last night in walking home a skulking vagabond addressed
> me,
> Says he, 'Pray, what's o'clock?' and, not intending
> any pun,
> Full in his ugly face I let out my left, and
> floored him,
> Observing as I did so, 'My dear friend, it's just
> struck one!'
>
> So, ruffians all, take warning now, and keep
> respectful distance,
> Or a bullet or a bowie-knife clean through your ribs
> I'll send;
> Well armed, we'll straightaway shoot or stab the rascal
> who attacks us,
> If SIR GEORGE GREY won't protect us, why, ourselves
> we must defend.
>
> (*Punch*, 20 December 1862)

It was not the only time that the Home Secretary, Sir George Grey, was identified as a sentimentalist. Colonel Joshua Jebb, the powerful architect of the prison system, was also implicated in the conspiracy, accused of selecting only the burliest convicts for release on 'ticket-of-leave'; and the well-fed convict feasting on turtle soup, rump steak, pudding and ale was another obvious target. Here and elsewhere, the police also came in for a fair amount of criticism — *Punch* portrayed London's genial giants Gog and Magog dressed as policeman, defending themselves from the wrath of the respectable populace — and there were perfectly sound reasons for such discontent. The fact that between 1866 and 1870 almost one quarter of the entire uniformed strength of the Metropolitan Police were dismissed because of misconduct gives some indication of the social organisation of

'NOTWITHSTANDING THE INSINUATIONS OF A CERTAIN STIPENDIARY',
asserted Mr Punch at the height of the garotting panic of 1862,
'JONES IS NOT AFRAID OF HIS SHADOW.'

ANTI-GAROTTE MOVEMENT
*Brown and Jones return home to the Suburbs with safety, taking front
and rear rank alternately.*

policing in this period.[27] The general drift of *Punch*'s enthusiasm, in fact, was that gentlemen should take steps to
arm themselves because of the uselessness of the police force.
It was occasionally recognised, however, that self-defence
might create more problems than it solved, as when Mr Punch

A SUBURBAN DELIGHT

Dark Party (with a ticket-of-leave, of course). Ay yer pardon, Sir—But if you was a-goin down this Dark Lane, p'raps you'd allow Me and this here Young Man to go along with yer— cos yer see there haint no Perlice about—and we're so precious feared o'bein' GAROTTED!'

recovered his wit and arranged for two anti-garotters to meet
one dark night in a lonely street:

> I won't trust to laws or police, not I,
> For their protection is all my eye;
> In my own hands I take the law,
> And use my own fists to guard my jaw.
>
> Is that a footstep behind my back?
> It must be one of the strangling pack;
> Is that a lurking villain I view,
> Crouched in the doorway of number two?
>
> Here's somebody coming! He'd best beware
> I'll give him a warm reception I swear.
> Where's my revolver? Good gracious! I see
> He's bringing his pistol to bear on *me*!
>
> Hold hard, put up your weapon, Sir, do —
> I am an anti-garotter too!
>
> (*Punch*, 6 December 1862)

As well as rumours of troops of infantry escorting respectable citizens to afternoon tea in the suburbs, and the recommendation that gentlemen at a loose end because of the
shortage of decent game reserves might turn their hand to
a new blood-sport — 'We have got together a splendid pack
this season, and the game is still so plentiful that I'll bet we'll
show you some really first-rate sport'[28] — the 'anti-garotte'
movement launched by *Punch* invented various kinds of anti-
robbery device. Metal collars with long steel spikes were
undoubtedly the favourite form of protection against throttl-
ing, although *Punch* (13 December 1862) also dreamt up
'great coats made a-la-porcupine ... with spring daggers at
the elbows and sharp spikes all up the back' in order to dis-
courage attack from the rear. Bowie-knives, sword-sticks,
bayonet-revolvers, protective head-gear and knuckle-dusters
completed the anti-garotte arsenal. 'Really,' sighed Mr Punch
when he had got it all off his chest, 'from the outrages which
have been late perpetrated, one might think that one was
living now in London as it used to be a hundred years ago.'
The Times agreed: 'It brings back Old London, unlighted and
without a police.'[29]

DO YOU WISH TO AVOID BEING STRANGLED!!

If so, try our Patent Antigarotte Collar, which enables Gentlemen to walk the streets of London in perfect safety at all hours of the day or night.

THESE UNIQUE ARTICLES OF DRESS

Are made to measure, of the hardest steel, and are warranted to withstand the grip of

THE MOST MUSCULAR RUFFIAN IN THE METROPOLIS,

Who would get black in the face himself before he could make the slightest impression upon his intended victim. They are highly polished, and

Elegantly Studded with the Sharpest Spikes,

Thus combining a most *recherché* appearance with perfect protection from the murderous attacks which occur every day in the most frequented thoroughfares. Price 7s. 6d, or six for 40s.

WHITE, CHOKER, AND Co.

EFFECT OF THE ANTIGAROTTE COLLAR ON A GARROTTEER.

Some examples of *Punch's* anti-garotte armoury

It is not necessary to go back a hundred years, however, in order to discover a London haunted by unusually similar fears about the leniency of the law and the terrors of the night. Only six winters earlier, respectable London had been awash with fears of violent crime. Lamenting 'the feeling of morbid sympathy with criminals which at the present moment undoubtedly exists', *The Times* (18 November 1856) had arrived at a sorry conclusion: 'Philanthropy, like crinoline, has become the fashion.'

The magnificence of crinoline and the billowing hoop-skirt were certainly exciting an interest of their own in the mid-1850s, as something symptomatic of the extravagant optimism of the period. Mr Punch had been in high spirits, too, in the summer of 1856, thinking that crinoline was a great joke. 'It is no longer correct to say "the height of fashion" . . . rather "she was dressed in the full *breadth* of fashion".' Recommending that hoop-skirts could be usefully converted into play-pens for children, *Punch* also pondered on whether Regent Street might have to be widened 'in order to accommodate the growing dimensions of the ladies' dresses'.[30] It was all lightness and air. But as the months passed and the winter fogs thickened, Mr Punch discovered a new source of inspiration in the hoop-skirt, transforming it into an ingenious anti-garotte device whereby its flowing dimensions could prevent a street robber from approaching his intended victim. Because, six years before the supposedly unprecedented alarms of 1862, Chokee Bill the Garotter was already practising his 'new' crime and the beacons of respectable discontent were already aflame warning of 'the social dragon of the hour, Ticketofleave'.[31]

The police were also hard pressed by criticism and ridicule in 1856. For example, that they were diligently enforcing bye-laws about where costermongers' barrows could be parked, while ducking their responsibilities to deal with ruffians and robbers. Or that London bobbies were too often to be found whispering sweet nothings to kitchen maids, and tucking into pastries in servants' quarters on foggy nights, when they should have been out walking the beat. When *Reynolds's Newspaper* (9 November 1856) tried its hand at

141

MR TREMBLE BORROWS A HINT FROM HIS WIFE'S CRINOLINE, AND INVENTS WHAT HE CALLS HIS 'PATENT ANTI-GAROTTE OVERCOAT', WHICH PLACES HIM COMPLETELY OUT OF HARM'S REACH IN HIS WALKS HOME FROM THE CITY.

a garotting song, it summed up the feeling well enough:

> 'Stand and deliver!' is a cry which England had forgot,
> But we have now a substitute for that in the *garotte*;
> And, if 'Your money or your life!' is heard no more, instead,
> A fellow with a life-preserver knocks you on the head . . .
>
> 'Oh where can the police be?' is the universal cry,
> And echo answers only with her regular reply,
> Whilst, for all that useful body, as they're said to be, of men
> We might as well be living in a lonely Highland glen . . .
>
> Let not old women's apple-stalls engross your manly rage,
> Ticket-of-leave men rather should your vigilance engage;
> To you from whom we look in vain our premises to guard,
> Then what can you be thinking of, ye men of Scotland Yard?

Perhaps the strangest think of all about the garotting panic of 1862 was that in the haste to describe the awful contours of the 'new' crime, the equally 'unprecedented' alarms of 1856 were almost entirely forgotten, although the same complaints and accusations had been well rehearsed. Mr Punch, for example, had already invented the spiked steel collar and the other improbable trappings of his anti-garotting campaign; and even the solemn judgements of *The Times* (10 November 1856) had been tempted from the paths of seriousness:

> Each stout-hearted citizen will have his rifle slung behind him ready to his hand, a six-shooter in his grasp, a bowie-knife at his belt, and round his neck a stout iron collar well garnished with spikes . . . The stern citizens will halt to reload, and then continue their stately march to their respective teas. Seriously, it is becoming unsafe for a man to traverse certain parts of London at night, save in company.

Who Holds the Whip Hand

Whether or not *The Times* did seriously entertain the possibility of vigilante self-defence, there were indeed serious considerations placed before its readers during the alarms of

1856. Hanging leaders were nothing out of the ordinary, and the Old Thunderer even confessed itself vexed by the 'over-magnanimous spirit of British law, which always presumes a man innocent until he is proven guilty'.[32] This placed an unfortunate obstacle in the path of the police who might otherwise, simply on the grounds of suspicion, make a 'clean sweep' of all known criminals — a policy that had been advocated for some years by Matthew Davenport Hill, the Recorder of Birmingham — as a sure means to guarantee the safety of the streets.[33]

Respectable England did not have the stomach for such a drastic curtailment of civil liberties, however, and although fearful of how to absorb the most noxious criminal elements back into society without the option of packing them off to the colonies, the deliberations of the mid-1850s bogged down in suggestions for more effective surveillance of 'ticket-of-leave' men, together with some wishful thinking about reviving transportation in some form or another. But the wishful thinking (suggesting the Falkland Islands as a possible convict settlement and, even more improbably, the Antarctic) remained wishful thinking. 'Be it so,' *The Times* grudgingly conceded, 'we must pay the penalty for our chivalry in the shape of daily outrage and nightly fears.'[34]

Amidst the 'garotting' agitations of 1862, however, those who were discontented with crinolined philanthropy and magnanimous justice discovered a much more amenable slogan around which to marshal their energies. Reintroduce transportation, they could not do. But bring back flogging — abolished as recently as 1861 — they could, and did. Stirred into action when a Member of Parliament, Mr Pilkington, was the victim of a garotting attack in Pall Mall while on his way to the Reform Club, a Security from Violence Bill was brought before the House of Commons to reinstate the penalty of flogging for robbery offences. Ignoring the advice of the Home Secretary Sir George Grey, who regarded the Bill as 'panic legislation after the panic had subsided', the House pressed ahead to implement the 'Garotter's Act' of 1863. The Act was destined to become something of a *cause célèbre* among successive generations of floggers who would fondly remember (although without a shred of evidence to support their claim) how flogging had put down the garotters, and could be relied upon to stop Hooligans or Teddy Boys.[35] Introduced so hastily after the original abolition of flogging, and remaining on the statute book until judicial corporal punishment was ended as recently as 1948, the Garotter's Act was thus a historic landmark of reaction; and it was quickly followed by measures to toughen prison discipline and to introduce a minimum penalty of five years of penal servitude for second offenders. The reformative principle was on the retreat.

In a recent analysis of the garotting panic of 1862, Jennifer Davis has argued that there was in fact no startling upsurge in crimes of violence which could justify the extent of the alarm. Moreover, that those increases in recorded crime which did occur came *after* the onset of the panic. The increase in arrests, in other words, was the result of increased police vigilance: the 'crime wave', such as it was, was created by 'the actions and reactions of the press, public, and various government agencies . . . rather than any significant increase in criminal activity in the streets'. This increased sensitivity to street crime, furthermore, was orchestrated into a powerful lobby of reaction against the reformative penal system: 'it was the mobilisation of public opinion during the panic', Davis writes, 'which facilitated the effective dismantling of the reformative penal system by its critics in the years following, and its replacement by a punitive model of convict treatment'.[36]

The issue which divided public opinion largely revolved around the ineffectiveness of the prison system and the ease with which convicts could bamboozle prison chaplains into believing that their characters had been reformed, thus securing their release on 'ticket-of-leave', and there was little room for the idea that the roots of crime might be found in social conditions. In this respect, however, *Reynolds's Newspaper* had devised an interesting prototype of what we might nowadays call 'anomie theory', arguing that crime was an inevitable result of the system of distribution of wealth and opportunity. The criminogenic nature of the social system, as it was described, was that honest labour was rewarded only with poverty-level wages and filthy cellar

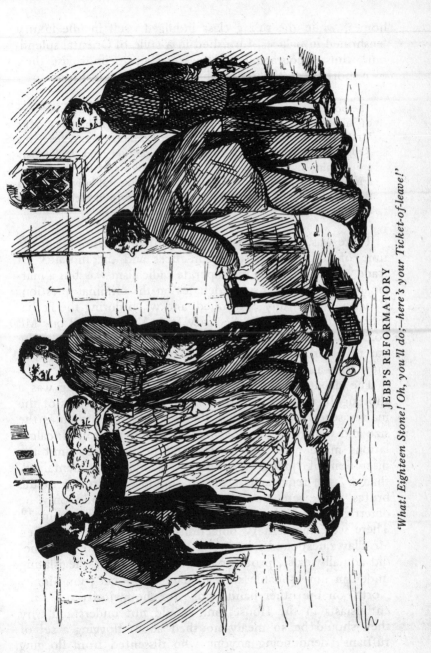

JEBB'S REFORMATORY

'What! Eighteen Stone! Oh, you'll do;—here's your Ticket-of-leave!'

homes, while the ruling class indulged itself in idle luxury 'enshrined in palaces, furnished in a style of Oriental splendour', thus encouraging the lower orders to improvise their own short-cut to the universal aspiration of acquisition:

> The poor, in seeking wealth and enjoyment without the preliminary of labour, are but following the examples of their betters . . . the Strahans, the Pauls, the Sadleirs, the Gordons, the Villiers, the Redpaths, and the rest of them . . . the garotters and the burglars are nothing but the rough and clumsy copyists of the fraudulent aristocratic bankers, the honourable blacklegs, the legislative swindlers that the last 12 or 18 months have brought forth in such appalling abundance.[37]

There was, indeed, a certain amount of questioning at the time of dishonest business practices and the morality of trade,[38] although this intemperate radicalism was but a marginal force in the ensuing debates on the criminal question. Reaction was firmly enthroned, and when during the Parliamentary debate on the Security from Violence Bill one MP voiced the belief that 'the want of employment was the parent of crime', this seems to have been regarded as little more than a sentimental eccentricity.[39]

The debate on the Bill to bring back whippping was a thoroughly undignified affair in which the principles of the matter seemed to count less than considerations such as the size and weight of the flogging instrument to be used: calculations made necessary no less by the desire to limit the discretion of 'judges infected by maudlin sentimentality', than by the requirement that it should measure up to the brutes who were 'so degraded, that they could only be deterred by forcible appeals to their fear of physical pain'.[40] There were momentary objections to the business, as when Mr Clay questioned whether an 'exceptional state of crime' did actually exist, protesting that the House was 'legislating under an unreasonable state of panic'. Colonel John Sidney North, on the other hand, spoke for the majority of *Punch* enthusiasts in the House, and 'could not understand why they should be so mealy-mouthed about flogging a set of ruffians', denouncing anyone who dissented from flogging

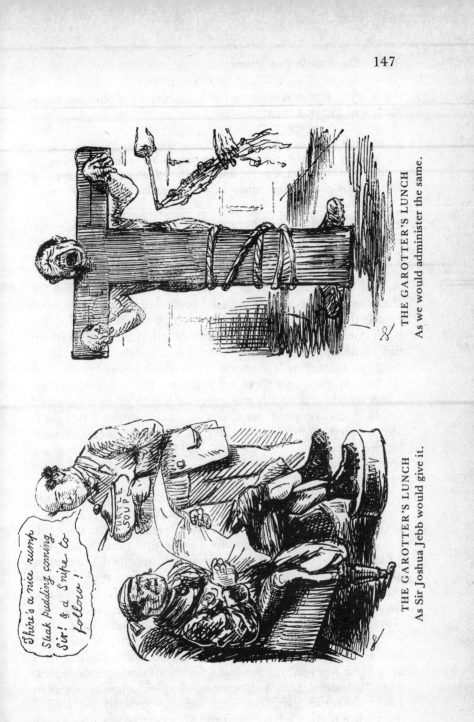

THE GAROTTER'S LUNCH
As we would administer the same.

THE GAROTTER'S LUNCH
As Sir Joshua Jebb would give it.

as 'a wretched old woman for his lenity'. Colonel North, in fact, was the star turn:

> See how the convicts were fed. These rascals had their roast meat, pudding, ale and porter — things which no honest labourer on Hon. Gentlemen's estates could get ... The whole country was justly indignant at the manner in which these ruffians were treated.[41]

The Garotter's Act became law on 13 July 1863 when, after a speedy passage through its readings, it joined the rump of archaic flogging laws which had escaped abolition in 1861. The names and dates tell their own story: the Treason Act of 1842, passed after an impotent attempt to frighten the sovereign by a young hunchback with a faultily loaded pistol; the Vagrancy Act of 1824 which allowed the flogging of 'incorrigible rogues', commonly elderly tramps, and which has come into more recent notoriety through the 'sus' laws; the Diplomatic Privileges Act of 1708 which offered protection to Ambassadors and their servants; and the Knacker's Act of 1786 which dealt with the irregular slaughter of horses and cattle.[42] In company such as this, the Garotter's Act must almost seem enlightened. After all, had it not been brought before Parliament by Mr C. B. Adderley 'in no retrograde spirit', but as something which merely followed 'the dictates of commonsense'?[43]

But why was the Garotter's Act passed? It trivialises the issue to say that it was merely the result of panic — although there was certainly panic in good measure. Because this conventionally liberal response to the prevailing mood disguises the fact that the themes which arranged themselves around the flogging solution reflected a much more mature retrenchment, and a much more solid base of opinion and material circumstance than is usefully summarised by the word 'panic'. *The Times* was certainly not panicking, as its editorials rattled off the press each after another, priming the fuse of Parliament's deliberations and heralding the garotters as something that signalled 'the failure of sentimental legislation'.[44] Indeed, it was in a mood of celebration rather than panic that the garotters were actually toasted for having 'taken upon themselves the duty of upsetting a whole fabric

THE GAROTTER'S FRIEND

'Let go, Bill, can't yer—it's our kind non-interfering friend, Sir George Grey!!!'

of amiable delusions' concerning the reformation of criminals, and further congratulated that through their 'inexcusable crime' they had made a salutary impact on public opinion and 'created a general belief that right and wrong are, after all, essentially distinct'.[45]

As we listen to these phrases that rolled so easily off the

tongue, and which have also rolled on down through history to our own time, we must make a special effort to remember very carefully just who the men were who engineered the Garotter's Act — what kind of men they were; what kind of times they lived in; and what forces helped to shape their upright moral certitude. Because these men who knew with such unquestionable certainty the difference between right and wrong, and who blithely described the garotters as creatures capable of responding only to the fear of physical pain, were people who knew a great deal about physical pain.

Floggings in the public school system, through which so many of these men had passed, had undoubtedly accustomed them in their youth to scenes of sordid violence, such as were everyday occurrences in these nineteenth-century centres of educational excellence.[46] Floggings in the army, and more especially in the navy, were another integral feature of the moral landscape of the rulers of Britain in the 1860s. At the very time that Parliament was debating the garotters, there had been a public sensation when *The Liverpool Mercury* exposed an eye-witness account of a brutal navy flogging on HMS Majestic in which it was alleged that the officer-in-charge had taken considerable pleasure from the proceedings.[47] The gentle mercies of the lash were used even more extravagantly for civilising the 'primitive' peoples of the Empire in the nineteenth century, and in one of its anti-garotting tirades *Punch* (6 December 1862) had good cause to remember the lesson of the Indian Mutiny of 1857 which had been put down in a sea of blood. 'Hang without mercy, hang like fun,' recommended Mr Punch, 'and you will check Garotters as effectually as Sepoys.' Flogging was reintroduced in India at this time by the Whipping Act of 1864, and even the bare statistical details of the numbers of floggings carried out by the British are enough to make the blood run cold. Tens of thousands of whippings were inflicted in India: 75,223 in 1878 alone, for example, and 64,087 in 1897.[48] What would 'the general belief that right and wrong are, after all, essentially distinct' have to say to this?

Again, the Morant Bay rising in Jamaica in 1865 was put down with savage majesty by Governor Eyre — 600 men, women and children indiscriminately massacred, many more

Whipping was commonly on the agenda when Britain looked to the rule of her Empire. Here we see Britannia, during the Afghan War of 1878, flourishing the birch-twigs against the Ameer of Kabul who is toying with his military supplies and the Russian Bear. Disraeli had said the Ameer was 'like a spoiled child' and *Punch* faithfully resorted to the Victorian maxim not to 'spare the rod'.

hundreds executed, and a thousand homes burned to the ground — as Eyre's troops went on a three-week orgy of hanging, torture, flogging and rape.[49] In the immediate aftermath of this squalid affair a former Stipendiary Magistrate of Jamaica, Mr H. Pringle, had felt obliged to lift the veil from the 'abominable and ferocious' treatment of black people in the Caribbean. And although, according to the conventions of the time, he acknowledged that 'the subject is quite unfit for women to think of', he nevertheless urged a loosening of convention, for 'it is absolutely necessary for the ends of justice, and a due regard for outraged humanity, that these things should be made known to the women of England'.[50] But it was not only the women of England, with their crinolined frailties, who needed to be shielded from the details. The punishments dealt out to the Morant Bay rioters were so hideous — it was reported, for example, that women were lashed on their naked buttocks, sometimes with piano wire — as to shock even lusty sexual flagellants such as Swinburne.[51]

The Governor Eyre controversy dragged on for a number of years, creating deep divisions within respectable society. An attempt to bring Eyre to justice on a trial of murder, spearheaded by John Stuart Mill, was to prove unsuccessful in spite of the Lord Chief Justice's eloquent support for his indictment. And when Parliament eventually turned back the tide of opposition to Eyre and voted financial support to the former Governor, it was poetically appropriate that those who had been most vocal in their support for the Garotter's Act — such as Mr Adderley and the rampant Colonel North — should be in the thick of it again, shouting their praise for Eyre's loyalty to the Crown and his firm action that had saved a colony. *The Times*, for its part, while maintaining a discrete silence when the fortunes of the case were in the balance, eventually brought its influence to bear against those who were understood as Eyre's malicious persecutors.[52]

The people who created the Garotter's Act, together with the gentlemen who egged them on from the sidelines helping to fashion the vocabulary of objections to penal reform which remain with us to this day, were thus the same men whose blunted moral sensibilities enabled them to preside over this magnanimous process of 'civilisation' without turning a hair. People, that is, who although they were scandalised by the outrageous behaviour of the garotters and roughs, lived nevertheless in an untidy moral proximity with systematic brutality, degradation and mass violence. Sometimes, as in the case of Governor Eyre's atrocity at Morant Bay, it was not even particularly systematic.

Two wrongs do not make a right, of course, although they must necessarily shift the balance in how we might approach such an inalienable moral precept as the 'general belief that right and wrong are, after all, essentially distinct'. And when we begin to gain, if only the merest glimpse of the deeply ingrained brutalities and prejudices embodied in what was judged to be 'right', then we can see more clearly that the Garotter's Act was not so much a moment of panic which led respectable England off its true course, but a mature expression of the existing social relations — including the self-assumption of the mighty, and their attitudes and actions towards the lower orders and the plebs.

This was, when all is said and done, class legislation: enacted by one class for the betterment of its lower brethren; not for the correction of its own bad habits. 'To a wealthy or aristocratic criminal the vengeance of the law is as a flea, which merely tickles', observed *Reynolds's Newspaper* which thought that as far as the Garotter's Act went 'only poor, plebeian criminals will be exposed . . . rich and aristocratic ruffians . . . are certain to be exempted from flogging'.[53] It was an entirely sound judgement. On the very day that the Garotter's Act became law, the essential distinction between right and wrong faltered appreciably in the pages of *The Times* where a disturbance was noted at Cremorne Gardens which had resulted in some upper-class rowdies being heavily fined. Admitting that 'a "row" at Cremorne on the night of Derby and Oaks day' was 'too ordinary an occurrence to deserve any comment', *The Times* nevertheless lingered over this scene of young gentlemen at play:

> We have no wish to curb these boisterous spirits which we are said to have inherited as a nation from our Northern ancestors . . . Shouting and hooting may all be very well, but when it comes to breaking windows and glasses by wholesale, hustling and insulting women, bonnetting the bystanders, striking right and left with sticks and umbrellas, and assaulting the police in the execution of their duty, the affair is beyond a joke.[54]

Given the habit of *The Times* to diagnose working-class violence as a deterioration of the national character, and to equate it with a Southern 'hot-blooded' temperament, this was an intriguing turnabout on the racial origins of upper-class ruffianism. And there was more to come. The respectable rowdies had set about their business with gleeful shouts of 'Now, boys, for a jolly spree!' and 'Go it, boys, go it!' doing damage amounting to £300 and causing the proprietor of Cremorne to pay out £500 in prosecuting the case. It is hardly surprising, then, that one observer thought this such 'a scene of riot, confusion, destruction of property, and injury to persons which would have been a disgrace to a savage land'. *The Times*, however, begged to differ: 'Knowing what we do of human nature, and of the licence claimed by young gentlemen in past times, we are inclined to take a somewhat less gloomy view of it.' So that, when young gentlemen were on the rampage, the past — instead of being used as a stick with which to beat the deteriorated present — became the justification for taking a lenient view.

The sequel, in which the young bloods of Derby and Oaks night received their rebuff, was that they were distracted from their other responsibilities by a four-day jury hearing which found them guilty of riotous proceedings, but not of riotous intent. Then, for four of the culprits there were whopping fines of £50 — which were paid immediately — plus even heftier sureties to keep the peace. *The Times* had no quarrel with this. These were people of means who could afford to foot the bill: no appeal to the fear of physical pain was needed here. The sentence, said the judge, was 'more for an example' for this was 'a matter to be dealt with with great leniency'. Indeed, he confessed that he was deeply troubled by having to pass sentence at all: 'It is with feelings of great pain that I pass sentence upon you, the defendants, and I can make great allowance for the youthful spirit which has been exhibited by you.'[55] Justice must be seen to be done, however, and when it had been seen to be done, the miscreants were cheered by a crowd assembled outside the court. Describing it variously as a lark and a spree, *The Times* was satisfied that although 'genteel ruffianism has met with a very decisive rebuff', the Cremorne affair was nothing more than something done 'on the impulse of the moment, and out of pure love of mischief'.

If the purity of the motive was not here in question, we can sorrowfully contrast the fate of Alfred Berry, an unfortunate young man of 18 years from Camden whose idea of mischievous fun was to make an annoying din in the open streets between three and four o'clock in the morning in late December 1862. There was no trial-by-jury for him, of course, and no *Times* leader. Nor had he spent the night at the opera, or at the Naval and Military Club, or feasting at Hummums Hotel as in the case of the respectable ruffians of Cremorne. But there were remaining points of similarity. When he appeared before the magistrate at lowly Clerkenwell, charged with 'willfully ringing several door bells and knocking at the doors in Upper Street, Islington, without lawful excuse' it was said that this kind of mischief — like the Cremorne Gardens affray — was a 'frequent occurrence'.[56] Alfred Berry also confessed that he had been drinking, and hoped that a lenient view would be taken of his misconduct. But here the similarities stopped. The magistrate could see no redeeming features in the case. He considered it 'very foolish for a young man to act in such a silly way' and 'What he did it for he could not tell, for there was no fun in it.' Unable to pay the ten shillings fine placed against him — a trifling sum, of course, compared with that paid out by the Cremorne merry-makers after their destructive binge — Alfred Berry was sentenced to seven days in the House of Correction. Here, moral certainty had found its feet again, secure in the knowledge that a short, sharp dose of discipline would curb the moral pauper and ensure the safety and the silence of the night.

7
The Artful Chartist Dodger

In these successive waves of anxiety about sudden upsurges in crime and violence, each pointing back to a previously untroubled era, we appear to glimpse a series of 'golden ages' nestling inside each other like a set of Russian dolls. And where must we look next in search of this stubbornly elusive era of tranquillity?

Writing in 1869 Matthew Arnold believed that the blame for 'the present troubled state of our social life' rested with 'our Liberal friends' and 'the thirty years' blind worship of their nostrums'.[1] It is certainly not the first time that we have met such reckoning which counts the onset of disorder in mere decades. On this occasion, however, it is especially difficult to resist the feeling that Arnold must have been joking.

Because in 1829, if we follow his judgement to the letter, with Queen Victoria only recently enthroned, the 'early Victorian' era was if anything even more ill-at-ease than either the mid-Victorian or late Victorian periods which we have seen to be such spectacular failures as exemplars of the golden mythology of Victorian stability and tradition. We would have to cope, for example, with the perilous details of London's criminal underworld depicted in Charles Dickens's *Oliver Twist* which first appeared in the years between 1837 and 1839, or the fearful imagery of the revolutionary mobs in *Barnaby Rudge* which made its appearance in 1841.[2] We would find the rebellious energies of Chartism coming to the boil in the late 1830s, to explode in the great wave of unrest which swept through the manufacturing districts of the North and Midlands in the summer of 1842: an insurrection of such devastating scale that in the North-West of England alone 1,500 labour leaders and strikers were brought to trial.[3] Nor would we find much comfort if we were to accompany Edwin Chadwick on his sanitary tour of smelly urban England in the early 1840s, whose sanitary observations on the labouring classes were repeatedly diverted from drains and sewers towards signs of dangerous social incohesion.[4] And although he was not setting out to offer comfort, nor should we ignore the opinions of the young revolutionary Friedrich Engels — recently arrived in Manchester, the burning focus of the world's first Industrial Revolution — who wrote in 1845 that 'the British nation has become the most criminal in the world': 'The contempt for the existing social order is most conspicuous in its extreme form — that of offences against the law ... In this country, social war is under full headway.'[5]

A Political Animal?

There had been a fitful preoccupation with mounting crime and disorder, and especially with lawlessness among the young, throughout the first half of the nineteenth century. Various 'crime waves' had been announced, and various signs of incohesion and demoralisation described: drunkenness, parental irresponsibility, heathen ignorance, promiscuity, the breakdown of the old traditions, and decreasing respect for order among the lower orders. In the 1840s, however, the question of juvenile crime burst into public awareness with a force previously unknown, spreading fear into the hearts and minds of the early Victorians of impending social collapse. The awful judgements scattered through the pages of the Reverend Henry Worsley's prize-winning essay on *Juvenile Depravity* (1849) sum up the consternation well enough:

> A bane to society, which like an ulcer on the body, is continually enlarging, and distributing far and wide its noxious influence ... a general and latent depravity, which a large extent of juvenile depravity

seems to indicate, is a state under which the manufacture of a nation must eventually decline, agriculture languish, and commerce disappear ... The numerous juvenile offenders, whose precocity in wickedness is subject of grief and alarm to every well-regulated mind ... the overwhelming mass of vice and crime, now deluging our land ... the increasing degeneracy of the juvenile population ... the current of iniquity which at the present sweeps through our streets.... The statistics of crime cannot develop in half or in a quarter of its fearful extent ... can never trace the monster roots of vice, how widely they spread and diverge themselves, or how deeply they penetrate the congenial soil.[6]

Faced with clouded and horror-struck language such as this, it is as well to say that Henry Worsley was not living in some far-flung lunatic fringe of early Victorian opinion. Rather, he occupied the turbulent centre and dozens of books and pamphlets on the question of juvenile crime appeared within the space of a few years, describing the same awful circumstances in the same terrified language. The metaphors of pollution and moral contagion, together with metaphorical allusions to the sewer, were the standard forms of expression in this era, conveying the fear of an oozing tide of poisonous violence and wretchedness that might burst from its subterranean home and sweep away the social order if not checked.[7] 'Human vermin', 'moral sewerage', the 'miasma of vice', 'the streams of pollution', 'the floodgates of moral pollution' were phrases which echoed through this monologue of fears, with the philanthropic mission also monotonously described as a sanitary endeavour by which 'the fountains must be purged of its impurities'; or as a quest 'to cleanse the polluted stream', to 'dry up the springs of juvenile depravity' and to 'fill up the defiling source'.[8] 'There was enough to excite not only sympathy,' wrote Thomas Beggs in his *Inquiry into the Extent and Causes of Juvenile Depravity* (1849), 'but apprehension and alarm':

A large proportion of the population were found to be grovelling in the veriest debasement, yielding obedience only to the animal instincts; brooding in spiritual darkness in a day of gospel light, and as much shut off from participation in the blessings of Christian privilege as if they had been the inhabitants of another hemisphere.[9]

The ignorance of the criminal classes, Alexander Thomson thought, was 'almost incredible — amounting often to something like the death of the mental faculties'.[10] Here was a population, lodging in the manufacturing districts of the world's first industrial civilisation, that often appeared to their contemporaries as sub-human. In 1846 Walter Buchanan thought that the parents of juvenile criminals 'care no more for their offspring than hyaenas for their whelps after they are suckled'; and casting his eye across 'the low-browed and inexpressive physiognomy' which was 'a true index to the mental darkness, the stubborn tempers, the hopeless spirits', Beggs reaffirmed his belief that 'the children who constitute the predatory hordes of the street . . . appear almost to belong to another race'.[11] And perhaps it goes without saying that so un-civilised, un-Christian and un-English were these young thieves and rascals that they were known flatly and uniformly in this era as 'street Arabs', 'English Kaffirs' and 'Hottentots'.

The most remarkable aspect of early Victorian perceptions of the criminal question, however, was the way in which juvenile lawlessness was believed to foreshadow the possibilities of political insurrection among the lower orders. Nor was this, by any means, solely the response of a prototypical Marxism such as that of Engels. The same political anxieties and predictions came to aid the wings of charity, and the philanthropic surge of the mid-nineteenth century repeatedly justified itself in the conviction that, unless a system of moral instruction were provided for the poor, then crime was a prelude to social revolution.

It was precisely in these terms that Lord Ashley, Earl of Shaftesbury, rose before the House of Commons in February 1843 to urge the necessity of a system of elementary schooling for the children of the 'dangerous classes'. Repeatedly reminding the House of the Chartist troubles of the previous summer, and freely mixing his references to the low state of morals in the manufacturing districts, crime and political danger, Ashley brooded over this 'fearful multitude of un-tutored savages' in the industrial towns which represented a problem 'so prodigiously vast, and so unspeakably important'.[12] Ashley was on his feet for a long time as he tried to give voice to the unspeakable. 'The morals of children are tenfold worse than formerly', he declared as he presented evidence from different parts of the country. In Wolverhampton 'their minds were as stunted as their bodies; their moral feelings stagnant'. In Warrington, they were 'alarmingly degraded'. In Leeds, 'the spirit of lawless insubordination' was 'a matter for painful apprehension'. In Birmingham, the 'arts of domestic economy' were at a low ebb, and 'sexual connection' began as early as 14 or 15 years of age. In the mining districts, there were girls who 'drink, swear, fight, smoke, whistle, sing, and care for nobody' and there was too much singing in other parts of the country where he noted 'the preposterous epidemic of a hybrid negro song'. In Nottingham, he remarked upon 'the vicious habits of the parents, many of whom are utterly indifferent to the moral and physical welfare of their offspring'. A clergyman from one of 'the disturbed districts' informed him that 'the moral condition of the people is as bad as it is possible to be . . . a spirit of disaffection prevails almost universally — magistrates, masters, pastors, and all superiors, are regarded as enemies and oppressors'. Another gentleman, 'whose opportunities of observation were, perhaps, unparalleled' according to Ashley, opined that the rising generation were 'more and more debased, I believe, than any previous generation for the last 300 years'.[13]

Everywhere that Ashley looked there was 'a wild and satanic spirit' abroad. In Manchester, 'a vast number of children of the tenderest years . . . are suffered to roam at large through the streets of the town, contracting the most idle and profligate habits'. In Sheffield, he found 'most vice and levity and mischief in the class who are between 16 and 19 . . . with dogs at their heels and other evidence of dissolute habits'. Although what was 'most deplorable' in Sheffield, as elsewhere, was that the young 'generally act as men' and in the 'Chartist attacks . . . a great number of young lads were among them' So, too, in the Midlands where he noted 'their low and degraded condition. Hence the disturbances and arson in the Potteries.' At which point Ashley's speech was greeted with a rousing 'Hear, Hear'.

And so it was that Lord Ashley, social reformer and

friend of boy chimney-sweeps, argued the case for 'diffusing the benefits and blessings of a moral and religious education among the working classes'. Education would instil a proper respect for law, property and order among the masses, and with the riotous events of the previous summer clearly stamped in his mind, he believed that while 'it is very well to rely on an effective police for short and turbulent periods; it is ruinous to rely on it for the government of a generation':

> This state of things is cruel, disgusting and perilous ... it breeds discontent and every bad passion, and then when disaffection stalks abroad, we are alarmed, we cry out that we are fallen upon evil times, and so we are ... The country is wearied with pamphlets and speeches on gaol-discipline, model-prisons, and corrective processes; meanwhile crime advances at a rapid pace ... the danger is wider, deeper, fiercer; and no one who has heard these statements and believes them, can hope that twenty years or more will pass without some mighty convulsion, and displacement of the whole system of society.[14]

Speaking on the very day before the great show trial of Feargus O'Connor and the other 58 leaders of the 1842 Chartist uprising began in Lancaster, Ashley had certainly chosen a dramatic and opportune moment to raise these matters in such terms before Parliament. Replying for the government, the Home Secretary Sir James Graham caught on to the idea readily enough. 'The late events were pregnant with a solemn warning', he believed, and 'now that the policemen and the soldiers have done their duty, the time has arrived when the moral and religious instruction of the rising generation must be attended to, and a sense of morality and Christianity implanted in their hearts.'[15] Not everyone was immediately pleased by these remarks. *The Times* confessed that 'we distrust the *animus* of one who associates with the education of the poor the ideas of the policeman's staff and the bayonet', although it conceded that 'it was remarkable that the better educated were not found among the insurgents in the late disturbances'.[16]

The assumed connection between Chartism and juvenile lawlessness had been given some immediate encouragement by the observation that young people had been particularly active in some of the more riotous happenings in the summer of 1842; and when Edwin Chadwick turned his attention to mob violence in his sanitary report he had also helped to propagate the view that among the mobs of Bristol, Bethnal Green and Manchester 'the great havoc ... was committed by mere boys'.[17]

There was, however, something altogether unbalanced in judgements such as these, for the Chartist ranks were built not so much out of the most down-trodden, but out of respectable artisans and working men, with a liberal sprinkling of shopkeepers, teachers, parsons, doctors, publishers and other worthy citizens within both the local and national leadership. Victorian England was also somewhat askew in its condemnation of the heathen inspirations of Chartism. The Chartist cause was infused with a radical and populist Christianity in its battle against wicked employers and tyrannical rulers, with Biblical war-cries as its texts and sermons. On more than one occasion for hungry people who were afraid they might 'pine away, stricken through, for want of the fruits of the field' the *Lamentations of Jeremiah* (4:9) informed their understanding: 'They that be slain with the sword are better than they that be slain with hunger.'[18] And nor could *Luke* (22:36) be counted on to inspire pacifism: 'He that hath no sword, let him sell his raiment and buy one.' During the Rebecca Riots which swept through rural Wales in the late 1830s and early 1840s, Biblical inspirations were again much in evidence, and Rebecca and her Children were as scrupulous as the Lord's Day Observance Society in their respect for the Sabbath.[19] The sources of their conviction, just as much as their organisation and leadership, marked out these popular insurrectionary movements as something more than a gang of ragged youths trailing dogs behind them or throwing stones at mill windows. Firm in the righteousness of their cause, the Chartists had marched into Halifax in 1842 singing 'Old Hundredth', with God on their side.[20]

But whatever we may think of this easy Victorian equation between crime and the supposedly heathen energies of Chartism, Ashley's warning of impending social revolution would be repeated tirelessly in the flood of philanthropic writings on the problem of juvenile lawlessness; and the unprecedented revolutionary current that swept through Europe in 1848 was not exactly a tonic for the nerves. 'Unless we are unmindful of the admonition given by the convulsions of 1848', Beggs cautioned, then steps must be taken to improve the moral condition of the poor, for 'safety can only rest on the morality of the people, and the wisdom of their rulers'.[21] Henry Worsley also saw moral leadership as a barricade against political disaffection, celebrating the example of a model pit-village built by Lord Ellesmere — which provided churches, a reading-room, a recreation ground, but did not permit a beer-house — where during the Chartist disturbances of 1842 Worsley rejoiced that the colliers had 'resisted the combination, refused to submit to the dictation of its leaders, and expressed their ardent attachment to Lord Ellesmere'.[22] C. F. Cornwallis, too, warned in 1853 of the dangers of the 'uncontrolled passions' of the labouring population: 'Robbery, fraud, violence, and finally murder, are the consequences if there be few persons in this condition; insurrection and revolution if there be more.'[23] Alexander Thomson echoed the sentiment: 'Unless effective and radical remedies be applied, the danger to the State must speedily become imminent.'[24] And so, even in the shadow of the industrial swagger of the Great Exhibition of 1851, and when already it was being trumpeted that Queen Victoria's illustrious power stretched across an empire so vast that the sun never set upon it, Micaiah Hill in another prize-winning essay on *Juvenile Delinquency* (1853) could neatly summarise the principle of mid-century philanthropy: 'Educate! Educate! is the cry of the day, or England's flag may be struck, and her sun set forever in a sea of blood.'[25]

Can these be Children?

The prevailing orthodoxy of mid-nineteenth-century philanthropy which identified the artful Chartist dodger as some kind of embryonic revolutionary cadre, although palpably false as a diagnosis of working-class unrest and political organisation in the 1840s, nevertheless spoke directly to the central dilemma of this era. If only as a metaphor pointing to another kind of revolution – the Industrial Revolution which had transformed the material basis of life in the space of a few decades – it accurately registered the feared consequences of this great social alteration which, while creating unimaginable wealth, had also upset what was often believed to have been a previously harmonious way of life in pre-industrial Merrie England. For here, in the crucible of the first industrial nation, we see emerging a mature expression of the modernisation thesis which understands crime and violence as a by-product of sweeping social change and the loosening of custom and tradition; a form of understanding which remains with us to this day as a dominant ideological tradition within European and American social thought.

Estimates of the rate of increase in crime varied, although they were in general agreement that the increase was considerable. 'It is too evident that our criminals are steadily increasing,' wrote Thomson, 'not only in absolute numbers, but in relative proportion to the rest of the population', and he estimated that there had been 'an addition of nearly 30 per cent' in the number of committals 'in the last twenty-one years'.[26] Beggs reckoned that one out of every 154 of the whole population were in prison, while Samuel Phillips Day arrived at the astonishing conclusion that the prison population had grown by 1,000 per cent since the beginning of the century.[27] Worsley calculated that in the same period 'crime generally . . . has increased five-fold', drawing attention to the age group from 15 to 20 years who 'form not quite one-tenth of the population, but . . . are guilty of nearly one-fourth of its crime' which was 'a feature . . . of crime in this country yet more alarming'.[28] 'A growing increase in the proportion that juvenile criminals bear to adults' also struck Cornwallis as one of the more frightening aspects of the problem.[29] Joseph Adshead estimated that 'nearly 7,000 youths are annually added to our criminal population', and working from the same kinds of statistical returns that were available to these native philanthropists Engels calculated a sevenfold increase in crime between 1805 and 1842.[30] It should be said that these early moral statisticians were somewhat cavalier in their use of crime statistics, and that their arithmetic was not always terribly sound, but the numbers only confirmed what the early Victorians already knew in their bones: that crime was advancing at a gallop.

The causes of the problem, as they were understood, were those which have already become wearily familiar. The cheap theatres, penny gaffs and two-penny-hop dancing saloons were regularly identified as incitements to crime and immorality among the young. 'The corruption of youth from spectacles, songs, etc., of an indecent nature' excited Cornwallis no less than others who described how the daring enactments of the outrages of Jack Sheppard, Dick Turpin and Claude Duval 'inculcate the same lesson, exhibit to admiration noted examples of successful crime' and thereby 'attract the attention and the ambition of these boys, and each one endeavours to emulate the conduct of his favourite hero'.[31]

The breakdown of family life was also described as a consequence of the Industrial Revolution, and working mothers were another source of moral outrage. 'The withdrawal of woman's attention from the care of her offspring, and from domestic duties' was 'an unnatural arrangement' and 'a stigma upon the social state'.[32] 'Young children are left at home under very inadequate conduct and almost without restraint', wrote Beggs, 'left to play at will, and to expand into every lawless form.' 'Ignorant of cooking and needlework ... unacquainted with all that is necessary to promote the comfort and welfare of a home ... slatternly and ignorant', Beggs feared that 'the unfortunate man who marries a woman of this class suffers also ... there is neither order nor comfort in the home ... his meals are irregular and ill-prepared, and his own fireside presents so few attractions that he is tempted to the beer-house.'[33] Worsley agreed: the failure 'to discharge the most common duties of a housewife' resulted in 'a house in the grossest disorder, and a home without comfort ... another inducement to seek refuge in the exciting pleasures of the theatre, the beer-shop, or gin-palace'.[34]

In the minds of so many of these mid-century philanthropists, all roads led back to the beer-house. Drink, as much as ignorance, was held responsible not only for the self-inflicted poverty and wretchedness of the working class, but also in Henry Worsley's words 'leaves them at the mercy of petty orators and selfish demagogues'. Drink was 'the cause of causes . . . the arcanum which is at the bottom of the whole superstructure of our national depravity': 'As long as the citadel of crime and iniquity remains fenced with the strong out-works of intemperance, it is impregnable.' Indeed, observing in words that are reminiscent of Karl Marx's judgement on nineteenth-century capitalism that 'All classes are merging in one of two, the indigent and the opulent', Worsley even feared that with the annihilation of the petit-bourgoisie and small traders, the only small business to survive 'is, it may well be feared, the publican's'.[35]

These fears of the demoralisation of the common people were also, quite predictably, gathered around what was seen to be the excessive independence of the young in the manufacturing towns, with the associated feeling of the increasing youthfulness of crime. 'Amid such a state of affairs,' Worsley thought, 'we learn without surprise that crime is precocious in an extraordinary degree'. 'Insubordination to parental authority, leading to insubordination to all authority, is stated to be very general':

> The social evils are aggravated by the independence of the young of both sexes . . . the child receives his own wages on his own account. In some cases, he will even remove from the parental roof . . . It is palpably a system fraught with innumerable evils . . . [especially when] we consider the early direction of the child's mind to the value of money, and the consequent temptation to procure it by illicit means.[36]

There were complaints in abundance about youths of both sexes mingling promiscuously in the cheap theatres and taverns, sometimes in the company of prostitutes, drinking, singing and swearing in a lewd manner, gambling for pennies in the streets, entertaining themselves with dog-fights, playing dominoes and bagatelle for money or drink, wearing coloured ribbons in their hair, or ganging together to commit robberies. Whereas Worsley had condemned the independence granted to young people through wage labour in the factories and mills, Beggs thought the 'absence of restraint' among street urchins even worse, recounting how 'by the proceeds of their irregular pursuits, they are enabled to lead a life of idleness and licentious freedom'.[37] Micaiah Hill was so shocked by the precocity of the young that he posed himself a startling question — 'Can these be *children*?' — arriving at the disturbing conclusion that 'we must regard them as diminutive men'.[38] Matthew Davenport Hill was another who was struck by the adult freedom of the young delinquent — 'He knows much and a great deal too much of what is called life . . . He is self-reliant . . . he submits to no control' — and must be reckoned as 'a little stunted man'.[39]

These worries about the precocity of the young, which perhaps reflected a larger fear of the growing independence of the working class, provided a focal point for the mid-century preoccupation with mounting lawlessness. It may be remembered that this was exactly what struck Oliver Twist when, on arriving in dangerous London, he bumped into a 'strange sort of young gentleman' whom he would come to know as the Artful Dodger. He was 'about his own age', but 'one of the queerest-looking boys that Oliver had ever seen': 'He was a snub-nosed, flat-browed, common-faced boy enough; and as dirty a juvenile as one would wish to see; but he had about him all the airs and manners of a man.'[40]

Was the Factory to Blame?

These familiar complaints against weakened family ties, irresponsible working mothers, demoralising popular amusements and the unbridled freedom of the young were knitted together within the dominant mid-nineteenth-century scheme of understanding as the consequence of the advance of the manufacturing system. 'The factory system,' said Samuel Smiles in 1843, 'however much it may have added to the wealth of the country, has had a most deleterious effect on the domestic condition of the people. It has invaded the sanctuary of the home and broken up the family and social ties.'[41] The assumed relationship between the rapid advance of crime and the Industrial Revolution was one which invited the traditions of pastoralism — with its persuasive juxtaposition of the quiet countryside and the noisy city, the familiar order of village life as against the disorderly anonymity of the town. 'Rather more than fifty years ago,' as Henry Worsley remembered it, 'farmer and labourers might be said with some truth to have formed . . . one united family'. But 'the associations of rural life were interrupted' by the 'money-making mania'. Now 'economy was the order of the day — more industry and less conviviality':

> Any candid judge will acknowledge the manifest superiority of the past century; and in an investigation of the causes which have conspired to produce such an unhappy increase of juvenile crime, which is a blot upon the age, the altered relations of village life cannot be overlooked . . . Is it not most agreeable to all our notions and reasonings, that . . . in the convulsions of social change . . . the working classes should have generally deteriorated in moral condition?

There can be little doubt that Worsley was too generous in his feelings towards the eighteenth century where, as he prettily described it, labourers 'nestled like birds under the manorial eaves' of the patrician squires.[42] But it was typical of mid-century philanthropy that it should hold up some vision of harmony between the classes, and the faded traditions of paternalism often served to organise early Victorian perceptions of urban disorder. 'Charity once extended an invisible chain of sympathy between the higher and lower ranks of society,' wrote James Kay-Shuttleworth, 'which has been destroyed by the luckless pseudo-philanthropy of the law.'[43]

If the growth of the anarchic towns was thought to have shattered the controls on the working classes, the new system of labour was also held accountable, as when one of the many government reports from the 1840s on employment conditions described how they had 'conspired to give a character of independence — something American — to this population'.[44] But if 'Americanisation' was already feared in this bygone age, more common allegations against the factory system suggested that it encouraged dissolute habits by bringing together men and women in the same workplace, and factory owners themselves were not above criticism for failing to exercise proper supervision over their workforce.[45]

Henry Worsley's prize-winning essay developed a particularly fierce moral indictment of the factory system, lambasting the early manufacturers as even worse than slave-owners, 'careless lookers-on, whose eyes glistened only at the sight of gold': 'in general the character of the early manufacturers has few parallels in the records of unfeeling oppression'. The inhumanity of the system was faithfully reflected in 'the new nomenclature which the rise of manufacture introduced': 'The "labour market", "so many more *hands* wanted", are they not terms and expressions which represent in some sort, the idea which the proprietors and masters had generally formed of those whom they employed . . . mere tools or instruments for the accomplishment of work.'[46] In Worsley's impassioned condemnation of the new order, the work of demoralisation began in the very heart of the system, the factory itself. For the children who worked there, amidst 'the contagion of vicious example and impure conversation . . . compelled to make one of a society which is continually exhaling the miasma of vice . . . breathing its pollution every moment', the factory was 'a school of iniquity'. 'No other term can fitly represent its abominations except "Hell" ', he wrote, and these were strong words from a vicar:

> The restless motion of machinery has begun; the continual clack of the several wheels . . . the inconceivable powers of steam are at work . . . There reigns in the work-rooms a Babel of confused sounds — the irreverent laugh, the open blasphemy, the licentious conversation . . . anger is stirred into acts of tyranny . . . In the heart of the factory — an assemblage of the vile of human beings, a fermenting mass of sin and vice, such as we may well doubt was ever before concentrated in one burning focus. It seems as if the mighty capacities of steam had lent an impetus, not only to the industry and ingenuity of man, but an equal impetus to all his faculties and contrivances of vice.[47]

Such hostility to the factory system drew on well-established critical traditions and controversies about whether the factories improved the character of the people or brought about their moral downfall: lines of argument already well aired in the eighteenth century.[48] Worsley's exceptionally severe criticism earned him rebuke in some quarters, however, where it was judged that he had gone over the top. Outspoken opposition to the new system of manufacture might politically endanger the philanthropic movement, while his attitude also encouraged fatalism by implying the impossibility of reforming the morals of the manufacturing population.[49] There were, in any case, reasons to believe that Worsley's criticisms were false to both the spirit and the realities of the manufacturing towns.

The opposing line of argument, developed most ambitiously in Thomas Plint's *Crime in England* (1851), set out 'directly to combat the prevailing theory, that ignorance and immorality are greatly on the increase'.[50] Showing far more statistical ingenuity than the philanthropists, Plint demonstrated that if allowances were made for the different age structures of the manufacturing and agricultural districts — a necessity if strict comparisons were to be made between their crime rates, because the towns tended to be more youthful — then the statistical basis of the common association between the growth of towns and the growth of crime was effectively demolished. He also made it embarrassingly clear that in their innocent attempts to calculate the rocketing crime rate, the philanthropists had committed some elementary arithmetical howlers.[51] Particularly annoyed by Worsley's *Juvenile Depravity*, Plint rounded against the writings of the philanthropic movement as a 'rhapsody of sentimentalism', 'mere rhetorical flourish' which was 'completely worthless'. The unregulated squalor and sprawl of the towns, he admitted, allowed criminal subcultures to thrive; but the factory system itself could be relied upon to produce disciplined habits in its workforce. The factory disciplines, he argued, together with the advent of the press and other regular associations of urban life, would do more to civilise the working class than the work of 'a knot of educators', for there was 'a teaching of them, by the daily circumstances and events of life, of which these charlatans were profoundly ignorant'. Taking together their 'gross arithmetical blunders' and their hasty moral judgements against the manufacturing system,

Plint found himself in radical opposition to philanthropic assumptions: 'The fact is now patent, which men, not blinded by prejudice, and not having their mental vision intercepted by foregone conclusions, have for sometime strongly surmised; viz., that the morality of the manufacturing population ranks above the agricultural.'[52]

It is the old problem of facts versus feelings which has dogged us every step of the way — complicated here, admittedly, by the sharp rivalries between those who had a material interest in industrial advance and embraced it warts and all, as against those who feared the anarchy of the new industrial system and wished to preserve the familiar moral order of the past. But although Thomas Plint may have been better at sums than the philanthropic heavenly choir, his moral calculations were adrift from the times: significant fractions of the English ruling class and middle classes were becoming disillusioned with the moral and political incohesion of capitalist manufacture as early as the 1850s.[53] As for the philanthropists, when they bothered to mention Plint's work at all, it was either coolly received as a 'needless dispute . . . sometimes repulsive, seldom beneficial', or poohpoohed as self-evident nonsense.[54]

Not Money, But Morals: Manchester De-Materialised

Once again, there are wide margins of disagreement within this history of respectable fears in which the factual considerations do not necessarily support the dominant preoccupations of the era. Even allowing for the niceties of statistical reasoning, however, no one was denying that crime was on the rampage. The appalling wretchedness of the manufacturing towns was also only too obvious, and there was every reason to fear the 'dangerous classes', no less than the violent epidemics of cholera which periodically swept through the insanitary cities with an uncheckable force. The social landscape of Britain had been torn apart in the first half of the nineteenth century by the explosive energies of the Industrial Revolution, and what had been left in its wake was not always a pretty sight.

Manchester was the symbol of this new age, and in the 1830s and 1840s it had become almost fashionable to do the 'grand tour' of the Northern manufacturing districts — Dickens, Disraeli, Carlyle, de Tocqueville all came to worship at the shrine of steam-power. Unless they were overcome by the glittering wealth that seemed to pour out of its black chimneys, however, these visitors to Manchester went home shocked and horrified by its brutality.[55] Their ears were not accustomed to the racket of machinery, nor to the factories trembling with their violent energy. Their eyes were not attuned to the beauties of rivers coloured in purple dye, nor to the impenetrable fog that hung over the town. 'Manchester is the chimney of the world', said Major-General Sir Charles James Napier when appointed to command the Northern district at the time of the Chartist upheavals, but 'some duties are not to be done voluntarily, and to live in a chimney is one'.[56] He might also have mentioned (others did) the stink of the polluted rivers and the excrement piled high in the streets; the squalid cellar homes whose occupants huddled together in maggot numbers; the meagre articles of diet which these unfortunate people scraped together; the physical exhaustion of the long working day under abominable conditions; the wasting industrial diseases that afflicted so many who worked in the mills; the armies of unemployed 'hands' standing about the streets during periodic moments of industrial slump. Here in Manchester was a combination of circumstances so terrible in their consequences that in Ancoats, a working-class district, as few as 35 children out of 100 born would survive until their fifth year.

It is an equally terrible judgement on the early Victorian mentality, however, that when the philanthropists finally addressed themselves to this abomination it was the moral details which held their attention more than the material circumstances of poverty and squalor. Victorian eyes looked upon the poverty of the common people, but often they did not seem to see poverty. The philanthropists certainly got close enough to smell the poverty of the rookeries and slums, registered in their obsessional use of the metaphors of sewerage and pollution, but they did not recognise these material conditions as a material force which could move men and women.

Nowadays a common form of response to the relationships between crime and material conditions, which has assumed the status of 'common sense' in the postwar years, suggests that whereas in days-gone-by poverty may have offered some form of justification for certain kinds of crime, under the present social arrangements these justifications have become redundant.[57] Crime, it is so often said, is now 'for fun' and not born out of any social necessity. But what this gesture towards the material disparities between social classes fails to acknowledge is that even in the 1840s the early Victorians gave little or no weight to the material circumstances of unemployment, wretched housing and poverty in their understanding of the crimes of the poor. In their visions of decay and reclamation, the problem of the industrial cities was de-materialised. So that when they gazed upon the 'Hungry Forties', the urgency of the temporal wants of the labouring classes was diminished in comparison with their spiritual failings.

'The filthy dwellings and squalid misery', wrote Cornwallis, 'are rather the indication than the cause of crime': 'Until the mind is raised to *wish* for something of decency and comfort, it is in vain that you provide better lodgings and higher amusements.'[58] 'Without corresponding good habits, higher wages are no advantage to the population', said Beggs echoing Chadwick's judgement on 'an uneducated population whose wages had advanced beyond their habits'.[59] For Thomson, the criminal classes could already 'afford to spend largely from their dishonest gains in riotous living and debasing indulgences', while a government commission had also explained how 'crime is caused by dissipation not by want': 'The notion that crimes against property are caused by blameless poverty or destitution we find disproved at every step.'[60] The object of reformatory schools, as outlined by the Reverend Joseph Kingsmill, the Chaplain of Pentonville, should thus be to teach 'that poverty is no disgrace, when it comes in the way of God's providence, but only when it results from one's own vice' and the boys should be encouraged to 'resolve to be at once poor and respected, rather than a thief'.[61]

There was not an entire consensus here, and Samuel Phillips Day expressed his astonishment that so many of his contemporaries could deny 'that pauperism is a prolific source of juvenile delinquency'.[62] Micaiah Hill, too, tended to place more weight on the material conditions of the poor, although he dithered somewhat. So that, while 'the moral reform of parents . . . will be defeated . . . unless a revolution takes place in the dwellings of the poor', when it came to possible improvements in the employment conditions of the working class he thought it 'very questionable' that this could change their lot 'without a simultaneous revolution in their mental and moral condition'.[63] And Henry Worsley, who had heaped such furious criticism against the manufacturing system and the 'pig-sty' dwellings of the poor, also changed his tune. Whereas earlier he had praised 'the manifest superiority of the past century', now he protested that 'My reasonings must not be misconstrued into opposition to the pursuits and arrangements of modern life': 'No man in his senses, could conceive it either possible or desirable, to turn back the tide of a nation's industry, and reduce things to the position in which they were in a past century.'[64] It would have been very easy to misread Worsley on this point. But too many enquiries into juvenile crime, he assured us, were 'very generally too superficial' as when 'we are repeatedly told, that "want of employment", that the "absence of the bare necessities of life", are the causes of precocious vice'. On the contrary, 'many of the miseries of the working man and his family are self-caused' and among these 'self-originating' problems, drink was the main enemy: 'Non-employment itself, the abject want and destitution, are in the majority of instances the necessary product of the intemperance of parents.'[65]

Once more it was Thomas Plint who provided the most systematic rendering of an alternative view, showing that the criminal statistics suffered from 'violent oscillations' which could not possibly result from variations in the moral state of the nation, although they did correspond to fluctuations in food prices and periods of economic distress. Plint thought that his statistical proofs were 'too complete and palpable to be met any longer by the flippant iteration of the cuckoo note, "that poverty does not increase criminal offences" ',[66] but there were more than enough cuckoos in the philanthropic nest. The Reverend John Clay, Chaplain of Preston Gaol, produced his own statistics to show that 'good times' produced more criminal hazards than 'bad times'. It was 'a grief and a reproach . . . that the material prosperity of the industrious classes should be so constantly accompanied by the moral degradation of a large portion of them': 'Want and distress, uncombined with dissolute habits, are rarely operative in producing crime.'[67] Matthew Davenport Hill worked along the same lines, arguing that if 'a flush of prosperity' increased wages, this only 'overwhelms the working classes with temptations to indulge in liquor – a cause of crime which is more potent for its increase than the diffusion of plenty for its dimunation'.[68] When asked by the Select Committee appointed to enquire into criminal and destitute children in 1852 whether 'You are of the opinion that fewer crimes are committed under the influence of actual want?' Hill replied: 'Exactly so; very few crimes indeed . . . so few, that I am almost afraid to state how few they are.'[69] Mary Carpenter bore witness to the same belief: 'It is from the mismanagement or low moral condition of the parents, rather than from poverty, that juvenile crime flows.'[70]

Mary Carpenter, who was perhaps the most articulate exponent of this de-materialised vision of the poor, elaborated the point in *Juvenile Delinquents* (1853) where she described how society could be divided into 'two great classes' – those who lived by human and divine law, and those who did not. 'These are grand moral divisions,' she explained, 'which are irrespective of physical conditions in society': 'Poverty and destitution alone cannot be regarded as the sole criteria; they are not themselves the cause, although often the consequence of the spiritual condition.' And although Mary Carpenter admitted that 'the line of demarcation between the two classes' was 'invisible to the eye' – or, at least, to the unpractised eye – yet it was 'as certain in its existence as that line . . . with which the astronomer, who views the earth in its relation to the heavenly bodies, divides the northern from the southern hemisphere'.[71]

This philanthropic vision thus afforded to invisible structures of morality the force of mass or gravity, whereas the observable and material marks of poverty vanished into inconsequence in the thin moral atmosphere. Indeed, Mary Carpenter had perfected a technique of looking at the rags of poverty in such a way that they actually disappeared, as she explained in her thesis on *Reformatory Schools* (1851):

> These children have been hitherto so despised, that they hardly know whether there is within them anything to be respected. They therefore feel no respect for others. Yet let them be treated with respect, with true Christian politeness, and they will give a ready response. Nor let it be imagined an absurd thing to treat these poor little dirty children with respect. Their rags will disappear before those who look at them as young immortal beings.[72]

It was no doubt an admirable sentiment, although it is unlikely that the poor would have found much to admire, and it is one that can easily lend itself to so much humbug. As an artful dodger, dressed in your mortal rags, you might think that you were thieving for the bread by which to live until tomorrow; but philanthropy saw through your mortal rags to an immortal contest which would be settled by other criteria, whether you lived until tomorrow or not. Within this Christian universe of immortal souls, moral destitution was emphatically more dangerous and more significant than physical wretchedness, an emphasis which *The Times* had seen fit to define as a sanctimonious delusion in its response to Lord Ashley's intervention of 1843:

> a delusion which people are too ready to adopt in practice, to suppose that we are repairing our misdeed by any degree of zeal in a system of national education . . . Has our zeal to make the poor man live well been preceded by a care of his 'whereon to live'? Is it not a mockery of his misery to approach him with an education scheme in one hand and the Poor Law in another? His children are starving, and you take them from him, and teach them their catechisms; they ask for bread, and you give them a stone.[73]

One further consequence of this moral emphasis was that, set against the engulfing fears which described the enormity of the problem of the poor, the mid-nineteenth-century philanthropists were sometimes staggeringly optimistic about the ease with which they might accomplish their self-appointed task of reclamation. We can see this already in Mary Carpenter's response, and Mr Power the Recorder of Ipswich also recommended 'a kind, gentle but firm' approach, 'one that recognises in them a reasoning power and a soul' and he believed that 'you will be enabled to show the country that the reformation of "the perishing and dangerous classes" of children is not only possible, but an easy task'.[74] Entertaining even more improbable and utopian hopes, Cornwallis thought that given a system of elementary education and moral instruction 'it might safely be predicted that were it carried out perseveringly, the next generation would find the office of criminal judge nearly a sinecure'.[75] More to the point – given the wretched and generalised poverty of the common people – it was not going to cost a great deal. 'A penny spent in teaching will save a pound in punishing' was Begg's motto of good moral house-keeping, and Alexander Thomson also found a cheerful coincidence between the pecuniary instincts and the philanthropic crusade:

> The object here is not to save money, but to save the child. Happily, however, it is true economy to save the child . . . While a child costs £20 a year in prison, he can be thoroughly educated in an industrial feeding school at a cost from £5 to £8 a year . . . therefore, on the whole, *prevention* is both easier and cheaper than *punishment*.[76]

Flighty optimism such as this was nurtured not only by the shift away from the weighty material crisis of the industrial cities towards the moral failings of the poor, but also one suspects by a certain amount of ignorance of the lives of the labouring classes. Because we cannot help noticing that the early Victorians were deliciously vague in their descriptions and responses to juvenile lawlessness and in what they imagined to be the consequences of life in the manufacturing towns. Compared with the writings of the late Victorian and Edwardian philanthropic movement – where we repeatedly encounter vivid illustrations of the lives of the poor, a detailed understanding of their problems, and occasionally a sensitive portrayal of working-class dialect which could only come from people who had spent many long hours in their company – there are few signs of intimacy in the relations between classes in this earlier period, and not even the vaguest indication of the nuances of working-class life and working-class speech. We can read through volumes of books and pamphlets issuing from the 1840s and 1850s, piled high with statistical tables alluding to the enormity of the problem, but only very rarely (if ever) do we confront anything resembling a self-actuating human being. We learn only the barest details of people's lives: this child's father was a drunkard; that one's mother was a whore; while another is said to be uncomprehending of the enormity of his crime. Scores of juveniles are listed who do not know the Saviour's name, but who do know (and are supposed to re-enact) the lives and crimes of Jack Sheppard and Dick Turpin, or who think that Goliath and Pontius Pilate were apostles. We read accounts of gentleman philanthropists venturing into the rookeries at night, usually in the company of the police, poking their noses into foul dwellings and counting the number of bodies crammed together in each sleeping place. The promiscuous mingling of these bodies in their tight holes is described to us as a terrible moral abomination, and the smell which hits the respectable tourists' nostrils does not go unnoticed. But as to what this child's actual relationship was with that drunken mother or father; how the adventures of Dick Turpin figured in the conversation and play of those juveniles; in what way Goliath's giant strength might have been thought to contribute to the coming of a new world; or what the people huddled together in a single room thought of their midnight visitors, or of each other, or of the fact that they were obliged to sleep in such verminous contact – all that is left to the imagination.

Reflecting the deep, uncharted divisions between the classes in this period of history we have already come across other evidence of these factual confusions: the erroneous identification of Chartism as a blind heathen force, the easy equation between crime and impending revolution, the shaky statistical reasoning that was used to indict the morality of the manufacturing towns, the obsessional use of metaphor in the place of simple description, and the carefree dismissal of the material realities and limitations imposed upon the working class. Here was a vagueness which allowed philan-

thropy to give a full rein to its own clouded imaginings of
what the problem signified, without any of the necessary
encumbrance of factual difficulty, thereby to reach a remarkable degree of clarity and agreement about what was (when
all is said and done) a vastly complex and unfathomed
subject. It was in this sense that the prize-winning essayist,
the Reverend Henry Worsley, was perfectly qualified to speak
for Victorian feelings (as opposed to Victorian facts) about
the monstrous people of the manufacturing districts: his
parish was not in Manchester, or anywhere near it, but in the
sleepy Suffolk village of Easton.

Willing Obedience: the Principles of Reform and Consent

Whatever its inexactitudes, the crowning achievement of mid-
nineteenth-century philanthropy and the focus for its agreement was the inauguration of the reformative tradition: this
era witnessed the creation of a separate system of juvenile
justice, for example, together with the beginnings of reformatory schools for young offenders and industrial schools for
children who were beyond parental control. Gathering
together the work of earlier generations of philanthropic
agitation, this marked a decisive break with the earlier
reliance on physical annihilation and terror (through hanging,
transportation, whipping or torture) and the arrival of a
recognisably modern foundation for criminal justice according to which wrongdoers should be re-educated back into
the ranks of conformity.[77] It was a necessary shift of emphasis,
moreover, within the broader context of the dawning principles of liberal democracy. For just as a willing consent
would be required from the population at large if it were to
be regarded as capable of self-government, so this aspiration
was mirrored (even anticipated) in the philanthropic ambition
to reach the hearts and minds of law-breakers.

The supreme ideologist of this reformative principle,
again, was Mary Carpenter. It was little surprise to her that
attempts to discipline unruly youths by whipping and force
should so often fail, for 'would we teach them to respect the
law of man' it would only be 'by making them *feel* the

brotherhood of man'.[78] Nor that the juvenile penitentiary at Parkhurst — 'with its impassable walls — its bolts and keys — its sentinels with loaded guns — and officers regarded by the boys with profound suspicion — its military discipline and solitary cells' — should be visited with so many outbreaks of disorder, assaults on officers, damage to property, arson and riot.[79] Defining a different principle upon which to found the reformation of character and the safety of the State, Mary Carpenter drew the lesson of the 'radical error of the whole system' of 'the mechanical and military discipline of Parkhurst':

> It attempts to fashion children into machines instead of self-acting beings, to make them obedient prisoners within certain iron limits, not men who have been taught how *to use their liberty without abusing it* . . . Such a system must fail; for the boy whose heart has never been purified and softened . . . will never give a *willing* obedience . . . where there is no softening power of love to subdue him . . . where he regards with profound suspicion the appointed agents of his reformation. It is utterly vain to look for any real reformation where the heart is not touched.[80]

'Love', then, 'must be the ruling sentiment of all who attempt to influence and guide these children . . . Love draws with human cords far stronger than chains of iron.'[81]

No doubt it is the rustle of crinoline, rather than the rattle of chains, that we hear as we listen to Mary Carpenter's soothing prose. But, if we are not to fall into the trap of viewing this principle of reform as merely the soft 'feminine' touch of slushy sentimentalism, she needs to be read alongside other accounts of the period: Engels's fiery Manchester, Dickens's fog-bound London, Chadwick's alarming sanitary excursion, and the urgent fears of the Chartist threat. Mary Carpenter, too, was well acquainted with the violent energies of the mob. In her early twenties she had witnessed the fearful Bristol riots of 1831 when after savage reprisals by the dragoons 500 people were left dead during three days of rioting in which prisoners were broken out from the lock-ups, buildings were burned, ransacked and looted, and the Mansion House invaded. Her father had been caught up in the disturbances, making representations to the authorities on behalf of some of those convicted in the riots, and the memory of the events stayed with her until her old age, no less than those of the cholera epidemic of 1832 which devastated Bristol. It was indeed in the aftermath of these two catastrophies that, in her diaries, Mary Carpenter had devoted her life to work amongst the poor.[82]

Well qualified by personal experience, then, to represent the twin fears of her age — the epidemics of revolution and disease — we can also hear in Mary Carpenter's gentle lesson of 'willing obedience' the echo of another great principle enunciated at this time: that which John Stuart Mill declared 'On the Probable Futurity of the Labouring Classes' in 1849. Writing in the wake of the European revolutions of 1848, 'in an age of lawless violence and insecurity, and general hardness and roughness of manners, in which life is beset with dangers and sufferings at every step', Mill understood the willing obedience of the working class as the key to the future prospects of liberal democracy: 'The prospect of the future depends on the degree in which they can be made rational beings.'[83] Beings, that is, who in Mary Carpenter's words could 'use their liberty without abusing it'. The agreement is clear: in the microcosm of the reformative principle of 'willing obedience' — the principal object of penal reform that has been contested by the floggers and diehards since the moment of its inception — we can see the larger democratic principle of 'rule by consent'.[84]

Of course, this did not mean (and does not mean) that the principles of reform worked in perfect harmony with all the competing definitions of democracy. Philanthropy was vigorously opposed to popular democratic movements such as Chartism, and the Chartists were not exactly enamoured of the philanthropically conceived version of education: 'Educationalists', said the *Northern Star* in 1848, were 'the pretended friends, but the real enemies of the people'.[85] Chartism embraced versions of democracy and education as worked and conceived 'from below'; philanthropy's alignment was with forms of democratic rule as might be imposed 'from above'. When they are placed in their proper contexts, however, the ambitions of philanthropy clearly had little to do with the caricature of soft-boiled sentimentality, and begin to look more like a system of discipline and regulation that was compatible with the requirements of 'rule by consent' to which the dominant elites of Victorian Britain were slowly beginning to accommodate themselves.

The mid-nineteenth-century preoccupation with the children of the dangerous classes so often seemed to act as a symbol of this larger political transformation. Indeed, the reformation of the rising generation was arguably the only means by which to maintain effective control over a fractious people. The education of the young would prevent the working class from reproducing itself in its present condition — vicious, criminal, heathen, drunken, dangerous and Chartist — because the adult population, it was commonly said, were beyond reclamation. 'A painful hopelessness comes over the mind', wrote Thomas Beggs, 'an impression that they are beyond any human instrumentality, and that unless God in his mercy breathes upon them . . . they must perish as they have lived.' As things stood, he warned, nothing could be expected 'but deteriorated men and women, each generation lower in scale than that which has preceded it'. 'To implant habits of order, punctuality, industry and self-respect', then, 'the work must begin with the young . . . They are the depositories of our hopes and expectations.'[86] This intermingling of hopes and fears was typical. 'Our hope must be to mend the parents through the children, and if this be impossible, to save the children from the parents.'[87] 'The young and the incipient criminals are the hopeful class . . . just as it is easier to bend to our mind the pliant twig than the stout sapling; the gnarled oak is beyond our power.'[88] 'Until a degree of education of the lower classes is attained, which is hopeless for the present generation at least', Edwin Chadwick thought, then other remedies would have to be applied, including 'one description or another of precautionary force' in order to quell 'a population that is young, inexperienced, ignorant, credulous, irritable, passionate, and dangerous'.[89] As an example of a golden age of order and stability the early Victorian era is not just a failure, it is a disaster area.

8

Merrie England and its Unruly Apprentice

I am one of the maddest Fellows about the Town, I sing, roar,
serenade, bluster, break Windows, demolish Bawdy-houses, beat
Bawds, scower the Streets . . . Ay madam, I am all Frolick, how
many Knockers of Doors do you think I have at home now, that I
twisted off when I scower'd, guess now.

THOMAS SHADWELL, *The Scowrers*, 1690[1]

As we approach the pre-industrial world of 'Merrie England',
we edge on to a large historical controversy. Namely, whether
the commercial and industrial revolutions had brought a
civilising influence to bear upon an ignorant and savage people.
Or, as was more usually supposed in the heat of the event,
whether the ordered familiarity of 'Merrie England' had been
ripped apart by these great transforming powers, creating
an unrivalled deterioration in the morality and conduct of
the common people. There are arguments on both sides.[2]

The world's first Industrial Revolution was not accomplished in the blink of an eye, and although the 1840s were
experienced as a time of quite unparalleled disorder, there
were many precedents to these alarms which accompanied
the advance of the industrial system. In the 1820s, for
example, fears of mounting crime and disorder had been
already much in evidence.[3] In one remarkable sermon on
the coming of *The Last Days* (1829), published in the same
year that the Metropolitan Police were established, the
Reverend Edward Irving a minister of the National Scotch
Church had surveyed in all their hideous detail the forces

conspiring to produce 'the amazing increase of juvenile depredations and felonies' which threatened the end of the world. And, naturally enough, he was to be found looking back to happier times 'which every Scotsman above thirty years of age remembereth'.[4]

Generally speaking, Irving believed that an unwelcome 'spirit of liberality — or what we might now call 'permissiveness' — had within a generation or so caused 'the relaxation of every bond and obligation, that we may follow our own mind, and do our own pleasure'. Nowhere was this more evident than among the young. The employment of children enabled 'the little nurseling of the workshop to emancipate himself from his father's restraint, and to earn a livelihood for himself'. The spirit of liberality had also invaded the classroom — 'the decline of authority which is daily going on . . . so as in some cases to have denied the authority and right of the parent to overrule and sway and direct' — although it was not, of course, John Dewey who had subverted 'almost all the school-books and nursery-books' but 'that eminent servant of the beast from the bottomless pit' Jean-Jacques Rousseau. Above all, it was 'the dislocation and corruption of family ties' which guaranteed that the 'perilous times' of the Last Days as prophesised by Timothy (2, iii, 1–6) had arrived:

> From this relaxation of parental discipline . . . doth it come to pass that children who have been brought up within these thirty years, have nothing like the same reverence and submission to their parents . . . This is the cause of juvenile depredation: this is a chief cause of the increase of crime, especially amongst children . . . Hence, also, the trustlessness of apprentices and of domestic servants . . . the domestication of man's wild spirit is gone . . . Oh, oh! what a burden hath the Lord laid upon his ministers, to stand amidst the wreck of a dissolving society, and, like Canute, to preach unto the surging waves![5]

With characteristic historical brevity, Irving recommended that, to discover the source of this momentous collapse, it was only necessary 'to transport yourself a generation or two back' to 'the times which every Scotsman above thirty years of age remembereth . . . when parents, being industrious and economical, would pinch themselves to send their children all year round to the parish school'.[6] And I think it will be agreed that we have to pinch ourselves, too, if we are to remember that these laments for the recently departed traditions — which would not be out of place within our own deliberations on the decline and fall of the old 'way of life' — were not issued yesterday, but 150 years ago.

Steady State: The 'Affluent' Footpad Makes His Entrance

There was a spark of originality in Edward Irving's formulation of the problem, in that he did at least admit that there were difficulties involved in striking comparisons between the present tense and the past perfect: 'You must make allowances for the hallucinations of age.'[7] Even so, it would be necessary to hallucinate away a great deal of conflicting evidence and opinion in order to make room for his nostalgia for the recent past. It is reasonable to suppose, for example, that someone over thirty years of age in 1829 would remember the fearful turbulence of the Peterloo era. The first report of the Society for Investigating the Causes of the Alarming Increase of Juvenile Delinquency in the Metropolis, founded in 1815, was already berating the deterioration of morals and the decline of parental responsibility; and the committee which reported *On the State of the Police of the Metropolis* in 1817 was particularly vexed by disorderly houses which were described as 'schools and academies for vice' producing 'that early depravity and extent of juvenile delinquency which every magistrate acknowledges to exist'.[8] There might even be a faint memory of the 'crime waves' that accompanied the Napoleonic Wars; or from those with enough grey hairs, of the first hesitant steps to provide for the rehabilitation of juvenile criminals by the Philanthropic Society which had been founded in 1788. The Philanthropic Society's description of its target population left the reader in no doubt as to the perceived shortage of controls upon the young:

They are a class which belongs to no rank of the civil community, they are excommunicates in police, extra-social, extra-civil, extra-legal; they are links which have fallen off the chain of society, and which going to decay, inure and obstruct the movements of the whole machine.[9]

The late eighteenth century had also witnessed the first penitentiary experiments in England, designed to shore up the faltering disciplines of society.[10] Joseph Hanway's *Solitude in Imprisonment* (1776) was transfixed by 'the host of thieves which has of late years invaded us', as well as 'robbers . . . more numerous, more daring, more skilful in the pernicious acts of plunder', a combination of circumstances which threatened the stability of the whole social order. It was 'impossible to govern a people without the exertion of parental authority' and 'we have been, for some years, in an undisciplined state'. As he strung together the rigid vocabulary of complaints that we have encountered so many times in other epochs, debasing amusements and 'false tenderness' towards criminals played their part in Hanway's diagnosis, while a root cause (perhaps more surprisingly) was described as the excessive prosperity of the common people: 'Nothing seems to be more certain than . . . that our immoral ebriety is produced by *affluence*.' 'And as to Newspapers, which let us into scenes of villainy, they are hurtful.'[11]

That belief that 'affluence' was a primary cause of lawless disorder, although laughable by contemporary standards, was by no means an eccentricity in eighteenth-century England. A generation or so earlier, Daniel Defoe had launched himself against it in *The Complete English Tradesman* (1738): 'There seems to be a general corruption of manners throughout the kingdom' and 'it must be next to a miracle if this flourishing nation is not reduced to some very low distress, in a short time, if some methods cannot be found to curb that spirit of luxury and extravagance that seems to have seized on the minds of almost all ranks of men.'[12] In his *Enquiry into the Causes of the Late Increase of Robbers* (1751) Henry Fielding would preach the same sermon against 'luxury among the vulgar' and 'too frequent and expensive diversions among the lower kind of people'. 'The vast Torrent of luxury which of late Years hath poured itself into this Nation, hath greatly contributed to produce among many others, the Mischief I here complain of.' The expansion of trade, Fielding asserted, 'hath almost totally changed the Manners, Customs and Habits of the People, more especially of the lowest sort'. And with considerations such as these preying on his mind, he was drawn compulsively to the lesson of the fall of Rome: 'from Virtuous Industry to Wealth, from Wealth to Luxury, from Luxury to an Impatience of Discipline and Corruption of morals'. The permissive revolution was already on the wing, and Fielding confidently predicted that, as sure as night followed day, public safety would soon be replaced by anarchy: 'In fact, I make no doubt, but that the streets of this town, and the roads leading to it, will shortly be impassable without the utmost hazard.'[13]

One of the ways in which Merrie England supplied itself with merriment, it may be remembered, was through the gin-shop and here in the shadow of the repressive Gin Act of 1751 was another source of grievous complaint against the lower orders.[14] There were large areas of disagreement between Fielding and his contemporaries on details of policy and severity, although the large volume of repressive legislation considered by Parliament at this time bears witness to the nervous dispositon of the rulers of England, and his accusations were reiterated in the sovereign's address to the opening of Parliament in 1752 where he urged 'some effectual Provision to suppress those audacious Crimes of Robbery and Violence' which 'proceeded in a great Measure from that profligate Spirit of Irreligion, Idleness, Gaming and Extravagance'.[15]

Faced with such outrage, Fielding composed his own pretty scheme of a 'golden age' of civility, gazing back across an eternity to King Alfred's day when the system of tythings and Frankpledge had supplied effective checks on the behaviour of the people; or a little more recently to the reign of William the Conqueror when 'there was scarce a Robber to be found in the Kingdom'.[16] Fielding was not unwise to enlarge his historical perceptions, even to this extraordinary degree, for there was little comfort to be drawn from the experiences of more recent history. From the late seventeenth century onwards, the country had been deluged by complaints of increasing wickedness, pleasure-seeking, crime and disorder.[17] From the early 1600s the streets of London and other cities had been terrorised by a succession of organised gangs – calling themselves the Muns, Hectors, Bugles, Dead Boys, Tityre Tus, Roaring Boys, Tuquoques, Blues, Circling Boys, Nickers, Roysters, Scowrers, Bravadoes, Hawcubites and Mohocks – who found their amusement in breaking windows, demolishing taverns, assaulting the Watch, attacking wayfarers and slitting the noses of their victims with swords, rolling old ladies in barrels, and other violent frolicks.[18] If a servant or waiter should happen to be killed in the act of wrecking a tavern, it was said to have been considered a great joke to inform the proprietor to 'Put him on the bill!' The gangs also fought pitched battles among themselves, dressed with coloured ribbons to distinguish the different factions:

> Sir quoth the *Youth*, most *Boyes* in all our *Parish*
> Such ribbans weare in honor of our *Morish*.[19]

The Nickers were said to specialise in window-breaking. So, too, the Scowrers who were celebrated in Shadwell's late seventeenth-century comedy which (among other improbable happenings) hinted at the entertaining prospect of glaziers growing rich as a result of this nightly vandalism.[20] There were other dramatic portrayals of these gangs, such as John Gay's comedy *The Mohocks* (1712) which held up to ridicule the exaggerated fears surrounding their exploits – 'All the ground covered with noses, as thick as 'tis with hail-stones after a storm' –and the extravagance of the rumours circulating around the Mohocks prompted some observers to question whether they existed at all, or whether they were not like the stories of hobgoblins and boggarts.[21] But they were real enough, and what little is known about these gangs and their detailed habits suggests that they were of upper-class extraction, with some affinity to the notorious 'Hell Fire' clubs. The 'Tityre Tu' gang, certainly, were unlikely to have been uneducated ruffians, in that they took their name from the opening phrase of Virgil's First Eclogue.[22]

Even in their barest detail these accounts of street robbers, thieves and pick-pockets, drunkenness, mob violence and the lawless antics of upper-class rowdies give the lie to simple-minded notions of an era of pre-industrial calm. The streets of Old London — which had neither an effective system of street-lighting nor a police — were perilous in the extreme. As to the allegedly quiet countryside of Merrie England, although the pattern of crime and disorder was appreciably different in ways that corresponded to the altered social landscape of the pre-industrial world, things were no better. The persistent interruption of food riots, the burning of hay-ricks and barns, smuggling offences, wrecking and coastal plunder, and crimes associated with poaching and trespass are all well documented in the eighteenth century.[23] The advent of machinery, together with the changing pattern of employment conditons which accompanied the emergence of a market economy and *laissez-faire* imperatives, were the focus of aggravated labour unrest and periodic bouts of machine-breaking. The enclosure of common lands, which eliminated popular rights of access to grazing and timber, were another source of discontent, unleashing waves of protest across many years. Attacks on enclosure fences, the maiming of sheep and cattle, the destruction of newly planted spinnies of woodland, or damage to the mounds of fish ponds that were attached to the country seats of the English gentry which were established during the process of enclosure — these were regularly the kinds of questions around which ruling elites organised their perceptions of popular disorder. Nor were they in a mood to take it lying down, as testified by the enactments of the eighteenth century's Bloody Code which caused an astronomical rise in the number of hanging statutes, introducing the death penalty for literally hundreds of common-or-garden crimes.[24]

The precise contours of these disagreements often remain necessarily vague, for they originated in the grievances of humble people who were voiceless and weightless in comparison with the forces of might that were brought down against them. But occasionally, as Edward Thompson has shown, the voice of Merrie England's discontent rings out loud and clear through the threatening letters visited upon the powerful; an act of anonymous protest itself made punishable by death through the Black Act of 1723 and further reinforced by a statute of 1754:

> This is to asquaint you that We poor of Rosendale Rochdale Oldham Saddleworth Ashton have all mutally and firmly agreed by Word and Covinent and Oath to Fight and Stand by Each Other as long as Life doth last for We may as well all be hanged as starved to Death and to see ower Children weep for Bread and none to give Them . . . if You dont amaidately put a Stopp and let hus feel it next Saturday We will murder You all that We have down in Ower List and Wee will all bring a Faggot and burn down Your Houses.

That was from the year 1762, addressed to a Justice of the Peace. The spelling was none too regular, often tuned to the vagaries of local dialect, but the threats were invariably momentous. Even so, sometimes, as in the following letter received by the Mayor of Nottingham in 1800, the tone was remarkably proper:

> If the Men who were taken last Saturday be not set at Liberty by tomorrow night, the Shambles and the Change and the whole Square shall be set on Fire . . . Hoping that you will take this into consideration.

On other occasions, as in an anonymous threat of the same year that warned Essex millers and farmers to lower their prices, it was not:

> this will all com true . . . kill the over Seeer . . . kill him for one . . . there is 4 more we will kill . . . Burn up all the Mills and du all the Mischefe as we can . . . Burn up all ever thing an set fier tu the Gurnray.[25]

With neighbours such as these to contend with, Merrie England was no place to be out alone on a dark night.

Apprentices and Fairs

> 'An apprentice is likely to be idle, and almost always is so.'
> ADAM SMITH, *The Wealth of Nations*, 1776.[26]

Where the young were concerned, the major focus of anxiety in the eighteenth century was the apprenticeship system, and there was a steady downpour of complaint that defective apprenticeship was a direct cause of what was coming to be called 'juvenile delinquency'. Adam Smith's view was somewhat unusual, however, although not because he believed apprentices to be idle — that was never in dispute. Rather, because in a pure ideological expression of *laissez-faire* principle he argued that it was apprenticeship *per se* which injured a young man's morals — by preventing him from freely selling his labour, as and how he wished, an experience which Smith believed would encourage more industrious habits — while at the same time damaging trade by raising the level of wages and placing restrictions on the free supply of labour to the capitalist labour market.[27] The much more common complaint abhorred the very process of *laissez-faire* that Adam Smith embraced, regarding the degeneration of youthful morals as a consequence of the decline of the strict system of 'indoor' apprenticeship by which an apprentice lived in the household of the master for a term of seven years under close supervision. The triumphant march of *laissez-faire* was not to be halted, however, and in the teeth of opposition from labour organisations the full rigours of the older apprenticeship system were abolished in 1814.[28]

Nevertheless, the Industrial Revolution cannot be wholly blamed for the demise of the system of 'indoor' apprenticeship. The idealised 'family' of interests between employer and employed, so much lamented by the paternalistic philanthropists of the 1840s, was already the cause of much weeping a century before. 'Fifty or sixty years ago,' Defoe wrote in 1738, servants and apprentices 'were infinitely more under subjection than they are now; they were content to submit to family government, and the just regulations, which masters made in their houses, were not scorn'd and contemn'd as they are now.'[29]

Defoe's remarks were double-edged, in that they were directed as much against the negligence of masters as the naughtiness of apprentices, and there were black marks on both sides. As for the masters, irregular usages had already crept into the apprenticeship system in the 1600s, contravening the Elizabethan statute of 1563 which had established the strict indenture system. Instead of being housed under the master's roof, apprentices were sometimes farmed out into lodging houses and it was frequently alleged that masters took on too many apprentices to be able to exercise adequate supervision and control; or that youthful labour was used as a cheap alternative to adult tradesmen and labourers. Apprentices were also sometimes the object of gross cruelty. Quite apart from over-work, regular beatings, starvation diets and sexual exploitation, some masters even went as far as murder and castration.[30] Parish apprentices — orphans who were bound to masters by the parish guardians — were undoubtedly the most vulnerable.

The apprentices, for their part, were described in a voluminous literature as idle, violent and profligate. In London the apprentices were so numerous that they were an identifiable 'subculture', with its own standards, codes of honour, literature and heroes.[31] Apprentices had thrown themselves into the thick of the revolutionary agitation of the 1640s, and the more extreme factions of the English Revolution were notorious for their youthfulness.[32] Feasts and carnivals also provided seasonal occasions for the apprentices to assert their riotous traditions. On Shrove Tuesday, for example, the London apprentices were accustomed to work off their energies by wrecking bawdy-houses (ostensibly to preserve themselves from temptation during Lent) and territorial disputes between apprentices from rival parishes were probably not uncommon.[33] In Dublin, too, the Sundays during Lent were a time for street battles between the butcher-boys of Ormond Street Quay and the tailors of the Liberties, when the fellows and students of Trinity College might also join in the 'roaring fun' on the side of the Liberty boys: for this was also religious warfare and 'fun' it might have been, but friendly it was not. The butchers, for their part, delighted in 'houghing' their opponents by cutting the tendon of the foot which lamed a victim for life, an ancient Irish practice; and on one occasion when the tailors were victorious it is said that 'they carried their fallen foes into the butcher shops, threw the meat off the great hooks and hung the Ormond boys up by their jaws, leaving each butcher struggling on a hook in his own stall'.[34]

Against a background of rumour and disorder such as this,

a running battle on the rights and wrongs of apprentices and apprenticeship stretched back across two centuries. The strict enforcement of the 'indoor' system bound apprentices to their masters in such a way as to prohibit them from contracting marriage or from owning personal possessions without the master's express approval. Various regulations banned apprentices from public houses and brothels, from participating in dice and card games, and even the playing of music was sometimes forbidden. In Manchester in 1609 football rowdyism had been frowned upon, and in other trades and localities football games were outlawed. The Merchant Adventurers had a rule of curfew which also forbad apprentices to 'knock or ring at men's doors or beat at windows', and by a regulation of 1697 in Newcastle they were not allowed 'to get to fencing or dancing schools, nor to music houses, lotteries or playhouses, neither to keep any sort of horses, dogs for hunting, or fighting cocks'.[35] Regulations controlled what clothes and fashions apprentices might (or might not) wear, and the length of hair was another area of widespread prohibition. An order of 1603 that they should not 'weare their haire long nor locks at their ears like ruffians' provoked a long drawn-out battle in Newcastle in which the apprentices were eventually triumphant — but only after forty years of struggle, during which some recalcitrant youths were committed to prison with shaven heads.[36] In 1692 apprentices were included in an Act that prohibited hunting. A statute of 1757 banned cards, dice, shuffle-board, mississipi, billiards, skittles and nine-pins. In 1766 another Act allowed masters to bind runaway apprentices to further terms of service, if and when they were caught, for it is hardly surprising that apprentices would sometimes try to flee from their bondage, and acts of defiance and violence against masters were entirely common. 'The theory that masters in general exercised a wholesome discipline over apprentices', Dorothy George dryly observed, 'seems to have been theory only.'[37]

The behaviour of apprentices, as well as the controls exerted upon them, needs to be understood against a radically different understanding of childhood and youthfulness in the pre-industrial world. Apprentices would usually begin their term at the age of fourteen years, or thereabouts, so that their ranks were made out of young men and boys in their teens and early twenties. They were not strangers to work when they began their apprenticeship, however, for there was no protected era of childhood such as we know it today, and children would begin to work alongside their parents (or be deposited in another household as servants) at a tender age. And although it was not until the systematic cruelties of the Industrial Revolution that young children would be worked in mines and factories for an inhumanly long working day, even toddlers were expected to make some contribution to the household economy: John Locke advocated in 1797, for example, that the children of the poor should begin some form of work when they reached the age of three.[38] The indifference shown by some masters towards the well-being of their apprentices takes on a somewhat different aspect when set against these more general and well-ingrained indifferences of pre-industrial family life.[39] But these considerations must also make nineteenth-century laments for the old days when the family was not yet defiled look faintly ridiculous.

Complaints against the disorderliness of apprentices, which in many respects appear to have been entirely justified, must also be set alongside the nature of pre-industrial work organisation — which nowadays would strike us as grossly disordered in itself. The ale-house was a common site for tradesmen and journeymen to contract business, as well as being the place where wages were paid; and judging by contemporary accounts of the amount of liquor consumed during a normal working-day, even some workshops must have been indistinguishable from ale-houses.[40] There were seasonal irregularities in the pattern of work in many areas, and workshops would be abandoned for weeks at a time during harvest. The ordered, time-clocked rhythms of work that would come to be enforced within the factory system were entirely foreign to the pre-industrial worker.[41] Periods of hard work, interspersed with bouts of idleness and drinking, were regarded as a more normal and natural rhythm to the working week. The traditions of 'Saint Monday', religiously observed in some trades, dictated that the week should begin with an extra holiday for drinking and social intercourse which would sometimes stretch into Tuesday, with the week's tasks crammed into the remaining days and rattled off at a cracking pace.[42]

Customs such as 'Saint Monday', while indicating quite radically different attitudes towards life and labour before the advent of the factory system, also point us back towards a host of ancient traditions associated with feast days and festivals in the pre-industrial world: Wakes and Revels, Plough Monday, Hock Tuesday, May Day, maypoles, Rush-bearing processions, Morris-dancing and hobby-horses, Whitsun Ales and Church Ales, fertility rites such as 'gang days' or 'cross days', Mummers, the Summer Lords and Ladies, and the Lords of Misrule. In the sixteenth century steps had been taken to curb such practices, which were viewed as relics of paganism or Popery, as well as occasions for popular debauchery and disorder.[43] Undoubtedly pre-Christian in origin, but often accommodated in Saint Days and Rogation Days, the traditions of carnival — *Fastnacht* in Germany, *Mardi Gras* in France — were spread throughout pre-modern Europe.

Sometimes we will be struck, necessarily, by the innocent charm of these rituals. In certain parts of France, for example, it was held that at Candelmas in early February a bear poked his nose out of the forest and predicted how long the winter would last: a beguiling form of long-range weather forecast for an agricultural community that would be nearing the end of its winter food stocks.[44] But feasts and carnivals were also associated with orgies of drunkenness and brutalising sports and pastimes: dog-fighting, bear-baiting, cock-fighting and pugilistic encounters such as those passed down in the North of England as 'purling' in which men engaged in mortal combat with iron-studded clogs. Feast days could also act as the tinder-box for riot, gang rapes, religious pogroms, or attacks on minority groups and foreigners as instanced by London's 'evil May Day' of 1517.[45]

Lewdness and violence alike were condemned by Puritans and Calvinists who frowned upon the singing of 'carnal songs' by boys and girls gathered beneath Maypoles, or the filling of children's shoes on the feast of St Nicholas with 'sweets and nonsense'. The Elizabethan Puritan Philip Stubbes in his *Anatomy of Abuses* (1583) regarded feast days as the source of all kinds of moral ruin: dancing was denounced as 'filthy groping and unclean handling'; football was attacked as 'a friendly kind of fight' and 'a murthering play'; and from many quarters it was alleged that 'popular songs too often presented criminals as heroes'.[46]

Apprentices and youths, as we might expect, were commonly at the centre of these festivities. Many of the traditions of carnival indulged in ritual mockery of the community's elders and betters, providing opportunities for licensed disorder. Formalised in some parts of Europe in the election of boy bishops who ridiculed their elders, in mock sermons and the ritual desecration of religious emblems, or in the absurd judgements of the Lords of Misrule, the folk imagery of pre-industrial Europe was saturated with fantasies of reprisal against the powerful and against existing moral codes. Numerous forms of role reversal and other theatrical devices were employed to this end. We see it in the figure of 'Mother Folly' — a man dressed as a woman — and in other reversals by which men and women exchanged clothing or turned their clothes back-to-front. We see it also among the London chimney-sweeps who covered themselves in flour on May Day; in a procession of mock priests carrying gaming-boards instead of prayer-books; and in the enormous variety of reversals portrayed in sixteenth-century pamphlets and engravings through which the traditions of carnival momentarily turned the world upside down:

A man straddling an upside-down donkey and being beaten by his wife. In some pictures mice eat cats. A wolf watches over sheep; they devour him. Children spank parents. The father, not the mother, wipes a baby's bottom. The cart goes before the horse; travellers pull a stage coach. Hens mount roosters; roosters lay eggs. The king goes on foot. The sick man cares for the doctor. The client advises the lawyer. The general sweeps the barracks courtyard. The fisherman gets caught. Rabbits trap a hunter. The goose puts the cook in a pot. The turkey roasts the farmer. A wheelbarrow stows a sack on a man's back. A maiden serenades at a man's window. Tigers in the zoo kill their keeper who was trying to eat them.[47]

There was an unhealthy spirit of insubordination implicit

in such imagery, and in the campaign to reform popular culture from the sixteenth century onwards there were any number of objections to the way in which carnival undermined religion, matrimony and much else besides. On occasion, ritual turned into reality, reminding us of the intimate relationships between the imagery of misrule and the actualities of social protest.

Forms of Protest: Ancient and Modern

> And now the cause of all their *fear*
> By slow degrees approach'd so near,
> They might distinguish diff'rent noyse
> Of *Horns*, and *Pans*, and *Dogs*, and *Boyse*.
>
> SAMUEL BUTLER, *Hudibras*[48]

A related stock of offensive ritual, again found in many parts of Europe, was reserved for traditional targets of communal resentment and hostility — lecherers, promiscuous women, wife-beaters, nagging wives or hen-pecked husbands, adulterers, swindlers and misers. Known in different parts of England as 'Riding the Stang', 'Skimmington', the 'Hooset Hunt' or 'Cool Staffing', these ancient traditions incorporated a variety of ridicule and abuse. The victim would be visited by a boisterous crowd who would sometimes have their faces 'blacked' or disguised, terrifying effigies might be paraded or burned, stink-bombs released and missiles thrown — all to the accompanying racket of 'rough music' played on crude instruments such as pots and pans, improvised drums and whistles, bells, rattles and jews' harps, with much wailing and screeching to add to the effect. 'The din of cleavers, tongs, tambourines,' as Thomas Hardy remembered the serenade of the 'Skimmity' in *The Mayor of Casterbridge*, 'kits, crouds, humstrums, serpents, rams' horns, and other historical kinds of music.'[49] In full cry the 'Skimmington' would parade an effigy of the ridiculed victim seated backwards on a donkey or a wooden pole; or the victim's own person would be hauled about and made to 'ride the Stang', in which case he or she might be roughly treated or ducked into a convenient pond or dung-heap. In all events, the indignities would continue until a customary fine was paid to buy off the persecutors. The pattern appears to have been much the same in the wider European traditions of *charivari, chevauchée, scampanate, cencerrada* and *katzenmusik.* The word 'Stang' was itself of Scandinavian origin, meaning 'pole' or 'stake', and in the same manner the *nid stöng* (or scorn-stake) employed a horse's head on a pole with a likeness of the victim attached to it.[50]

Especially where sexual misconduct was concerned, role reversals again appear to have been much in evidence. In Samuel Butler's seventeenth-century description of the English 'Skimmington', there was 'A Petticoat displayed, and Rampant' carried by the procession's standard-bearer to signify the discomfort of a humiliated husband and the dominance of his spouse, 'The Proud Virago-Minx' and 'Amazon triumphant'.[51] In Andrew Marvell's account, this was the purpose and origin of the Skimmington:

> A punishment invented first to awe
> Masculine Wives, transgressing Natures law
> Where when the brawny Female disobeys,
> And beats the Husband till for peace he prays . . .
> . . . the just Street does the next House invade,
> Mounting the neighbour Couple on lean Jade.
> The Distaff knocks, the Grains from Kettles fly,
> And Boys and Girls in Troops run houting by;
> Prudent Antiquity, that knew by Shame,
> Better than Law, Domestick Crimes to tame.[52]

But although husband-beating seems to have figured prominently in these customs, the tactic of reversal had a much wider application within the traditions of misrule, and so grotesque were some of the spectacles of emasculation held up to public ridicule that they suggest a celebration (rather than a denigration) of feminine vengeance. Natalie Davis, whose historical researches have elaborated the subversive undertones of what she calls 'political transvestism', has described some of the awesome theatrical devices employed to stand the world on its head:

> The festive organisations mounted floats to display the actual circumstances of the monstrous beating: the wives were shown hitting their husbands with distaffs, tripe, sticks, trenchers, water pots; throwing stones at them; pulling their beards; or kicking them in the genitalia.[53]

It was, then, with rude and violent pantomime such as this that pre-industrial communities circumscribed the boundaries of their far from rigid ethical codes. In a somewhat jollier frame of mind, similar customs allowed that the houses of marriageable girls should be wreathed with the 'May Bush'; or a holly bush might be left to declare a secret love. But young ladies of immodest virtue would be visited on 'Mischief Night' with the gorse bush, also known as the 'Smelly Bush', which makes the meaning of the ritual clear enough.[54]

Here was a universe of boisterously profane pre-modern ritual and imagery, providing an arena for licensed disorder, merry-making, mischief and protest which was only displaced in the course of many generations. As E. K. Chambers describes it, these customs stood 'on the border line between play and jurisprudence', and the relationships between misrule and the possibilities of political disaffection were also always intimate. At Dijon in 1630, for example, *Mère Folle* and her *Infanterie* rioted against royal tax officers, and within the traditions of 'riot' which were so well established in pre-industrial England the rituals of misrule and Skimmington were also put to political uses in food riots and in some eighteenth-century labour disputes.[55]

In Wales, the custom was known as *ceffyl pren* (the wooden horse) and as late as the Rebecca disturbances of the 1830s and 1840s — where the figure of Rebecca, a man dressed as a woman, was herself reminiscent of 'Mother Folly' — the *ceffyl pren* once again rode the Welsh hills. We have a detailed account of the practice from an informant to the Home Secretary in 1837:

> The figure of a Horse made of wood is carried by four or six men and on it is carried a man in disguise. Ten or eleven o'clock at night is usually the hour chosen for this exhibition which is accompanied

> by a large concourse of people, not fewer perhaps than four or five hundred — many carrying torches, some guns, and others having their faces blackened and their person disguised and not unfrequently using obscene and disgusting exhibitions. They proceed . . . in a tumultous and noisy manner to the residence of the person for whom the effigy is intended and there the Man on the Horse delivers an oration or 'preaches' as it is called against him, full of abuse, and sometimes in language obscene and disgusting. This is repeated for three successive weeks, one night in each week, and at the conclusion, that is to say in the third week, the effigy is burned in some public place amidst the shouts and noise of the people accompanying it.[56]

Magistrates, urgently trying to suppress these customs and the associated use of 'squibs, rockets, serpents or other fireworks', were most alarmed that the *ceffyl pren* — long used against sexual malpractices — was being turned to new political uses. So, an anonymous letter announcing an attack on the tollgate at Penlone Blaenant warned employers to 'send all your workmen and come there with Guns or Pickaxes or Mattocks or Swords or music and dress in Women's clothes — the meeting is to begin at 9 o'clock — or else', signed 'Rebecca'. Another note, this time from Llechryd, reminds us of the religious convictions which supported these popular discontents:

> The poor asked for Bread, but fools gave stones
> Behold Christ's cross and holy Crown
> Now he casts guilty Nations down
> And gives the poor a good release
> Who Government shall never cease
> *The New Jerusalem*
> As it was in Noah's day so shall it be again.[57]

Worried magistrates also reported that the *ceffyl pren* had been carried against people who had informed against poachers and given evidence in cases of taking timber from plantations — typically contested rural 'crimes' which the poor held to be their 'rights' — and at Llangoedmor an attempt was made to dissuade a farmer from enlarging his holding by burning him in effigy.[58] A more direct way of levelling an enclosure fence, admittedly, was to make a feast-day the occasion for a monster football match, to be conducted by several hundred disgruntled villagers across the disputed tract of land.[59] This was itself a tactic that once again married the festive traditions to sources of popular grievance, although Becca and Her Children were probably the last historical instance of a knowing intersection between the ancient rites of misrule and social protest: when as well as attacking tollgates, fish-weirs and workhouses, Rebecca also found time to return to some of her more traditional haunts — settling scores with wife-beaters, intervening in family feuds, and returning illegitimate children to their rightful parents.[60]

The traditions of misrule have been displaced from the active centre of public life over the centuries, although they have taken a long time dying. 'Riding the Stang' is almost certainly related to the American 'Wild West' custom of punishing wrongdoers by 'riding them out of town on a rail', and to the ritual degradation of 'tarring and feathering'. Nationalistic enthusiasms have come to express themselves in these ways, as when at the time of the Crimean War an anti-Russian effigy was paraded on Guy Fawkes Day 'under a rather formidable escort of juveniles'.[61] Pointing back towards the more ancient contours of festive misrule, from the same Guy Fawkes celebration in 1856 we also hear of an 'effigy of a bishop in full Canonicals, under the guard of a host of boys . . . attacked by a brigade of other boys, wearing badges of green ribbons and armed with staves . . . and despite smart resistance, the effigy was destroyed, and portions of it carried away by the attacking party'.[62] Perhaps, a few decades after Rebecca, we can again glimpse the lingering traditions of Skimmington in the attacks of the 1880s on Salvationists by the 'Skeleton Army' who in the West Country were decked out in coloured tinsel and other carnival attire.[63] Then, from working-class London at the turn of the century we hear of a local protest against a police informer which showed its displeasure by burning him in effigy.[64] We have already seen how effigies representing 'Hooliganism' were burned on Guy Fawkes Night in 1898, when in other localities the Khalifa — Britain's foe in the Sudan campaign — was roasted. In the aftermath of the terrible London water shortage of that year popular socialist feeling also availed itself of the tradition, and the people of the East End warmed their hands by bonfires with a Guy in 'an old top hat, a large white paper waistcoat, and a dog-chain for a watch-guard . . . intended to represent a director of a well-known water company'.[65]

No doubt we can see other lines of continuity within the traditions of protest, ancient and modern. In political demonstrations, for example, which regularly involve the burning of effigies, the carrying of banners and emblems, the use of fancy-dress and other theatrical devices of public mockery, chants and slogans which ridicule the mighty, and the throwing of rotten eggs: where the carrying of fresh eggs in procession was once an ancient symbol of fertility, and addled eggs the sign of something else. Some of these time-honoured customs and seasonal festivities are preserved in the language and folklore of children.[66] And although their origins are no longer remembered, the bawdy, sexual role-reversals of carnival peep out at us in the characters of the Old Dame and the Principal Boy in the seasonal English pantomime. Misrule still has a toehold in the modern world in the form of student rags, in the tincans irreverently attached to the carriages of newly weds, and through initiation ceremonies such as 'black balling' whereby ritual humiliation has for centuries signalled the acceptance of an apprentice into his trade. Within this enlarged historical vision of what we now so easily slap down as the 'permissive' deluge of mindless 'hooligans' and 'yobbos', we might also reflect on the continuities between the riotous traditions of carnival and the ritual confrontations between football rowdies with their own 'rough music' medleys; or the outbreaks of seasonal disorder at those modern feast-days, the Bank Holiday excursions. We might also feel some obligation to reassess the excitements that have accompanied the Caribbean carnival in London which has so often been portrayed as an 'alien' intrusion within British public life. Usually we think of disturbances such as these as a break with tradition; but perhaps they are more usefully understood as tradition itself.

A BRITON IN THE TIME OF PEACE
From a sketch taken at Notting Hill.
(from *Punch* 1856)

PART FOUR

Making Sense of 'Law-and-Order' Myth

A class of morbid philanthropists, whose sentimentality swallows up all sense of the rational, and obliviates the distinction between right and wrong . . . All sympathy expressed for the offender, and none reserved for the innocent victim.

A County Magistrate (Anon.), *Juvenile Delinquency*, 1848

We need to consider why the peaceful people of England are changing . . . Over the 200 years up to 1945, Britain became so settled in internal peace that many came to believe that respect for the person and property of fellow-citizens was something which existed naturally.

The Daily Telegraph, 11 March 1982

A myth is, of course, not a fairy story. It is the presentation of facts belonging to one category in the idioms appropriate to another. To explode a myth is accordingly not to deny the facts but to re-allocate them.

Gilbert Ryle, *The Concept of Mind*

We must begin to retrace our steps. History is not usually written backwards, of course, although the logic of this history of respectable fears — repeatedly accusing the here-and-now present of succumbing to an unprecedented deluge of crime and immorality, while gazing back fondly to the recently and dearly departed past — has insisted that we follow it step by step, leafing back through the pages of history in search of the still unlocated 'golden age'. A golden age, it is so often said, where, by its emphasis on 'traditional' discipline and the unswerving distinction between right and wrong, the 'British way of life' kept the hooligan wolf from the door.

What this historical journey has revealed to us, by contrast, is a seamless tapestry of fears and complaints about the deteriorated present; a long and connected history that makes plain the shortcomings of the more usual view of our cultural inheritance which is severely limited by its simple nostalgia for the old 'way of life'. What is less clear, is the extent to which we can make reliable comparisons between different epochs, and thereby judge the historical realities of crime and violence.

Taken in its own terms, this history of respectable fears describes to us a moral downfall among the British people of landslide proportions. But can it be taken in its own terms? This is a question surrounded by the utmost difficulty.

The Vocabulary of Decline: Everything Changes, Nothing Moves

I should say at once that I am not trying to promote a 'flat earth' version of history according to which nothing ever changes: social circumstances do change, and undeniably. Nor am I trying to re-invent a primitive theory of the 'historical wheel' which rolls on through the ages, as if events move in cycles and periodically repeat themselves. Even so, in trying to make sense of this history we must take as a central plank of our understanding its formidable stability. A stability, what is more, which repetitiously identifies some aspect of 'social change' as the cause of the loosening of tradition, but which is itself paradoxically immune to change.

If we accept these accusations at face value, then generation by generation, crime and disorder increase by leaps and bounds. Parental care plumbs increasing depths of irresponsibility, while the shortage of authority in the home is said to be mirrored by the excessive leniency of the law and the interference of sentimentalists. As the rising generation soars to new heights of insubordination and depravity, working mothers are reliably identified within this otherwise predominantly masculine discourse as a primary cause of these 'new' outrages — whether by reference to the mill-hands of the 1840s, the deterioration of motherhood in the Edwardian years, or the careless guardians of the 'latch-key' kids in the postwar years. Abuse is piled against mass education from its beginnings in the Ragged Schools, via the 'Bored Schools' of the early 1900s, to the 'permissive' jungle of the modern comprehensive system. Spectator football is also associated with violence, rowdyism and un-sporting behaviour from the moment of its inception, while on a wider front popular entertainments of all kinds have been blamed for dragging down public morals in a gathering pattern of accusation which remains essentially the same even though it is attached to radically different forms of amusement: pre-modern feasts and festivals; eighteenth-century theatres and bawdy-houses; mid-nineteenth-century penny gaffs; the Music Halls of the 'Gay' Nineties; the first flickering danger-signs from the silent movies; the Hollywood picture palaces between the wars; and then television viewing in our own historical time. Each, in its own time, has been accused of encouraging a moral debauch; each has been said to encourage imitative crime among the young. Another accusation that echoes across the centuries, sometimes involving quite improbable justifications, alleges that the common people are living in a condition of unbridled freedom and luxury. Once again, the youth are seen to be the worst afflicted by the weakening temptations of 'affluence'. And nor does it matter a great deal, in the way in which the

complaint has been phrased, whether this refers to the 'affluence' of the eighteenth century, the young factory slaves of
the Industrial Revolution, the Edwardian van-boy, the irresponsible pleasures said to have been heaped upon the young
during the 1930s depression, or the dazzling entrance of the
'war babies' in their Teddy Boy suits, and the other monstrous
apparitions that constitute this history of the British Hooligan.

The crystallising focus for this immovable preoccupation
with the erosion of social discipline and the corruption of the
national character is the awesome spectre of crime and violence, perpetually spiralling upwards. The fact that young
people are over-represented in the criminal statistics is repeatedly rediscovered in each successive wave of concern as a
particularly 'new' and shocking feature of the problem. While
at the heart of the matter stands the 'un-British' crime of
violence, its supposedly alien presence asserting itself time
and time again in 'new' and unparalleled forms: the lawless
tribes of 'street arabs' of the 1840s; the ungentlemanly garotters of the 1860s; the degenerated 'un-English' Hooligan of
the 1890s; the Hollywood-inspired motor-bandits and bag-
snatchers of the 1930s; the new streak of violence shown by
the 'Americanised' Teds; the 'foreign' importation of street
crime by the black muggers. This recurring belief in the alien
interruption of violence into Britain's domestic affairs, which
must be counted as a dominant aspect of the British political
culture, shows not the slightest sign of abating itself. 'Since
the war', says the Hytner Report on the Moss Side disturbances
of 1981, 'the means used to manifest violent feelings have,
beyond doubt, become uglier', providing a clear restatement
of the principal element of the myth: 'At one time to kick in
the head somebody lying on the ground was regarded as "un-
British" as was the use of a knife in a fight.'[1] The awkward
fact, however, is that a hundred years ago when the notorious
'Scuttlers' kicked and hacked their way to territorial supremacy against rival gangs, the citizens of Manchester were saying
exactly the same thing.

Novelty and Continuity: the Foundations of Myth

What are we to make of this relentless history of decline?
Without a shadow of doubt, each era has been sure of the

truthfulness of its claim that things were getting steadily worse, and equally confident in the tranquillity of the past — although, significantly, there have always been those who questioned whether the problem had become enlarged in the public mind. Each era has also understood itself as standing at a point of radical discontinuity with the past. But when we reconnect these bursts of discontent into a continuing history of deterioration, must not the credibility snap — unless, that is, we judge ourselves to be in a worse condition than the poor, brutalised human beings who suffered the worst effects of the Industrial Revolution? If we listen to the documentation of history, rather than the pulse of our contemporary anxieties, is it not a little fanciful to believe that Britain's well-policed streets in the 1980s are more perilous than Henry Fielding's disorderly London, Engels's fiery Manchester, or the turbulent street life known to the original Hooligans? Or, in order to guarantee the fears of the present in the terms in which they are presented, must we discount the fears and facts of the past?

The recurring allegations against the decline of the family must also invite suspicion. Not least because they invariably issue from that well-heeled section of the community which segregates its own children away from the family in private schools and preparatory schools, as soon as it is decently possible to do so. But equally, we must ask where — just where? — did the family exercise such a dominant influence in the lives of the mass of people? The historical record registers centuries of complaint against weakened family ties. Were those who complained in the past, therefore, wrong to complain? Had they lost their sense of perspective? And if so, why could they not see what can now be seen so clearly: namely, that in their time (which is our past) the family was alive and well? The historical record also reminds us that in the past the conditions of life were commonly so wretched as to offer no material basis on which a decent family life could be built. So that, if we mean by 'the family' the kinds of shared pursuits and beliefs, together with the careful nurturing of children, which might be thought to characterise the modern family when it is fulfilling its functions, then unquestionably the family today is stronger — both as a material force and as an ideology — that at any time in remembered history. Indeed, whether we attend to the apparently ever-increasing problem of lawless violence and unsafe streets, the perpetual decline of the family, or the barrage of criticism against popular amusements, we must be tempted to discount this history — which invites the accusation 'Cry wolf!' or 'The record is stuck!' — as nothing more than a litany of hallucinatory fears that bears little or no relation to reality.

Nevertheless, we must proceed with caution. It is clear, I think, that we are dealing with a form of moral dodo-ism, marked by its inability to keep pace with a moving world and to adapt its complaints to sometimes dramatic social alterations. But it is an unusually lively dodo: one that keeps escaping from the museum, and which is currently on the rampage in the vigorous shape of the 'law-and-order' movement. It is therefore not enough to shrug off these fears and doom fantasies as mothball reaction, or to say that they signify nothing. Because, while we might wish to redress the historical dimension, crime and violence are indisputably immediate social realities; and the fears which circulate around the criminal question are a potent cultural and political force. How is it, then, that this antiquated vocabulary of accusations, which was fashioned under such manifestly different social conditions, is still capable of moving men and women in the contemporary world?

In trying to make sense of what this history says to us, we face an immediate point of confusion. There is, on the one hand, a repetitious and rigidly immovable vocabulary of complaints and fears; while at the same time this ages-old tapestry is held up as something entirely new and unprecedented: both in terms of the complaints themselves, and the problems to which they direct our attention. Historical realism insists that we must find some way of holding on to the realities and specificities of street violence, and the anxieties that surround it, while throwing out the claim of novelty. Within the present climate of opinion this is not easy, because if the worries of the present day are at all diminished — as they are, most directly, by showing that they are in no way unparalleled — then the inevitable complaint will be raised that, 'You are not taking the problem seriously.' I will argue, against this, that if the spurious novelty is discarded, this must actually incline us to take the problem *more* seriously and not *less* seriously.

In order to begin to untangle the mythical nature of this history of respectable fears, it will be useful to adopt Gilbert Ryle's distinction between myths and fairy stories. 'Law-and-order' enthusiasts who perpetrate the belief in a pre-existing era of tranquillity certainly tell fairy stories about the past: because they get their facts wrong and thus talk nonsense. But the preoccupation with lawlessness is not itself nonsense, because the facts of crime and violence are evident enough. In Ryle's terms, however, it is not facts that are at issue in the creation of myth, and the doom fantasies of 'law-and-order' are mythological not because there are *too few* facts to grapple with, but *too many*. 'Law-and-order' myths restrict attention to the facts of the immediate present, while turning a blind eye towards the over-flowing evidence of the past.

Where myth enters, to follow Ryle, is in 'the presentation of facts belonging to one category in the idioms appropriate to another', and in order to combat myth the task is 'not to deny the facts but to re-allocate them'.[2] The twin mythologies of 'law-and-order' and 'permissive' rot thus arise out of the way in which the facts of disorder are paraded within a historical idiom of decline and discontinuity. Whereas, if we reinstate the facts of the past it becomes clear that the preoccupation with lawlessness belongs more properly to a remarkably stable tradition. Rather than being cast in the historical idiom of *change*, that is, the facts of crime and disorder must be re-allocated within the idiom of *continuity*.

The continuities are abundant: both in the actualities of crime and hooliganism, and in the ways in which the problem is perceived and understood. We can see them in the conflicts between generations; in the conflicts between classes; in the perpetual tendency to view the past nostalgically; and also to see the future as posing a threat. Then, there is the continuing social reproduction of an under-class which as the traditional location of riotous discontent is repeatedly the object of fearful scrutiny within this unfolding history. There should be nothing staggering in the discovery that crime and violence are not new, but it is the continual reappearance of these ancient preoccupations as if they were 'new' and unrivalled in their enormity that renders it necessary to state the obvious. Here in the abundant confusion between what changes and what is constant, the basis of myth is laid — myth granted numerical certainty by the criminal statistics which, obeying their own grammar of continuity, spiral relentlessly upwards across centuries and obligingly confirm our worst fears of social ruin. In surveying the continuities within hooligan history, I will start with the crime statistics.

Painting by Numbers

> It is, I say, from such wretched data as these that the melancholy conclusion is drawn, that the progress of civilisation, so far from amending public morals, has even been productive of a positive increase of crime!
>
> FREDERIC HILL, 1853.[3]

Criminal statistics are notoriously unreliable as measures of the actual extent of criminal activity, to such a degree that it is not unknown for historians to discount them altogether.[4] The reason for their notoriety is that they are complicated by a number of factors other than real changes in levels of crime. The growing size of the police force and its supporting apparatus is the most obvious and general factor. Changes in the routines of law enforcement, the increased mobility of the police, changes in what the law counts as crime, fluctuations in the vigour with which the law is applied, and shifts in public attitudes and tolerance — these must all be counted within the hidden dimensions of the manufacture of crime figures.

To take just one example of where a naive reading of official crime statistics will lead us, Chief Constable James Anderton in his 'Crime Top Growth Industry' speech of 1978 pointed to the apparently disturbing fact that 'crimes recorded in England and Wales in 1900 stood at 77,934; by 1976 that figure had reached 2,135,713'. 'In the same period', he added for good measure, 'convictions rose from 45,259 to 415,471.'[5] It is all too obvious what conclusion Mr Anderton would like us to arrive at. But having spent a little time among the disorderly streets of the early 1900s — the home of the original

Hooligans — what sense can we possibly make of these numbers?

Between 1900 and the late 1970s, to adopt Mr Anderton's timescale, even allowing for unknown and hypothetical alterations in the nature and scope of criminal activity, we are asked to strike comparisons between such different styles of law enforcement as to make little sense. First, in the earlier period there were wide margins of discretion within an extremely informal mode of policing — the proverbial clip around the ear, or the dreaded flick of the Edwardian policemen's rolled cape — which has been replaced by the more likely possibility of prosecution, or the issue of a formal caution. And a formal caution, unlike a clip around the ear, goes into the record book as a 'known crime'. We have also seen how in earlier times people involved in acts of gross disorder would commonly be charged only with simple assault or drunkenness. Responding to a sharp increase in recorded offences in his annual report of 1899, for example, the Metropolitan Police Commissioner thought it 'satisfactory to note that the arrests were mostly for offences of a trivial nature, such as drunkenness, disorderly conduct, offences against the Police Acts, common assaults etc.', and he was at pains to distinguish between these 'trivial' matters and the proper affairs of his criminal department.[6] In other words, at a time when a quarter of London's police were assaulted each year in the course of their duties, street violence was too much of an everyday occurrence to count as 'real' crime. There was also a tendency not to record incidents which could not be cleared up. Until the 1930s, for example, it was a routine practice for the London police to record thefts reported to them by the public as 'lost property'.[7] When this practice was changed, recorded levels of property crime soared: but, obviously, as a consequence of changes in policing and not as a result of changes in crime.

In overall terms, between 1900 and the present day, the State apparatus for collecting and storing criminal information has changed so dramatically that we must question whether it can supply us with a valid measuring stick with which to compare the two periods. The cluttered informality of the Edwardian local police station with its rudimentary procedures for record-keeping has been replaced by elaborate computer-assisted systems of information retrieval. And whether or not they enhance the efficiency of the police, they certainly expand the crime statistics. When we remember that the capacity to store and retrieve information is precisely what is meant by a 'crime statistic' then clearly the expansion of telecommunications systems, together with the increasing use of motorised transport and radio, have enlarged the possibilities for the accumulation and storing of information by unimaginable dimensions in the twentieth century, and particularly since the Second World War. To ask us to strike meaningful comparisons across such a technological gulf is like trying to compare a theory of the origins of the universe based on observations through Galileo's lens with one facilitated by the radio telescope. It simply will not do.

This kind of questioning of the usefulness of official statistics, although it has come to have a particularly forceful relevance in the era of telecommunications and sophisticated information-retrieval systems, has its own history running alongside fears of mounting crime and disorder. It was already well in evidence in the mid-nineteenth century when the use of social statistics was in its infancy. In 1851 Thomas Plint made it unmercifully clear, for example, that a number of the calculations pointing to enormous increases in crime were based on 'gross arithmetical blunders'. Even where the arithmetic was sound, there was a tendency to ignore 'changes in the law' and the 'greater activity of the police' which Plint thought 'may have had much to do with the increased ratios of detected crime' and would 'lessen the proof of greater criminality amongst the general population'.[8] Frederic Hill, a barrister and ex-inspector of prisons, although less assiduous in his refutation of the 'crime wave' of the 1840s, adopted the same view that the 'wretched data' of the crime statistics took no notice of 'the greater efficiency of the police, the increased willingness to give evidence . . . a less reluctance to prosecute . . . and changes in what the law declares to be crime'.[9] Mary Carpenter was another sharp-eyed observer who saw the defects in these 'wretched data', especially the way in which the fluctuating popularity of summary jurisdiction had produced an artificial instability in the statistical returns.[10] The Juvenile Offenders Act of 1846 which allowed summary trial for juveniles under 14 years of age charged with larceny, the Act of 1850 which raised the age limit to 16 years, and the Criminal Justice Act of 1855 which further extended the scope of summary trial, all contributed to this instability. The effect of these legal alterations, as analysed by David Phillips, 'was not simply to transfer to the Petty Sessions those larcenies which had been previously tried at Quarter Sessions . . . but also to increase by a vast extent the number of such larcenies which were tried at all'.[11]

Legal and administrative changes such as these continued to produce rippling 'crime wave' effects in subsequent epochs. The Probation Act of 1907 and the Children Act of 1908 both increased the likelihood that young people would be brought before the courts, producing a sharp increase in the number of committals — a fact that was often enough noted during the next great legislative 'crime wave' produced by the Children and Young Persons Act of 1933. It was 'not that children have suddenly become more wicked', said *The Times* in response to the 'crime explosion' among juveniles in the mid-1930s, 'but that the legal machinery has become more efficient': 'The statistics really reflect the growth of confidence in the system as reformed.'[12] In 1939 A. E. Morgan explained the position in some detail:

> Many a young person is brought before the court today whom formerly the police would have hesitated to indict . . . When the alternatives were to risk smirching a boy's character by a police court appearance or letting him off with a smart warning, wisdom and clemency alike dictated the lenient course. But as the juvenile courts became more and more a place of help and reform these deterrents were removed, and it seemed wiser and more merciful to make a case . . . which showed itself in the sudden rise in the figures.[13]

Leo Page was another who, in 1937, felt it necessary to protest against the idea that young people could 'suddenly become 30 per cent more depraved in a single year'. 'It would be merely absurd', he thought, 'to explain the rise by suggesting that children who formerly had obeyed the law had learnt of the alteration of procedure and began to disobey the law as a consequence'.[14]

Absurd or not, the accusation was made and we can sorrow-fully reflect that nowadays it is part of the staple wisdom of the 'law-and-order' lobby that young people have made a sudden quantum-leap into a new level of depravity as a con-sequence of the leniency of the Children and Young Persons Act of 1969. The fact that juvenile justice in the 1970s has become much more severe (and not less severe) and that increasing numbers of young people have received custodial sentences in Borstals and Detention Centres appears not to have registered itself in the minds of 'law-and-order' enthusi-asts.[15] Nor that the increasing use of formal cautions in the 1970s, as opposed to the more informal system of unregistered cautioning, has also contributed to recent increases in official crime figures. The precise effect of the use of the formal caution is necessarily a matter for speculation, although it is generally agreed that it has not simply diverted work away from the courts — which was its intention — but has added substantially to the volume of recorded crime and recorded police activity.[16] Among boys under 14 years of age, for example, the increased use of the formal caution is enough to account for the whole of the increase in recorded crime for this age-group during the 1970s.[17]

It is not only across broad expanses of time, then, that comparisons of crime levels are hedged about with difficulty, but even in the short run the crime statistics are complicated by changes in law enforcement. The case of vandalism — a favourite hunting ground for 'law-and-order' critics — is par-ticularly interesting, in that recent changes in record-keeping have produced an altogether dizzying statistical effect on the crime figures. Until 1977 a distinction had been made between 'major damage' and 'minor damage', whereby only those cases which resulted in damage above an arbitrarily agreed sum of £20 (itself vulnerable to the ravages of inflation) were entered in the official statistics. From 1977 this distinction was abandoned, and all criminal damage incidents were re-corded as 'known crimes'. In a single year, this simple admin-istrative change produced the statistical illusion that vandalism had more than doubled, adding at a single stroke *a sixth of a million* indictable offences to the criminal records.[18]

To give some indication of the scale of this totally fictitious 'crime wave', it adds to the annual returns more indictable offences than the total number of offenders cautioned in a whole year. It is a number equivalent to almost one-half of all criminal convictions on indictable charges. It adds twice as many new recorded crimes than there are known cases of violence against the person; or twelve times the number of known robberies. Or, to offer one final and appropriately absurd comparison to match Mr Anderton's beguiling statistical reasoning, it adds to the crime figures four times the total number of criminal convictions in 1900. It is worth saying, moreover, that while this remarkable feat of statistical levitation can be deduced without any difficulty from the official publication of the crime figures, it is the kind of thing that goes unmentioned in the sensational pronouncements by our politicians and newspaper editors and, more regrettably, by some of our senior police officers.

But the argument can bite both ways, and we must add one final complicating difficulty to these already dense folds of complication that surround the interpretation of crime statistics. What is usually known as the 'dark figure' of crime — illegalities that go unnoticed, or ignored, or unreported, or unrecorded — is such an imponderable that all statements about movements in the levels of crime (whether up or down) are largely a matter of guesswork. We neither know with any useful degree of certainty what proportion of the 'dark figure' is reflected in the crime statistics, nor how this proportion might fluctuate across time. The only certainty is that the crime statistics are but a pale shadow of the total volume of illegalities. Estimates of the size of the 'black economy', for example, suggest that it dwarfs conventional theft; and more generally some informed guesses put the proportion of crime revealed by official sources as low as 15 per cent.[19] But there is no way of reliably counting on the size of this 'dark figure' and hence no way of making sure-footed judgements about whether movements in recorded crime reflect actual alterations in criminal activity; or shifts in public tolerance; or changes in policing; or some messy permutation of any of these factors. Statements about rising crime (or about falling crime) can neither be regarded as true nor false in this strict sense. Instead, we must regard them as logically *undecidable*.

That is, unless we totally disregard these long-standing and deep-rooted controversies about the interpretation of crime statistics and accept a naive view of them as straightforward reflections of criminal activities.

If we reject these myths of numerical certainty, as I think we must, then the strictly regulated operations of rational thought can only supply us with a quicksand of indecision when we attempt to strike comparisons of the state of lawlessness in different historical times. The only guarantee is that the continually mounting crime figure cannot be used to lend some objective status to feelings of historical decline. Computer-assisted quantum-leaps in the crime rate, while they certainly reflect massive changes in the scope and organisation of policing, tell us nothing much worth knowing about the historical realities of crime and violence. In which case, we might be well advised to return to the sure-footed terrain of human feelings.

Youth and Age: a 'Timeless' Dispute?

> 'And sigh that one thing only has been lent
> To youth and age in common — discontent'
>
> MATTHEW ARNOLD, 1852.[20]

Human feelings tell us, reliably across the ages, that the world is a less comforting place than it was in our youth and that the sun is setting on the happier times of the past. 'I think morals are getting much worse', a 60-year-old woman, Charlotte Kirkman informs us. 'There were no such girls in my time as there are now', she adds, continuing her indictment of parents nowadays. 'When I was four or five and twenty my mother would have knocked me down if I had spoken improperly to her.' It is a familiar enough complaint, and one frequently encountered in the modern fast-moving world. But there is the increasingly familiar difficulty: Mrs Kirkman's lament was voiced more than a century ago, as part of the evidence marshalled by Lord Ashley to meet the crisis of the 1840s.[21] The grumbling of older generations against the folly of youth — in which the rising generation is accused of breaking with the 'timeless' traditions of the past — has all the appearance of being a 'timeless' phenomenon itself.

Nostalgia is clearly an active ingredient in these great land-locked debates, and the complex emotional and cultural energies of nostalgia insert themselves in a number of ways into social perceptions of the criminal question. It is a matter for little surprise (although it is of enormous social conse-quence) that it is elderly people who are most prone to nos-talgia, and who also most fear crime and violence.[22] Research on the victims of crime tends not to confirm their fears — showing, by contrast, that old people are among those least victimised by crime, and particularly by violent crime.[23] But it would be difficult to pretend that old people are treated with uniform respect in contemporary Britain, and the old remain one of the most vulnerable sections of the community. A knock on the head or a street scuffle, which might be a matter to joke or brag about among young men, can be a shattering experience for someone who is old and frail. There is also material substance in nostalgia in that old people find increasing difficulty with increasing age in adapting to social changes, whether for good or ill — although this is itself prob-ably a 'timeless' aspect of the ageing process.

We can admit that the recurring preoccupation with social change, quite necessarily, asks what social arrangements inherited from the past might have enduring strength, and what can be discarded or needs to be renewed. Where nostalgia enters into these elementally important questions about cultural direction, however, inevitably it judges what is new (or apparently new) as also bad. So that debates across genera-tions, while they might have real and vital implications, are watered down into matters of little consequence. So that unless the 'hallucinations of age' that the Reverend Edward Irving warned about 150 years ago are perpetually guarded against, generational disputes will be settled in favour of the past, thus making for utmost difficulty in establishing a plat-form of standards against which to judge such things as the contents of popular amusements, the safety of the streets, or the morals of the young.[24]

Nostalgia is a perplexing human phenomenon (I will freely

confess that, in spite of the historical realism that I am arguing here, I sometimes suffer from it myself) but although it holds an authoritative position within numerous public controversies, it does not offer a royal road to either historical or moral certainty. We might perhaps think of it, whatever its complex social and emotional roots, as one of the raw materials of the human condition out of which the immovable preoccupation with declining standards and mounting disorder is fashioned. The predominant involvement of young men and boys in so much of this hooligan history is another of these 'raw materials', providing evidence of the biological characteristics of youthfulness as well as possible indications of male aggressiveness and persisting cultural definitions of manliness and machismo. Across the centuries we have seen the same rituals of territorial dominance, trials of strength, gang fights, mockery against elders and authorities, and antagonism towards 'outsiders' as typical focuses for youthful energy and aggressive mischief. Even under vastly different social conditions there are striking continuities between the violent interruptions to pre-industrial fairs and festivals, and the customary eruptions during modern Bank Holidays or the weekly carnival of misrule at contemporary football games — where the modern football rowdy, with his territorial edginess, mascots, emblems and choral arrangements in the 'rough music' tradition, must seem like a reincarnation of the unruly apprentice, or the late Victorian 'Hooligan'.

Comparisons between late twentieth-century disturbances among youths and the riotous accompaniments to festivals in early modern Europe may seem to be stretching a point too far, however, in that they blur across too many social alterations. Surely, while there may be some momentary resemblances there is more to separate the unruly apprentice and the modern football hooligan — in terms of language, custom, material benefits, cultural horizons, and even bad habits — than to bring them together as instances of the 'same' phenomenon? But the point can be stretched even further, back into ancient history. There are truly astonishing similarities, for example, between football rowdyism and the violent disputes between hostile factions at the theatres and hippodromes in Byzantine Rome and Constantinople when, more than a thousand years ago, the 'Blues' and the 'Greens' chanted their support for rival champions in chariot races, each faction grouped at opposing 'Ends' of the stadiums. Some of these continuities are pointed out by the Latin historian Alan Cameron:

> Theatre rowdies had been causing trouble for centuries in relative anonymity, usually in small groups of fluid composition . . . But once they acquired the notorious title of Blues and Greens, wearing appropriately coloured jackets, they became instantly recognisable and were bound to be singled out more and more often – by the law as well as by the historian . . . This increased publicity may well have played a part in actually increasing both the violence and the number of such disturbances. The growth of parallel phenomena in our own day has shown that punitive fines and excessive press coverage tend to reinforce and exacerbate the violence they purport to condemn. Once one set of Blues and Greens had begun to acquire their deplorable 'Byzantine' reputation, others would emulate their achievement, unwilling (like soccer fans today who defiantly chant 'we are the famous football hooligans') to disappoint public expectation by not living up to their stereotype. A spurious 'solidarity' was created; we hear, for example, of the Blues of Constantinople avenging a wrong done to the Blues of Tarsus.[25]

Other forms of organised rowdyism were found in both Roman and Greek civilisations when, much abused by their elders, gangs of young bloods adopted such nicknames as Triballoi, Autolecythoi and the rampant Ithyphalloi.[26] Disorders around popular entertainments in Rome during the first few centuries after the time of Christ were a particularly grievous matter, however, commonly ending in bloodshed. Around 500 AD, when Emperor Anastasius had found it necessary to ban wild beast shows and pantomime dancing in order to quell faction violence, one of the more terrible theatre riots resulted in no less than three thousand deaths.[27]

The more modest punch-ups of our own time hardly bear comparison with such a spectacular disregard for human life. Even so, faced with formidably ageless continuities such as these we must be tempted to conclude that these problems are indeed one of the 'timeless', if more regrettable, aspects of the human condition. But whether we care to phrase such an appeal in terms of eternal human folly, or evil, or the age-less chemistry of the demon drink, or in terms of a built-in aggressive impulse and an upsurge of youthful instinctual energy, we must take care not to write off history at a stroke of the pen. It is one thing to wriggle free of the ageless myth-ologies of historical decline. It is quite another to leap into the arms of the equally pernicious social doctrine that nothing ever changes.

There are a number of detailed objections that must be brought against these kinds of formulae. What, for example, would a theory basing itself upon an upsurge of youthful instinctual energy as the root cause of street violence have to say to the following case:

Mugger, 85, told: Give up Crime
Pensioner, William . . . , 85, mugged an 81-year-old woman . . . for her weekly groceries.
   And yesterday an Old Bailey Judge told him: 'You are a very silly old man. You ought to know better at your age. It's about time you forgot about crime.' (*The Daily Mirror*, 7 April 1977)

Another unusual headline — 'A RED CARD FOR SOCCER HOOLIGAN, 68!' — points to the same dilemma. Shouting, 'He cost us the match, I will kill him', this 'old-age soccer rowdy' had attacked the referee after a game in which his local club had been (as he saw it) unfairly treated. A Barnsley fan for fifty years, photographed in an unrepentant mood grinning from ear to ear with an emblem of his club held aloft, he explained his motives: 'I'm football daft and I always get involved in the matches. The referee was too lenient and Doncaster were clogging our lads out of the game. I just ex-ploded' (*The Daily Mirror*, 7 March 1978).

   I would not wish to pretend that these elder statesmen of hooliganism are indicative of an uncovered 'dark figure' of mindless grandads. But their presence makes a simple point in a complex argument, which must reduce our confidence in the view that there is something exclusively 'youthful' about hooliganism or its motives, and call into question even more emphatically the simple-minded thesis that 'permissive' child-rearing is the root of all evil.

The predominance of young people in the criminal statistics has certainly been one of the strikingly consistent features for more than a century. But is it because young people are more uncontrollable? Or is it that the lives of young people are subject to more public regulation, so that the kinds of illegalities that are classified as 'serious crime' and which consume the large part of the energies of the police and courts, bias the crime statistics towards the young? There are many areas of criminality where young people are only marginally involved. By virtue of their age they figure hardly at all in motoring offences, for example, which constitute a body of largely 'respectable' crime – even though the motorcar kills and maims far more people than muggers and street rowdies. Nor are they implicated much in organised conspiracies, embezzlement, fraud and other 'fat cat' crimes. Nor in the great uncounted recesses of the 'dark figure' of tax-dodging and theft-from-work, and all the other fiddles and favours in the legal twilight of the 'black economy'. The prevailing definitions of what is 'serious crime' – which are quite laughable when the size of the 'black economy' is calculated by comparison with conventional theft – together with the social opportunities for certain types of crime and not others, must be counted as determining conditions that produce the disproportionate appearance of young people in the official reckoning of crime.

The 'peak age' for known criminal offenders, hovering as it does around the mid-teens for boys in contemporary Britain, provides more tempting evidence in favour of a biologically inspired view of youthful misconduct. But if this 'peak age' points to a phase of instinctual turbulence in adolescence, then it must be one of the more remarkable aspects of our instinctual equipment, in that it can be altered at the whim of Parliament. When the school-leaving age was raised from 15 to 16 years in 1972, in fact, the criminal statistics revealed that this 'peak age' rose obediently to accommodate itself to these new circumstances.[28] It is the social transition from school to work (or dole) that most usefully explains the phenomenon of the 'peak age': a line of social continuity that can be traced in twentieth-century Britain from the Edwardian 'boy labour' problem down to our own time.

There are any number of qualifications that must be arranged around simple equations between youthful misconduct and a 'timeless' biological impulse. So, too, with those forms of argument which identify an exclusively male biology as the seat of violence and aggression, or which harness biology to the supposedly 'racial' origins of Britain's social problems. It is indisputably true that the males of numerous animal species display more inclination towards aggressiveness and dominance, although in the case of the human animal matters are further complicated by the cultural reinforcements of patriarchal social arrangements and pervasive images of macho masculinity, and the emphasis on an exclusively male problem fails to encompass the known contours of either biology or history. Females of numerous species display forms of aggression, notably in the case of 'brood defence', and nor is male dominance either culturally or historically a universal human phenomenon.[29] It is all very well for a judge in 1977 to confess himself 'frightened by a new aspect of crime . . . "the emergence of the female mugger" ', as if this indicated a novel departure for the gentle sex. 'The thing that frightens me', he went on, 'is that here are three young women behaving like common footpads from the eighteenth century.'[30] Quite so. In earlier chapters we have encountered girl garotters in the 1860s, as well as 'Hooligan Girls' in the 1890s throwing their weight about in the streets in a manner that was entirely indistinguishable from their Hooligan brothers. In early modern Europe, moreover, women were generally regarded as more disorderly than men, when they figured centrally as organisers of the violent festivities of Misrule and commonly acted as instigators of food riots in eighteenth-century England.[31]

As for the 'racial' thesis, our hooligan history has equipped us well to understand and combat it, revealing a long and dishonourable tradition of British belly-aching against the 'racial degeneration' of the common people and its supposed manifestation in 'unprecedented' violence and outrage. This inclination to invoke 'racial' metaphors of social incohesion must be counted as a dominant theme within the British political culture — according to which violence and disorder have been repeatedly disowned as an alien intrusion into the peaceful ancestry of the 'British way of life'. It is wonderfully convenient, of course, that this accusation can now be brought against an actual black presence in Britain's cities, thereby making it all the more powerful. But the fact that this 'racial degeneration' thesis pre-dates the immigration of the postwar years by decades, and that it was first fashioned as an accusation against the British people themselves — most fearfully articulated in the pseudo-Darwinian speculations on the fate of the 'Imperial Race' at the turn of the century — refutes the scientific credentials of racist ideology, no less than the 'golden age' mythologies inscribed upon the past.

Having said all this, it would be wrong to deny that the biological sciences have a place within human self-understanding. While biological determinism is justly viewed with suspicion in many quarters, on the moral grounds that it has served to legitimate numerous atrocities by humankind against itself — whether through racial bigotry and genocide, the oppression and elimination of 'inferior' peoples, or the patriarchal domination of women as 'natural' consequences of human nature — we must be careful to distinguish moral principle from observable evidence. It is not only the dogmas of biology that have legitimated the infliction of pain and suffering on other human beings. The opposing scheme of human self-understanding, first propagated by the Enlightenment, that human nature is infinitely malleable, has been associated with its own history of human cruelties — from the earliest penitentiary experiments with prolonged solitary confinement, through to modern brain-washing and behaviour-modification techniques — in the quest to master our own nature.[32] It would be folly, in any case, to deny that human beings are animals (we are certainly not plants!) or that our animality is a determining circumstance of our existence which sets material limits to what can be humanly accomplished.[33] It is flat denials such as these which continue the deception that humankind is somehow 'above nature', and under-write a further tendency to deny that there is any human intelligibility in troublesome behaviour, and to categorise certain classes of people (criminals and hooligans, for example) as sub-human 'savages' and 'animals'.

When we say that human violence is 'biological' or 'animal'

we not only do an injustice to the larger animal kingdom —
which is often remarkably ordered and stable — but we also
misunderstand what human violence and self-destruction
largely consists of. In violent rituals of territoriality, for
example, what is often thought of as the utter primitivity and
animality of 'unsocialised' aggression is invariably directed
against culturally prescribed targets — scapegoats and 'outsiders' of different kinds — so that violence is marshalled in
the service of some version of community, brotherhood and
belonging which is thereby confirmed and celebrated. Viewed
in this light, culture is to be seen not so much as a control
upon violence, but as an 'incitement' to violence: a form of
regulation, to be sure, but a regulation that defines, promotes,
organises and channels violence. There is a subtle interlacing
of biology and culture throughout the range and history of
humankind's violent potential against itself — from the petty
skirmishing of 'Mods' against 'Rockers', say, through racial
bigotry and religious riots, to the ultimate savagery of civilised
warfare which is invariably organised around symbolic crusades
which champion one notion or another of 'freedom', 'civilisation' and other 'just causes'. 'Better dead than red!' goes the
war-cry of the human lemming whose capacity for symbolic
fanaticism — rather than some primitive biological realm
untouched by 'civilising' influences — lies at the root of the
bulk of human self-destructiveness and hatred. Nor is this a
particularly novel recognition: Swift's satire of the people of
Lilliput, where the 'Big-Enders' and the 'Little-Enders' fought
holy wars over at which end an egg should be broken, reminds
us of its enduring strength.[34] So, too, as when Erasmus argued
that war was a specifically human and most 'unnatural' phenomenon: 'Whoever heard of a hundred thousand animals
rushing together to butcher each other, as men do everywhere?'[35] We talk blithely about the 'beast within', but as
Mary Midgley has so persuasively argued, why not accept that
it is the 'human within' that confronts us in these all-too-
human problems?[36]

The accusation that hooligans are 'animals' is usually followed by the instruction that their sub-human energies should
be beaten out of them. But if hooliganism were biological —
and it is a big 'if' — then we could no more hope to eliminate

it entirely than we might expect to eliminate the biological tendency for human beings to grow old. The biological tendency for old people to progress towards helplessness and senility does not lead (except perhaps in Erewhon) to the view that frail old people should be caged in disciplinary camps to be drilled or whipped into submission. So, the biological dimensions of hooliganism, if it were only 'biology' that confronted us in these disputes, might be expected to teach us a lesson in tolerance. And they should also remind us that flighty utopian notions of human self-perfection sometimes need to be held in check, in that they can all too easily lead to excessively zealous applications of the law and discipline, if not to some kind of eugenic purge — as if, ignoring the limiting circumstances of our biology, human nature could be entirely mastered and expunged.

An anthropology of human conduct that remains faithful to the history of human conflict must encompass the material circumstances of our biology, although to admit the biological sciences into our reasoning is not to admit fatalism.[37] The doctrine that human beings are 'naturally' violent and bellicose, like the opposing faith in the 'naturally' peace-loving instincts of the new-born infant, begs far more questions than it answers. An exclusive reliance on biology does not provide us with anything like a sufficient explanation of the human problems of crime and violence, nor their encircling social preoccupation. No more, in fact, than the idea of the 'natural' tranquillity of the 'British way of life', or the tired usages of nostalgia.

Future Conditional: the Moral-Political Agenda

'Brixton is the iceberg tip of a crisis of ethnic criminality which is not Britain's fault — except in the sense that her rulers quite unnecessarily imported it.'

PEREGRINE WORSTHORNE, *The Sunday Telegraph*, 29 Nov 1981

'For mischief is a lechery to some,
And serves to make them sleep like laudanum.'

JOHN OLDHAM, 1682.[38]

The terms and limits within which the problems of lawlessness are understood and acted upon are established within a form of public discourse which has been with us for generations, each succeeding generation remembering the illusive harmony of the past while foreseeing imminent social ruin in the future. The 'timeless' raw materials of the human condition — whether the feelings of nostalgia or the facts of youthfulness — provide some basis on which it is possible to understand how the immovable vocabulary of 'law-and-order' complaint is able to construct and re-construct itself across these broad acres of time. These raw materials do not constrain human possibility by universal decree, however, and nor do they predetermine the formidable constancies of this preoccupation with social ruin. Rather, they are recruited and harnessed in a much more specific way within public discourse — as ideology. The turbulent energies of youthfulness, for example, rather than being seen as a curse can sometimes appear in a more hopeful light: as in the romanticism of the interwar years that was inherited, in part, from the Edwardian response to its troubles. Nor does nostalgia operate uniformly in all spheres of human concern, and there are some public issues — and certain historical times — where it is more agreeable to think of the past as a time of barbarism and ignorance. Equally, there are different measures of emphasis in the way in which these 'raw materials' are mobilised within different national cultures. A dominant characteristic of the European and American intellectual tradition is that it harbours misgivings about the effects of urbanisation and industrialisation, and we have seen how these surface within the social preoccupation with declining standards and mounting disorder.[39] But whereas America, to take one instance, glories in its 'Wild West' inheritance and France often seems to relish its revolutionary traditions, the British political culture appears to be peculiarly unique in its total amnesia for signs of trouble in the past. If similar societies to our own are able to sustain themselves without reference to the illusions of the past, however, we might hope to relinquish at least a little of the humbug surrounding the traditions of the 'British way of life' without immediately endangering the 'social fabric'. The very fact that respectable fears of imminent ruin, reprocessed and embroidered for generations, have repeatedly failed to confirm themselves should also offer some encouragement. The end of the world has been announced with sufficient regularity to sustain the belief that it will not end just for a while — or, at least, that its end will not come from the quarter of street crime.

Even so, these fearful preoccupations have led such a charmed life within the British political culture that if we expect to wrench ourselves instantly free from their suffocating vision, then we will undoubtedly suffer instant disappointment. But what form of more limited escape is available to us — one that might enable some more light to be brought into 'law-and-order' controversies?

It can hardly escape notice that, although the fixed vocabulary of complaint rumbles on through British history almost without interruption, it comes into a sharp crystallising focus at moments of more general anxiety. The preoccupation with mounting disorder seems to serve a specific ideological function within British public life, as a convenient metaphor for wider social tensions which attend the advance of democratisation. Thus, the preoccupation with lawlessness gathers itself to meet the Chartist threat of the 1840s; then amidst the political tremors that accompanied the electoral Reform Bill in the 1860s; then during the rise of the New Unionism and the socialist upsurge at the turn of the century; and so on, down to our own historical time when the 'law-and-order' movement is indelibly associated with authoritarian tendencies within the political culture. On each occasion, this preoccupation returns to a cluster of themes bearing upon the production and reproduction of consent and social discipline among the working class — and more particularly among the rising generation, the bearers of the future. On each occasion, the same metaphorical appliances spell out that 'things have gone too far', that the common people have gained 'too much freedom', and that the reins of government must be held more firmly. This ideological sketch of the ebb and flow of hooligan history may explain why in the interwar years, when the working class was firmly under the heel, 'law-and-order' enthusiasms carried less weight than at other times.

The preoccupation with mounting lawlessness possesses its own rigid continuities, then, but it is not at all 'timeless'.

Rather, it moves in fits and starts, geared to the urgencies of a much wider social apprehension. Some elements of this preoccupation, undoubtedly, are inherited from the eighteenth century; but it was not until the question of the mass franchise was placed firmly on the political agenda by the Chartist movement that it attained its fully elaborated and recognisably modern contours. The philanthropic 'reform' movement of the 1840s, emerging as a specific mode of response to this crisis of consciousness, aimed to implant a new form of discipline in the hearts and minds of the labouring classes, a form of discipline compatible with democratic rule. Subsequently, the criminal question has been haunted by the ghost of the pre-democratic past which urges that reformative principles should be discarded in place of the 'short, sharp shock' to render the public body docile. The preoccupation encircling the criminal question thus bears directly on the central ideological problems of liberal democracy: the opposition between rule-by-might which is essentially pre-democratic, and rule-by-consent which is the hallmark of democratic forms of government. The recurring waves of reaction against reform, correspondingly, must be understood as a continuing struggle within (and against) democratic forms of rule and the precepts of 'willing obedience'.

Where the past is glorified in such a way as to suggest that the difficulties of the present will be solved by turning back the clock, it is to be expected that the forces of reaction will be to the fore. But reform can also present itself in the guise of a return to the past. Amidst the present crisis of policing in the British cities, where consent is once more at issue, the celebration of the old-fashioned beat bobby is a splendid example. Historical realism disappoints backward-looking reformism no less than reaction, however, failing to offer any substance to the belief that in days-gone-by the police were universally loved as 'friendly British bobbies'. It was only in the course of decades that the police gained such consent as they did in working-class communities, and this was by no means complete. We have seen more than enough evidence of fierce hostility towards the police, not to mention the fact that the police themselves were not always terribly friendly. If the British police nowadays have earned a reputation for occasional brutality and a disregard for civil liberties, it is difficult to uphold the view that this itself represents a novel deterioration. Strong-arm tactics against demonstrations of the unemployed were common in the interwar years, and the policing of 'rough' districts has always been a rough affair. The 'Flying Squad' which broke up the Sheffield gangs of the 1920s was notorious for its methods, and at the time of the original Hooligans — when the police were widely condemned for observing 'no-go' areas and keeping clear of trouble — there were calls for a 'Flying Squadron' to deal with 'this class of animal', and fond memories of the Tottenham Court Road police who had been known as 'The Butchers' because of the way in which their neighbourhood gangs had been 'kicked from pillar to post'.[40] The campaign to institute 'community policing' in contemporary Britain is in many respects an admirable ambition: but it is one to be built in the future which cannot be founded upon the illusions of the past.

Historical mythology is invoked in any number of ways to support different ideological constructions of the criminal question, each playing across a wider range of social issues in a figurative or metaphorical sense. The 'anti-permissive' thesis, for example, clearly identifies itself as a revolt against modernity and against what is understood to be the excessive liberty of the common people. Perhaps the most archaic form of conservative moralising, with already more than a century of doom-laden prophecy behind it even in Henry Fielding's day, it has weathered the storms of social change so well that its time-honoured prescriptions are preserved intact to this day. Regarding crime as only one symptom of a much larger process of moral decay, the themes and arguments of the 'permissive' thesis are figurative precisely in the sense that crime and violence excite the attention largely as a means by which to indict those wider social arrangements that are found objectionable.

A different line of argument, more usually associated with the liberal humanitarian tradition, voices its opposition to economic *laissez-faire* on the otherwise similar grounds that it has undermined what are imagined to have been previously harmonious social relationships. Opposition to *laissez-faire* has been deeply ingrained in the English liberal conscience since the mid-nineteenth century.[41] In the criminal sphere, *laissez-faire* is accused of producing a number of undesirable results such as destroying paternalistic class relations, apprenticeship schemes, community spirit and the old 'crime-free' neighbourhoods. Opposition to *laissez-faire* and opposition to 'permissiveness' share clear family resemblances, although this does not guarantee their agreement, for they tend to come out of different political stables. We see this in the contemporary 'law-and-order' movement where the so-called New Right opposes 'permissiveness' in the moral sphere, while embracing the principles of *laissez-faire* economics — which amounts to wanting to have your cake and eat it.

Another of these metaphorical appliances, which finds its constituency within the socialist tradition, points to crime and disorder as an indictment of the social order which is seen as unjust and criminogenic. One way of phrasing these relationships between crime and the wider social structure is to say that crime flows directly from the egoistic imperatives of 'possessive individualism' which characterise capitalist market philosophy.[42] Another line of argument relates crime to social distress, so that unemployment, poverty, slum housing and unequal opportunity are seen as the root causes of crime. A form of response most clearly represented within contemporary sociological enquiry, it is a mode of socialist critique that was already established in the 1850s.[43] It should also be said that it is not without its own considerable difficulties as an explanation of crime, in that while the real despair and anger generated by unemployment cannot be doubted, attempts to show strict correlations between crime levels and unemployment are notoriously hazardous.[44]

We see, then, different ideological formulae constructed around the problems of lawlessness. Each tradition employs the existence of crime in a figurative or metaphorical sense to indict some aspect of the social order and to champion its own social causes. None of them is without difficulties as a scheme of understanding, although each enjoys considerable authority within their different intellectual and political constituencies, resulting in some quite bizarre contradictions. What are we to make of the fact, for example, that at different times (and often simultaneously) it has been held to be incontrovertibly true that both poverty *and* affluence are the cause of lawlessness — except to recognise that unless the contested ground of these moral-political disputes can be shifted, then we seem doomed to repeat the failures of the past?

Our confusion is only deepened by the way in which marriages of convenience are commonly struck between these separate traditions. We have already seen how conservative moralising hedges its bets on the consequences of 'permissive' *laissez-faire*. The British socialist movement, on the other hand, has frequently indicted the criminogenic nature of unemployment and poverty, while harbouring some misgivings about the 'good old days' when poverty is said to have encouraged communal solidarity in poor neighbourhoods. The Labour movement also has its own traditions of suspicion towards 'permissiveness', and opposition to *laissez-faire* is another broad church: the uncontrolled sprawl of industrialisation and the lurchings of the 'free market' economy have more than once put fear into Tory politicians and industrialists.[45] When former Conservative Prime Minister Edward Heath launched against the criminogenic nature of monetarist economic policy in his prescient remarks only a few days before the outbreak of the July riots of 1981, he even appeared to borrow wholesale the clothes of socialist argument: 'Of course, if you have one million unemployed young people hanging about the streets all day, you will have a massive increase of juvenile crime . . . Of course you will get racial tensions when you have young blacks with less chance of getting a job.'[46] Then, we have Tory fears of criminally inspired insurrection which — unlike the socialist tradition which has tended to discount the political significance of the *lumpenproletariat* — are surprisingly close to anarchist and libertarian assumptions of 'spontaneous' revolt in the margins of society.[47] By contrast, pastoral sympathies of spontaneous harmony insert themselves into every nook and cranny of our social and political life — whether in the new-breed libertarian utopias of the simple-living, small-is-beautiful 'Green' movement which is not so well represented in Britain as in other European countries; in the pastoral under-current within

British socialism, most notably in the traditions of Ruskin and Morris; or in various permutations of Tory and Liberal paternalism. So, when the Conservative Party set out on its postwar 'law-and-order' crusade against 'permissiveness' in the mid-1960s, it spoke to a broad (if deluded) consensus:

> We live in times of unprecedented change — change which often produces stress and social breakdown. Indeed the growth in the crime rate may be attributed in part to the breakdown of certain spontaneous agencies of social control which worked in the past. These controls operated through the family, the Church, through personal and local loyalties, and through a stable life in a stable society.[48]

We have seen enough of these 'spontaneous' territorial loyalties, embodying their own fierce traditions of resistance to law and authority, to be able to blow a little fresh air into these dusty memories — of a moment when the world stood still and silent, all of one piece, without tensions, without fractures, and essentially without change. We have also seen the testimony of successive generations of men and women, living in a moving world, who felt themselves to be besieged by 'unprecedented' change which often left them wondering what the world was coming to.

To give one final instance of this thicket of alliances and blurrings within criminal discourse, we can take the radical feminist critique of male violence which, through its campaign against pornography as a licence for sexual violence has often appeared to move in the company of the 'anti-permissive' thesis; which in its own terms would confound the very object of feminism, confine women even more fundamentally to the home, restrict the right to abortion, and so on. 'Reclaim the Night!' says the feminist slogan, confronting us yet again with that nagging difficulty: because it is not clear where we can locate historically a time when women were, in fact, free to walk the streets without the possibility of harassment or molestation. The safety of the night is not a 'thing of the past': it is a prospect for the future. Indeed, in spite of all their different points of emphasis, these varying ideological deployments of the criminal question agree on one thing: that there was in the past a haven of tranquillity. Thereby, whatever else we might wish to say about their differences, these moral-political responses to lawlessness are grounded in the impotent premises of myth.

The way to challenge the foundation of myth, to repeat, is not to deny the facts of violence and disorder. Rather, it is to insist that *more* facts are placed within the field of vision: that is, the abundant facts of crime and hooliganism that pulse through British history, proving them to be such stable features of an otherwise changing society. When the cobwebs of historical myth are cleared away, then we can begin to see that the real and enduring problem that faces us is not moral decay, or declining parental responsibility, or undutiful working mothers, or the unparalleled debasement of popular amusements — or any other symptom of spiritual degeneration among the British people. Rather, it is a material problem. The inescapable reality of the social reproduction of an underclass of the most poor and dispossessed is the material foundation to these hooligan continuities. And I say this not as a way of harking back to a simple causative model that poverty causes crime — the ample evidence of 'respectable' crime, taxdodging and the 'black economy' shows that material deprivation is not a necessary condition of the criminal question — but as a way of saying, quite simply, that it is those crimes that are associated with the materially disadvantaged underclass which have provided the continuing thread within this history of respectable fears.

The continuities show through in every grain of our social being. The home of this under-class was once known as the rookeries, then the slums, now the 'inner city'. The underclass is recruited disproportionately from successive generations of migrant workers; not merely the black migrant settlements of contemporary Britain, but in an ingrained tradition of conflict and controversy that reaches back to the Irish presence in eighteenth-century London. Then, as now, there were riots against migrant workers and lofty accusations that 'the uncontrolled importation of Irish vagbonds' had led to an increase in footpad crimes — together with a rather familiar complaint that the Irish had brought with them the foreign habit of resistance to street arrest.[49] Continued through waves of immigration from Ireland in the nineteenth century, the relationship is stamped into our language by the sudden and sustained popularity of the word 'Hooliganism' itself.[50] Structural dislocations in employment opportunities for the young, associated with the progressive development of machine technologies, describe another continuing dimension in the material reproduction of this under-class, and not — as it is so often thought to be — a novel phenomenon of the 'micro-chip' era. Historical myth proposes that our contemporary problems are a break with the past. Historical realism shows that they are not. Indeed, when a government such as Mrs Thatcher's indulges in some old-fashioned class warfare, which will necessarily bite hardest against the under-class, we might even judge it historically appropriate that it should be visited with some old-fashioned 'riot'. Although it is also in keeping with the time-honoured traditions that class warriors should disown their corporate responsibilities in the reproduction of the problem and, while denying the material foundations of our difficulties, should pin the blame on weakened family ties or on the conspiratorial activities of modern-day Jacobins stirring up the mobs.[51]

To recognise the persistent nature of these respectable discontents, stretching back as they do across more than a century, is neither to deny the reality of the anxieties themselves, nor the material foundations of the problem which have disfigured our history. It is certainly not my intention to suggest that criminal violence is a figment of the imagination — a way in which almost any questioning of the gravity of 'law-and-order' wisdom is slapped down — although it must be allowed that the imagination lends more than a spice of colouring to public images of hooliganism. Nor to suggest that we should abandon forthwith all efforts to clarify and elaborate our extremely fragile understanding of these troublesome questions and the public response to them. We must admit, however, and very forcibly admit, that our understanding and our actions are constrained in a large measure within the blinding certainties of myth.

Nor is the importance of the moral-political disputes that have been engaged and re-engaged repeatedly — principally in the lines of opposition between 'reform' and 'reaction' — called into question. A recognition of the historical depth of these controversies reveals the hollowness of the allegation that reformative ambitions are merely the child of 'new-fangled' sentimentality. But reform is not without its own difficulties and limitations — whether we think of what I have described as the essentially vague origins of early Victorian philanthropy, the continuing difficulties of its application and the failure to hold in check those moral panics which mobilise support for authoritarianism, or the inherent tendency for 'reform' to embody itself in an enveloping machinery of intrusive surveillance and manipulation.

The fundamental opposition between reaction and reform, nevertheless, resists qualification: whether it is better to defeat the problem by force; or to attempt to win consent through a constructive educational dialogue. As matters are usually stated, reform is equated with weakness, while its opponent is imbued with virile strength. What can be reclaimed from this history, however, is that the boot is on the other foot. It is reaction that is an admission of weakness, in that the refusal to enter into dialogue and to attempt to persuade wrongdoers that there are good and tangible reasons why they should lead good and useful lives is tantamount to a failure of faith in the system of rewards, regulation and law itself. Weakness, not strength, lies behind the command that reformative principles of 'willing obedience' should be relinquished in favour of the 'short, sharp shock'.

There are grounds for self-doubts, certainly, in that consent has never been won in a thoroughly popular sense that reaches through every sinew of British society, and it is unlikely that truly popular consent could ever be won in an unequal and divided society. Nor is it the first time that ruling elites have themselves shown signs of faltering when it comes to upholding the democratic principles of consent, especially in the workings of the criminal justice system. But consent, if it is to be won, is not won on a once-and-for-all basis. It must be repeatedly negotiated and re-negotiated on the shifting grounds of material circumstance and public opinion. It would be wrong, moreover, to reduce all the social pressures that bear on the reproduction of consent to the question of 'law-and-order'. If mass unemployment should threaten consent, for example, then what is fundamentally important is not whether unemployment causes crime and riots, but that mass unemployment is an evil in itself. This is why I have laboured the figurative and metaphorical dimensions of the arguments that are arranged around the criminal question, because of the way in which they focus our perceptions in such a way as to diminish whole areas of social experience, except in so far as these are thought to cause crime and disorder. The argument that unemployment leads directly and mechanically to crime and unrest has always been suspect — not least because the experience of unemployment can just as easily induce apathy and despair — but this should be no reason to discount the importance of unemployment as a public issue. So, too, if mass entertainments are sometimes shabby and impoverished, then this is a matter of vital cultural importance in its own right: whether or not television-viewing, for example, offers incitements to crime. The argument is no less significant in the sphere of 'race relations' where institutional racism is an affront to human dignity — whether or not it encourages disrespect for law and authority. So, too, when and if educational provision fails the young. Or if there is a failure to reproduce a decent housing stock and to build viable communities in which men and women, the poor and the privileged, young and old alike, can find public space in which to move. Too often matters of vital public importance — jobs, homes, schools — are swallowed up in the maw of 'law-and-order' discourse, and publicly addressed as if the only important consideration was whether these social deficiencies might lead to crime, vandalism and hooliganism. Certainly, these matters bear on the reproduction of consent. But if we reinstate these problems in their own terms, and in all their enormity in contemporary Britain, then the preoccupation with 'hooliganism' must begin to pale in significance.

Finally, what about a war as the answer to our problems? War is commonly identified as *the* historical moment when consent draws us together in its cohesive embrace. When the drums begin to roll, we tell ourselves, our hearts beat in unison and domestic peace descends, our internal differences set to one side in the face of a common enemy. But only the most truncated version of history could support these heroic assumptions. The age of Palmerston's gun-boat diplomacy, for example, was not exactly noted for its domestic harmony, in that it happened to coincide with the first wave of the 'garotting' panic in Victorian London. Indeed, Lord Palmerston's pledge to 'protect the humblest British subject in the most distant quarters of the globe' earned him a rebuke in the columns of *The Times* where it was thought to be 'of far more moment to a Londoner that he should be able . . . to walk in safety about the streets of London . . . than that there should be the most perfect security within the Tropics or the Polar Circles': 'A man cannot return to his home at night without imminent danger of being throttled, robbed, and if not actually murdered, at least kicked and pommelled within an inch of his life . . . If the police cannot or will not protect us, we must learn to protect ourselves.'[52]

The argument was repeated at the time of the Boer War, when imperial skirmishes across the globe meant that Britain was on an almost permanent war-footing, although this did not have the slightest effect on the massive social anxieties with street crime and violence – nor on the conduct of the 'Hooligan' gangs. The age of total war might be expected to have had a more congealing effect upon the temper of the nation, and on some accounts the onset of the First World War may have lured some of the original Hooligans away from their street-fighting habitat, to learn a new kind of butchery in the trenches. Nevertheless, the Great War was accompanied by a perceived upsurge in juvenile lawlessness, especially among boys under 16 years of age, which 'spread through the country like a plague'.[53] Nor did the war interrupt the established pattern of respectable complaint, and with a relentless predictability the juvenile 'crime wave' was regularly associated with weakened family ties and the war-work of mothers – 'some whose heads have been turned', according to one authority, 'by their new-found economic independence' – as well as the break-up of communal feeling, the excitements of the cinema, and youthful 'affluence' that was said to have resulted from buoyant wartime employment conditions. An alternative line of reasoning suggested that the unnatural excitement and blood-lust of war itself had a deteriorating effect that led to increased crime. But whether or not the war did foment the passions of youth, the excitement turned a few heads in the magistrates' courts where there was an unparalleled enthusiasm for whipping young offenders.[54]

The Second World War, in its turn, was visited by any number of internal difficulties: widespread racketeering in the 'black market'; episodic fears of violent crimes by deserters from the armed forces who numbered in tens of thousands; and outbreaks of hooliganism that were laid at the door of street-lighting restrictions during the black-out. Writing in 1941, Hermann Mannheim noted that 'thieving from the docks, bag-snatching, assaults on police or on women, and other forms of hooliganism' were prominent in the news headlines.[55] Epidemics of looting in London, Sheffield, Manchester, Coventry and elsewhere in the aftermath of air-raids also excited considerable alarm. Children and youths, who were brought before the courts for looting and vandalising household belongings in bomb-damaged dwellings, formed one part of this picture. The most scandalous aspect of the problem, however, was that people in positions of public trust — ARP wardens, rescue workers, auxiliary firemen, war-reserve policemen, demolition squads, bomb-disposal units and mortuary assistants — figured prominently in looting cases.[56] In 1941 no fewer than 2,763 looters were found guilty under Defence Regulations alone, when some swingeing penalties of penal servitude were imposed, and in the same year it was reported that 4,584 looting cases had passed through the London courts by one means or another — and this in the winter of Britain's 'Finest Hour'.[57] If there is an excess of sentimentality in our appreciation of the criminal question, it is nowhere more in evidence than in that 'old chestnut' of commonsense reasoning which equates war with domestic peace.

An Admission of Failure

The working class boy is a critic, and by no means a gentle one.

CHARLES RUSSELL, *Manchester Boys*, 1905. [58]

This has been a history of myth and tradition, in which there are no historical bolt-holes in which to hide from the difficulties of the present or to clothe ourselves in the achievements of the past. It is also a story of failure. A failure in the development of British society to win the consent of substantial proportions of its people, and to find a secure and trusting place in the social fabric for its youth, no less than a failure of rational thought to dispel the illusions of the past. And although we should not overestimate the problem of crime and hooliganism in British society — the monumental crime-rate in America, the freest of all the nations of the Free World, stands as a perpetual corrective to our 'law-and-order' jeremiahs — nevertheless the continuing presence of the hooligan in our midst serves to remind us of the incapacities of our accustomed habits of thought and practice.

The urgent problems facing Britain seem to insist on urgent remedies, and no doubt there will be objections in some quarters that a historical narrative such as I have offered here does not supply any immediate balm to the problems of crime, violence and disorder. While a sense of urgency governs our attention, the pale shadow of time is no match for the instant photo-flash of the present. Indeed, by introducing some of the necessary complications into the criminal question, and into our understanding of the social beliefs which surround crime and violence, it may be thought that I have placed the possibilities of a solution even further out of sight.

If so, then it seems to me that this is entirely the right kind of response. If this long, connected history of respectable fears tells us anything at all, then it is surely that street violence and disorder are a solidly entrenched feature of the social landscape. Hence, they are going to be much more difficult to dislodge than if we imagined that they had suddenly sprung from nowhere in the past twenty years or so; or since the war; or because of the arrival of black people in Britain; or because of recent changes in the law; or as a result of 'new-fangled' educational philosophies, or television violence, or any other symptom of 'permissive' modernity.

Such commonplace formulae as these, which refuse to grapple with the problems that have exercised the minds and actions of generations before us, trivialise the problem. Long-standing social difficulties and disputes are not solved by short, sharp remedies. No more, perhaps, than a short, sharp history lesson can be expected to dislodge the stubbornly immobile myths of 'law-and-order'. Our collective misunderstandings of both the past and present shape of our difficulties are so well entrenched that we cannot expect them to vanish overnight. Historical realism is a sobering companion for those who wish to set the world right, and a history of hooliganism may well seem a queer way to address contemporary 'law-and-order' problems. So, why history? Not, certainly not, to perpetuate the all-too-common view that our contemporary dilemmas can be resolved by somehow bringing the past back to life — whether by reference to the old 'carefree' neighbourhoods, or a new Riot Act. Rather, in the belief that we are so entrapped within the grief-stricken myths of the 'British way of life' that it will help first to repossess the past, if we are to understand the present and build the future.

Notes and References

The lines quoted in the Dedication on p. v are extracted from P. N. Furbank, *E. M. Forster: A Life* (Secker & Warburg, 1979) p. 100.

Chapter 1 Present Tense: Moderates and Hooligans

1. Enoch Powell, BBC Television, 28 May 1981.
2. *The Daily Mail*, 7 July 1981.
3. *The Daily Express*, 7 July 1981.
4. Austin Haywood, Deputy Chief Constable of West Yorkshire, *Bradford Telegraph and Argus*, 17 April 1976, and Mr James Jardine, Chairman of the Police Federation, *The Daily Telegraph*, 16 March 1978.
5. Sir Keith Joseph, *The Guardian*, 21 October 1974.
6. A. Clarke and I. Taylor, 'Vandals, Pickets and Muggers: Television Coverage of Law and Order in the 1979 Election', *Screen Education*, August 1980.
7. Quoted in *Social Work Today*, 29 April 1976; and *The Daily Mirror*, 11 October 1978.
8. *The Daily Mirror*, 28 June 1978.
9. *The Times*, 26 April 1978.
10. *The Daily Telegraph*, 31 May 1979.
11. R. Mark, *In the Office of Constable* (Collins, 1978) p. 286.
12. *The Daily Telegraph*, 26 April 1978.
13. *Report of Her Majesty's Chief Inspector of Constabulary, 1975* (HMSO, 1976) pp. 1–3, 38–9.
14. *The Guardian*, 4 July 1979.
15. R. Mark, *Minority Verdict* (Police Federation Occasional Papers, 1973) p. 1.
16. *The Daily Express*, 6 October 1977.
17. T. A. Critchley, *The Conquest of Violence* (Constable, 1970) pp. 193, 199.
18. *Public Order* (Conservative Political Centre, 1970) p. 26.
19. *The Guardian*, 22 September 1979.

20. *The Guardian*, 21 October 1974.
21. *How to Spot a Red Teacher* (National Front, 1977).
22. Quoted in *Social Work Today*, 29 April 1976. Cf. R. Boyson, *Down with the Poor* (Churchill Press, 1971); T. Russell, *The Tory Party* (Penguin, 1978) pp. 103ff.
23. 'Flog the Girl Thugs', *The Sun*, 13 February 1976; 'Bring back stocks for hooligans, MP says', *The Guardian*, 14 March 1981.
24. Cf. G. Pearson, *The Deviant Imagination* (Macmillan, 1975) ch. 7 and Chapters 4, 5, 7 and 8 of the present work.
25. P. Morgan, *Delinquent Fantasies* (Temple Smith, 1978) p. 191.
26. *The Daily Telegraph*, 25 October 1979.
27. *The Daily Mail*, 30 August 1977.
28. The Diana Dors Column, 'Sex is getting out of hand!', *Revue*, 8 February 1980.
29. 'Rees attacks "dangerous" Maggie', *The Daily Mail*, 24 February 1978.
30. Merlyn Rees, BBC Television, 31 October 1978.

Chapter 2   Twenty Years Ago: Teds Under the Bed

1. *The Daily Mirror*, 12 October 1978.
2. *78th Annual Conference* (Conservative Political Centre, 1958) pp. 95–102.
3. Ibid, pp. 97, 101–2.
4. Ibid, pp. 96–9.
5. *Hansard*, 27 October 1959.
6. *Hansard*, 10 March 1960.
7. *Hansard*, 6 May 1954 and 5 November 1959.
8. *Youth Astray* (Conservative Political Centre, 1946) p. 42.
9. *The Responsible Society* (Conservative Political Centre, 1959) p. 60.
10. Ibid, pp. 59–62; *Crime in the Sixties: A Bow Group Pamphlet* (Conservative Political Centre, 1963) pp. 13, 26–8; *Crime Knows No Boundaries* (Conservative Political Centre, 1966) pp. 11ff.
11. A. Bryant, Foreword to P. Jephcott, *Some Young People* (Allen & Unwin) pp. 6–7.
12. *The Adolescent* (British Medical Association, 1961) p. 5.
13. Ibid, pp. 5–6.
14. King George's Jubilee Trust, *Citizens of Tomorrow* (Odhams, 1955) pp. 49, 52.
15. T. R. Fyvel, *The Insecure Offenders* (Penguin, 1963 edn) pp. 18, 24, 63–5, 147, 212. Emphasis added.
16. *The Adolescent*, pp. 5–6.

17. Fyvel, *The Insecure Offenders*, p. 40.
18. Quoted in *The Daily Express*, 17 August 1977.
19. Mr R. A. Butler, addressing the *78th Annual Conference*, p. 102.
20. *Hansard*, 6 May 1954.
21. For accounts of the Teddy Boy phenomenon, see Fyvel, *The Insecure Offenders*; P. Rock and S. Cohen, 'The Teddy Boy' in V. Bogdanor and R. Skidelsky (eds), *The Age of Affluence, 1951–1964* (Macmillan, 1970); H. Hopkins, *The New Look* (Secker & Warburg, 1964); T. Jefferson, 'The Teds: A Political Resurrection' in S. Hall and T. Jefferson, *Resistance Through Rituals* (Hutchinson, 1976).
22. R. Hoggart, *The Uses of Literacy* (Penguin, 1958 edn) p. 248.
23. Ibid, p. 246.
24. For example, *Hansard* (3 February 1949, 16 February 1950, 9 March 1950, 23 March 1950, 9 November 1950, 24 July 1952 and 31 July 1952) where we hear of 'lustful and savage acts of cruelty and violence', 'this terrible wave of crimes', 'citizens . . . robbed, maimed and murdered daily in our towns and cities' and that 'the degree of violence employed is becoming more brutal', etc., as well as allegations that army deserters were at the heart of the trouble, and that military training was responsible for increasing violence. On army service, see also note 27 below.
25. Mass Observation, *Puzzled People* (Gollancz, 1947) p. 7; B. H. Reed, *Eighty Thousand Adolescents* (Allen & Unwin, 1950) pp. 173ff.
26. Mr Frank Beverley, Recorder of Bradford, in *Bradford Telegraph and Argus*, 11 July 1951. And here, another eye-catching headline: 'BLITZKRIEG BY BRADFORD CHILDREN: greenhouses and gardens wrecked at Rooley Lane', *Bradford Telegraph and Argus*, 5 June 1951.
27. King George's Jubilee Trust, *Citizens of Tomorrow*, p. 17; *Social Problems of Postwar Youth* (Economic Research Council, 1956). Cf. J. Trenaman, *Out of Step: A Study of Young Delinquent Soldiers in Wartime* (Methuen, 1952).
28. H. D. Willcock, *Report on Juvenile Delinquency* (Falcon, 1949) pp. 46–50.
29. *Bradford Telegraph and Argus*, 8 August 1977.
30. *The Daily Mail*, 4 September 1956.
31. *The Daily Mail*, 5 September 1956.

Chapter 3   Since the War: Past Perfect

1. G. Orwell, *Coming up for Air*, 1939 (Penguin, 1962 edn) pp. 27, 168.

2. Ibid, pp. 106—7.
3. 'The Lion and the Unicorn' in G. Orwell, *Collected Essays, Journalism and Letters*, vol. 2 (Penguin, 1970) pp. 79, 82.
4. 'The Decline of the English Murder' and 'Raffles and Miss Blandish', both in G. Orwell, *Decline of the English Murder* (Penguin, 1965) pp. 12, 67—8.
5. Orwell, 'The Lion and the Unicorn', p. 75.
6. M. J. Wiener, *English Culture and the Decline of the Industrial Spirit, 1850—1980* (Cambridge University Press, 1981).
7. T. S. Eliot, *Notes Towards a Definition of Culture* (Faber, 1962 edn) pp. 26—7, 103—8.
8. Q. D. Leavis, *Fiction and the Reading Public* (Chatto & Windus, 1932) pp. 151, 211, 231.
9. C. B. Cox and R. Boyson (eds), *Black Paper 1977* (Temple Smith, 1977) p. 5.
10. F. R. Leavis, *Mass Civilisation and Minority Culture* (Minority Press, 1930) pp. 6—7; F. R. Leavis and D. Thompson, *Culture and Environment* (Chatto & Windus, 1933) p. 87.
11. R. and T. Calvert, *The Law-Breaker* (Routledge, 1933) pp. 60—1.
12. W. Elkin, *English Juvenile Courts* (Kegan Paul, 1938) p. 292.
13. A. E. Morgan, *The Needs of Youth* (Oxford University Press, 1939) pp. 166—7, 190—1.
14. *The Times*, 4 January 1937.
15. *The Times*, 2 January 1937.
16. *Reynolds's News*, 8 November 1936. Forty years later, when Queen's Park Rangers fans staged a similar protest against the sale of a star player amidst Britain's 'winter of discontent', *The Sun* (24 February 1979) splashed a headline that contrived to get 'strike news' even on to the sports page: 'Soccer's first picket line'.
17. D. Russell and J. Reynolds, 'Sport Between the Wars', Bradford History Workshop, March 1980; R. Pardoe, *The Battle of London: Arsenal versus Tottenham Hotspur* (Stacey, 1972) p. xii.
18. *Reynolds's News*, 29 September 1935.
19. By comparison, there is ample documentation of football disturbances before the First World War. See Chapter 4, notes 35—9.
20. A. J. P. Taylor, *English History 1914—1945* (Penguin, 1970) pp. 237, 392.
21. Leavis, *Mass Civilisation*, p. 9; G. Orwell, 'Review of "The Pub and the People" ', 1943, in *Collected Essays*, vol. 3, p. 61.
22. C. E. B. Russell, *The Problem of Juvenile Crime* (Oxford University Press, 1917) p. 6
23. National Council of Public Morals, *The Cinema* (Williams & Norgate, 1917) pp. xxxiv, xxxviii. For early enquiries into the cinema, see

Commission on Educational and Cultural Films, *The Film in National Life* (Allen & Unwin, 1932).

24. H. Redwood, *God in the Slums* (Hodder & Stoughton, 1932) 16th edn, p. 43.

25. H. A. Secretan, *London Below Bridges* (Bles, 1931) p. 85. Secretan also entertained a somewhat unusual fear that the Hollywood talkies were corrupting the true Cockney dialect. Cf. pp. 86—7.

26. Morgan, *Needs of Youth*, p. 242

27. *Reynolds's News*, 15 December 1935.

28. H. Fielding, *An Enquiry into the Causes of the Late Increase of Robbers* (Millar, 1751) p. 3.

29. *Reynolds's News*, 1 November 1931, 17 November 1935 and 20 December 1936.

30. *Criminal Statistics for England and Wales 1928*, Cmd. 3581 (HMSO, 1930) p. xiv.

31. Ibid, pp. xii—xiii.

32. *Criminal Statistics for England and Wales 1935*, Cmd. 5520 (HMSO, 1936), pp. xviiff; *Report of the Departmental Committee on Corporal Punishment*, Cmd. 5684 (HMSO, 1938); *Corporal Punishment*, Cmnd. 1213 (HMSO, 1960) p. 31. Following a great upsurge in birching during the First World War, its use rapidly decreased and by the 1930s it was virtually abandoned in the cities, and birchings were almost entirely ordered by courts in small towns and country districts. See also Chapter 5, note 92.

33. *Hansard*, 8 March 1933.

34. *Hansard*, 30 June 1933.

35. R. Mark, *In the Office of Constable* (Collins, 1978) pp. 28—9.

36. R. Samuel, *East End Underworld* (Routledge & Kegan Paul, 1981); J. P. Bean, *The Sheffield Gang Wars* (D & D Publications, 1981).

37. See, for example, complaints about 'socialist hooliganism' at the meetings of National candidates reported in *Reynolds's News* (10 November 1935) beneath the headline 'HOOLIGAN LIE'. Or Oswald Mosley's justification of the use of counter-force against 'red terror' in *The Greater Britain* (BUF, 1934) pp. 186—8. Mosley poured scorn on the leaders of established parties who 'creep in by back doors, under police protection, to well picketed meetings', no less than hecklers at his own meetings 'who ran howling, when counter force was employed, for the protection of the police': 'When we have been attacked, we have hit back.' The General Election campaign of October 1931 was accompanied by particularly determined rowdyism: Beaverbrook was howled down at Glasgow, Churchill faced trouble at Peckham and MacDonald had

a bruising campaign at Seaham. Cf. 'Rowdies at it Again in Bradford
... Another meeting wrecked', *Bradford Telegraph and Argus*,
22 October 1931 'More Rowdyism in Leeds' and 'Rowdies Busy in
Newcastle', *Yorkshire Post*, 16 October 1931 and 22 October 1931.
A meeting of Mosley's 'New Party' at the Rag Market in Birmingham
was halted by a 'wild riot' in which 'a shower of chairs' was thrown
on to the platform (and thrown back by the speakers) whereupon,
with a great show of reluctance, the leaders were escorted under
police protection through a rear exit. *Yorkshire Post*, 19 October
1931.

38. Public Record Office, Home Office Papers, HO 45/11032/423878.
39. *Yorkshire Post*, 2 October 1931 and 3 October 1931; *The Times*,
    2 October 1931 and 17 October 1931; W. Hannington, *Unemployed
    Struggles*, 1936 (EP Publishing, 1977 edn); J. Stevenson and C.
    Cook, *The Slump* (Quartet, 1979).
40. J. White, 'Campbell Bunk: A Lumpen Community in London
    between the Wars', *History Workshop*, no. 8, 1979. See also the
    brief account of riotous eruptions on Peace Night in 1919 which
    coincided with race riots at seaports, in J. White, 'The Summer
    Riots of 1919', *New Society*, 13 August 1981. For the destruction
    of property during riotous Peace Celebrations, see also Public
    Record Office, Home Office Papers, HO 45/11068/372202.
41. Mass Observation, *The Pub and the People* (Gollancz, 1943) p. 248.
42. S. F. Hatton, *London's Bad Boys* (Chapman & Hall, 1931) p. 129.
43. J. Butterworth, *Clubland* (Epworth, 1932) pp. 37–9.
44. Hatton, *London's Bad Boys*, p. 169.
45. B. L. Q. Henriques, *The Indiscretions of a Warden* (Methuen,
    1937) pp. 240–4.
46. H. S. Bryan, *The Troublesome Boy* (Pearson, 1936) pp. 31–2.
47. Hatton, *London's Bad Boys*, pp. 14, 17; Butterworth, *Clubland*,
    pp. 47–8; Secretan, *London Below Bridges*, p. 87.
48. W. Hannington, *The Problem of the Distressed Areas* (Gollancz,
    1937) p. 90; W. F. Lestrange, *Wasted Lives* (Routledge, 1936)
    p. 124; R. H. Tawney, *The School-Leaving Age and Juvenile
    Unemployment* (Workers' Educational Association, 1934).
49. J. J. Findlay, *The Children of England* (Methuen, 1923) p. 188;
    Hatton, *London's Bad Boys*, p. 202; Butterworth, *Clubland*, p. 21.
50. D. Thompson, 'Advertising God', *Scrutiny*, vol. 1, no. 3, 1932,
    p. 246.
51. 'The School and Society', 1899, in J. Dewey, *The Child and the
    Curriculum* (Chicago University Press, 1956 edn) p. 34.
52. R. Baden-Powell, *Aids to Scoutmastership* (Jenkins, 1919) pp. 14,
    21, 27. Here and elsewhere, Baden-Powell's romanticism was

interlaced with large doses of anti-socialist philosophising, and no small amount of humbug. So, at the time of dole cuts in 1931 he urged youth 'to assist in the national economic emergency' and to 'keep the national keel steady' by developing 'the habit of thrift' and consuming only 'home and Imperial produce'. Above all, they were 'to carry out the principle of cheerfulness': 'Gloom and pessimism are having too much their own way just now, and never ... was there greater work for real happy grins to do' (*The Times*, 16 October 1931). A few years earlier, he had urged the necessity of 'developing the movement among our poor London lads and putting up a barrage of Scout ideals against the Communism that stalks in our midst' which led to a rather unfriendly exchange of letters with the Young Communist League. See *Baden-Powell Exposed!* (Young Communist League, 1927).

53. H. N. Casson, *The Teacher's World*, no. 710, vol. 20, 18 December 1918.
54. *The Teacher's World*, no. 711, vol. 20, 25 December 1918.
55. Ibid.
56. L. Le Mesurier, *Boys in Trouble* (Murray, 1931) pp. xv-xvi.
57. Quoted in W. Elkin, *English Juvenile Courts*, p. 288.
58. A. M. Carr-Saunders *et al.*, *Young Offenders* (Cambridge University Press, 1943) p. 47.
59. *Report of the Departmental Committee on the Treatment of Young Offenders*, Cmd 2831 (HMSO, 1927) p. 23.
60. *The Times*, 4 January 1937 and 25 October 1937.
61. *The Times*, 4 May 1935.
62. N. Walker, 'Crime and Penal Measures' in A. H. Halsey (ed.), *Trends in British Society Since 1900* (Macmillan, 1972) table 15.1; D. H. Thorpe *et al.*, *Out of Care* (Allen & Unwin, 1980) table 1.3; New Approaches to Juvenile Crime, *Briefing Paper No. 3: Some Facts About Juvenile Crime*, January 1980.
63. Butterworth, *Clubland*, p. 22.

Chapter 4   The Traditional 'Way of Life'

1. Wilfred Owen, 'Anthem for Doomed Youth', *Collected Poems* (Chatto & Windus, 1967) p. 44.
2. G. Winter, *The Golden Years, 1903–1913* (Penguin, 1977).
3. F. H. McClintock and N. H. Avison, *Crime in England and Wales* (Heinemann, 1968) p. 18; T. R. Gurr *et al.*, *The Politics of Crime and Conflict* (Sage, 1977) part II; V. A. C. Gatrell and T. B. Hadden, 'Criminal Statistics and their Interpretation' in E. A. Wrigley

(ed.), *Nineteenth Century Society* (Cambridge University Press, 1972) p. 374.

4. *Juvenile Offenders* (Howard Association, 1898) pp. 22—3.
5. Ibid, pp. 5, 9; *The Times*, 16 August 1899.
6. *Juvenile Offenders*, pp. 21—2.
7. H. Bosanquet, *The Family* (Macmillan, 1906) p. 310; M. G. Barnett, *Young Delinquents* (Methuen, 1913) p. 6.
8. *Report of the Inter-Departmental Committee on Physical Deterioration*, vol. 1, Cd 2175 (HMSO, 1904) pp. 4—5, 92. With some shattering evidence placed before it on the physical and moral degeneracy of the population, the committee thought that this only related to the lowest of the low, because of the way in which army recruitment attracted large numbers of men who were 'loafers' and 'rubbish'. The committee thus hoped that their report would 'have some effect in allaying the apprehensions of those who ... have made up their minds that progressive deterioration is to be found among the people generally'.
9. R. Baden-Powell, *Scouting for Boys* (Horace Cox, 1908) p. 208.
10. R. Baden-Powell, '"Boy Scouts" in connection with National Training and National Service', *Royal United Services Institute Journal*, vol. LV, 1911, p. 595.
11. J. Gorst, *The Children of the Nation* (Methuen, 1901) p. 213.
12. W. J. Braithwaite, 'Boys' Clubs' in E. J. Urwick (ed.), *Studies of Boy Life in Our Cities* (Dent, 1904) p. 189.
13. *Physical Deterioration*, vol. 2, Cd. 2210, qu. 2107; C. E. B. Russell and E. T. Campagnac, 'On the Physical Condition of Working Class Children in Ancoats, Manchester', appendix XXII to *Physical Deterioration*, vol. 3, Cd. 2186.
14. Anon, 'Religious Influences on the Adolescent' in J. H. Whitehouse (ed.), *Problems of Boy Life* (King, 1912) p. 263.
15. R. A. Bray, 'The Boy and the Family' in Urwick, *Boy Life*, pp. 23—5; R. A. Bray, *Boy Labour and Apprenticeship* (Constable, 1911) pp. 102—3, 205.
16. *Report of the Departmental Committee on the Employment of Children Act, 1903*, Cd. 5229 (HMSO, 1910) p. xxviii.
17. C. Booth, *Life and Labour of the People in London*, 17 vols (Macmillan, 1902); B. S. Rowntree, *Poverty: A Study of Town Life* (Macmillan, 1901).
18. T. N. Chamberlain, 'The Station-Lounger: A Study' in Whitehouse, *Boy Life*, gives a particularly harrowing account of the conditions of young street urchins. Also, E. T. Campagnac and C. E. B. Russell, 'The Education, Earnings and Social Condition of Boys Engaged in Street-Trading in Manchester', Board of Education, *Special Reports*

on Educational Subjects, vol. 7, Cmd. 835 (HMSO, 1902); C. E. B. Russell, 'Some Reflections on Home Office Schools and Juvenile Street Trading', *Charity Organisation Review*, November 1910; O. W. Hind, 'Juvenile Street Trading', *Shaftesbury Magazine*, November 1910. On common lodging-houses, A. Paterson, *Across the Bridges* (Edward Arnold, 1911) pp. 222—39.

19. *Minority Report of the Poor Law Commission 1909*, ed. S. and B. Webb (Kelley, 1974) part II, pp. 269, 273.

20. Bray, *Boy Labour*; S. J. Gibb, *The Boy and His Work* (Mowbray, 1911); C. E. B. Russell and E. T. Campagnac, 'Report on the School Training and Early Employment of Lancashire Children', Board of Education, *Special Reports on Educational Subjects*, Cd. 1867 (HMSO, 1903); F. Keeling, *The Labour Exchange in Relation to Boy and Girl Labour* (King, 1910); F. J. Leslie, *Wasted Lives* (Tinling, 1910); A. Freeman, *Boy Life and Labour* (King, 1914); A. Greenwood, 'Blind-Alley Labour', *Economic Journal*, June 1912; W. S. Churchill, *The People's Rights*, 1909 (Cape, 1970 edn) pp. 136—7.

21. F. Keeling, *Child Labour in the United Kingdom* (King, 1914) offers the most useful summary of the messy complexities of the law. The failure to enforce a uniform school-leaving age had various causes: the continuing desire of employers to use child labour at cheap rates, the vagaries of the 'half-time' system, and the disputed question of whether Education Act bye-laws could override the Factory Acts. It is a sorry reflection on the indifference of Victorian legislation that Keeling found it had 'not even been possible to enforce the apparently unconditional minimum age of 10, which was established by the English Act of 1876' (p. xxi).

22. H. Bosanquet, *The Standard of Life* (Macmillan, 1898) p. 178.

23. Preface to S. J. Gibb, *The Problem of Boy Work* (Wells Gardner, 1906) p. ix. For moral and hygienic crusades which focused on girls, see C. Dyhouse, *Girls Growing Up in Late Victorian and Edwardian England* (Routledge & Kegan Paul, 1981) and A. Davin, 'Imperialism and Motherhood', *History Workshop*, no. 5, 1978.

24. Quoted in *Minority Report of the Poor Law Commission 1909*, p. 274.

25. S. Meacham, 'The Sense of an Impending Clash: English Working Class Unrest before the First World War', *American Historical Review*, vol. 75, no. 5, 1972.

26. D. Marson, *Children's Strikes in 1911* (History Workshop Pamphlet, 1973).

27. S. L. Hynes, *The Edwardian Turn of Mind* (Oxford University Press, 1968); G. Dangerfield, *The Strange Death of Liberal England* (MacGibbon & Kee, 1966).

28. E. J. Hobsbawm, *Industry and Empire* (Penguin, 1969) p. 164.
29. 'Hooliganism and the Halls', *The Times*, 26 September 1898. Compare the lively riposte in the trade magazine, *Music Hall and Theatre Review*, 7 October 1898.
30. A. Wilson, 'Music Halls', *Contemporary Review*, vol. 78, July 1900, p. 138.
31. C. E. B. Russell, *Manchester Boys* (Manchester University Press, 1905) p. 94.
32. Barnett, *Young Delinquents*, p. 8.
33. *The Times*, 12 April 1913.
34. *The Times*, 25 October 1913.
35. T. Mason, *Association Football and English Society 1863–1915* (Harvester, 1980); J. Hutchinson, 'Some Aspects of Football Crowds before 1914', *Society for the Study of Labour History Bulletin*, vol. 32, Spring 1976; W. Vamplew, 'Ungentlemanly Conduct: The Control of Soccer Crowd Behaviour in England, 1888–1914' in T. C. Smout (ed.), *The Search for Wealth and Stability* (Macmillan, 1979).
36. *The Centenary A–Z of Albion* (Matthews & Mackenzie, 1979) p. 67.
37. Quoted in Mason, *Association Football*, p. 162.
38. *Football Field and Sports Telegram*, ed. 'Olympian', 27 September 1884.
39. E. Ensor, 'The Football Madness', *Contemporary Review*, vol. 74, November 1898, pp. 751–60. Cf. C. Edwardes, 'The New Football Mania', *Nineteenth Century*, vol. 32, 1892; Anon, 'Some Tendencies of Modern Sport', *Quarterly Review*, vol. 199, 1904; Anon, 'Are We Going Down Hill?', *Twentieth Century*, vol. 3, November 1901.
40. H. Perkin, 'The "Social Tone" of the Victorian Seaside Resorts' in *The Structured Crowd* (Harvester, 1981); J. Walvin, *Beside the Seaside* (Allen Lane, 1978); 'Alarum: Excursions', *Punch*, 30 September 1882; and W. Besant, 'From Thirteen to Seventeen', *Contemporary Review*, vol. 49, March 1886, p. 419 for a glimpse of 'those foul-mouthed young Bacchantes and raging Maenads of Hampstead Heath . . . sallow-faced lads with long and ugly coats and the round-topped hats'.
41. H. Bosanquet, 'Cheap Literature', *Contemporary Review*, vol. 79, May 1901, p. 672.
42. E. B. Turner, 'Health on the Cycle', *Contemporary Review*, vol. 73, May 1898.
43. Dr Lewis Hawkes, *Physical Deterioration*, vol. 2, qu. 13080.
44. *The Daily Graphic*, 17 September 1897 and 18 May 1898; *Reynolds's Newspaper*, 26 July 1897; *Leeds Mercury*, 8 August 1898;

The Daily Mail, 8 August 1898 and 18 August 1898; *News of the World*, 11 September 1898.

45. Such events were a cause for amusement in *Punch* (15 October 1898): 'Prove by example that the mean velocity of any given cyclist varies directly with the imagination of the nearest policeman.' But not in the cycling press where, 'tired of being lectured' by 'a stiff-necked lot', there were complaints of police harassment and 'bucolic magistrates' prejudice against cyclists'. *Bicycling News*, 27 July 1898, 31 August 1898 and 7 September 1898. *The Times* (28 January 1899) thought that, 'The early bicyclists complained that they were treated like early Christians.'

46. *The Daily Graphic*, 5 April 1898; *News of the World*, 7 August 1898; *The Daily Mail*, 8 August 1898. *Bicycling News* (17 August 1898) retorted with a cartoon: 'An Obstreperous Jury: Old Gentlemen Sometimes Die from Natural Causes.'

47. 'The ladies . . . as we know by sad experience . . . are only too often rash to a degree. It is the lady, as a rule, who cuts just under the bus horses' noses, who shaves the corner most finely, and who rides fast in traffic' (*The Daily Mail*, 18 August 1898). 'It is the female cyclist who does the rash and venturesome thing . . . riding about with an indifference to death that is positively Dervish-like' (*Manchester Evening News*, 8 September 1898). *The Times* (17 August 1898) implied that the ladies were not 'real' cyclists at all: 'Most real cyclists . . . would consider that a lady on a bicycle is utterly out of place in . . . any great artery of traffic . . . no one likes to see a woman taking unnecessary risk.' But some of them obviously were real cyclists and liked taking risks: 'Female "Scorcher" Cyclist . . . wearing the rational costume' (*Illustrated Police News*, 13 August 1898). *News of the World* (11 September 1898) had discovered a new angle on the female cyclist, however, offering 'Bicycles for Barmaids' in a popularity poll among Londoners.

48. A Clarion song from 1895, quoted in D. Prynn, 'The Clarion Clubs, Rambling and Holiday Associations', *Journal of Contemporary History*, vol. 11, 1976, p. 68.

49. B. Semmel, *Imperialism and Social Reform* (Allen & Unwin, 1960); G. Stedman Jones, *Outcast London* (Oxford University Press, 1971).

50. W. Booth, *In Darkest England and the Way Out*, 1890 (Knight, 1970).

51. J. Springhall, *Youth, Empire and Society* (Croom Helm, 1977).

52. K. H. Pearson, *National Life and Character* (Macmillan, 1894) pp. 189, 362.

53. Anon, 'Sport and Decadence' *Quarterly Review*, vol. 212, 1909, p. 487; Anon. In Whitehouse, *Boy Life*, p. 257.

54. T. Hodgkin, 'The Fall of the Roman Empire and Its Lesson for Us', *Contemporary Review*, vol. 73, January 1898, p. 70.

55. *Scouting for Boys*, p. 338.
56. C. F. G. Masterman (ed.), *The Heart of the Empire* (Fisher Unwin, 1902) pp. 7–8.
57. J. London, *The People of the Abyss* (Arco, 1963 edn) pp. 39, 137.
58. R. A. Bray, *The Town Child* (Fisher Unwin, 1907) pp. 145–6.
59. For an analysis of 'Mafficking' and the jingo crowd, see R. Price, *An Imperial War and the British Working Class* (Routledge & Kegan Paul, 1972).

Chapter 5 Victorian Boys, We Are Here!

1. *South London Chronicle*, 15 October 1898; *Reynolds's Newspaper*, 2 October 1898; and notes 22 to 33 below.
2. *Music Hall and Theatre Review*, 26 August 1898.
3. Clarence Rook tells us in *The Hooligan Nights* (Grant Richards, 1899) that the gangs took their name from Patrick Hooligan who lived in 'Irish Court' in the Elephant and Castle, 'a leader among men' who 'established a cult'. Earning his living as a chucker-out, and famed for his lawless daring, Mr Hooligan is said to have died in prison after killing a policeman. Rook likens his career to 'the lives of Buddha and Mahomet' (pp. 23–4). *The Hooligan Nights* is a skilful journalistic portrayal of the life and times of the original Hooligans, but if 'Patrick Hooligan' was a legend in his own time, then it is odd that no one other than Clarence Rook seemed to have heard of him. The press, for example, while using the word 'Hooligan' freely enough, were totally bemused about its origins.

   Other stories in circulation suggested that the name had been taken from a comic character in *Nuggets*; or from a music hall turn called 'Brother Hooligan' or 'The Hooligans', although the music hall trade magazine had never heard of any acts by these names. 'Like many other things,' it said, 'the word comes from America.' The word's similarity to the American 'hoodlum' was noted elsewhere, and Australia was also mentioned as its birth-place. Yet another story said that the word had been derived from two brothers named Hoolehan who were prize-fighters, and that in a court case involving them a foolish policeman had mispronounced their name as 'Hooligan'. The policeman's famous mispronunciation also figured in accounts which gave it as a corruption of 'Hooly's gang' or 'Hooley's gang' which is the version accepted by the *Oxford English Dictionary*. Cf. *Music Hall and Theatre Review*, 26 August 1898; *The Daily Mail*, 18 August 1898; *South London Chronicle*, 20 August 1898; J. Trevarthan, 'Hooliganism', *Nineteenth Century*, January 1901, p. 84; E. J. Urwick, *Studies of Boy*

Life in Our Cities (Dent, 1904) p. 300; *Notes and Queries*, 9th Series, no. 2, 17 September 1898, p. 227 and 15 October 1898, p. 316; 9th Series, no. 7, 19 January 1901, p. 48.

There was indeed a Mr Hooley in the headlines at the same time as the Hooligans in August 1898, but he was not a 'Hooligan'. Mr Edward Terah Hooley was a high-class villain and bankrupt who had been paying 'slush money' to bicycle manufacturers, and in the course of an absorbing corruption scandal he seemed hell-bent on implicating almost the entire ruling class of England as beneficiaries in his schemes. Mr Hooley's enterprise earned him even more column inches in the press than the terrible Hooligans, and numerous jokes contrived to link the two news stories. So that we hear of 'Hooleyans', 'Hooleyism', 'Hooleybaloo' and 'Hooleyiana', with 'Mr. Terah Boom-de-Ay Hooley' himself described by *Punch* as a 'Hooley-gan'. Cf. *Bicycling News*, 3 August 1898 and 24 August 1898; *The Daily Mail*, 18 August 1898; *Punch*, 6 August 1898 and 12 November 1898; and a *News of the World* (7 August 1898) cartoon, 'Hooley's Game of Skittles', which shows him bowling down the House of Lords with his evidence in the bankruptcy hearing.

It is a fair guess that it was these long-forgotten jokes which helped to secure the authority of 'Hooley's gang' as the origins of 'Hooligan'. There certainly were street gangs who took their name from a local hard man in such a way, but the Hooligans were not a local gang. Rather, as I will show, they were a well established 'youth culture' in working-class London, with affinities with similar subcultures in other cities, and we find youths from many parts of London adopting the title of 'Hooligans'. If it had not been for the energies of the press in promoting the new word, however, then no doubt 'Hooligan' would have passed into obscurity along with the unfortunate Mr Hooley and much else of late nineteenth-century London slang.

4. *The Daily Graphic*, 31 August 1898; *The Sun*, 7 August 1898; *South London Chronicle*, 27 August 1898, 3 September 1898 and 15 October 1898; *News of the World*, 2 October 1898.

5. *Hansard*, 8 August 1898; *South London Chronicle*, 6 August 1898; 'The Police Court and its Problems: An Interview with Mr. Thomas Holmes', *The Young Man*, vol. 15, 1901, p. 327. Charles Booth's survey found agreement: 'Hooliganism has been exaggerated by the Press . . . So say our witnesses.' *Life and Labour of the People in London: Notes on Social Influences* (Macmillan, 1903) p. 139.

6. *Manchester Evening News*, 18 August 1898; *The Echo*, 11 August 1898; *The Sun*, 3 August 1898.

7. Quoted in *The Daily Graphic*, 22 August 1898.

8. *The Sun*, 3 August 1898 and 6 August 1898; *The Lancet*, 20 August 1989; *The Daily Mail*, 11 August 1898; *News of the World*, 7 August 1898.

9. *South London Chronicle*, 13 August 1898; *The Sun*, 3 August 1898 and 11 August 1898; *The Daily Graphic*, 6 October 1898.

10. *The Clarion*, 20 August 1898.

11. So, Robert Blatchford's view on the frequently condemned drunkenness of the poor was that it was a consequence of their low state of physical health, and not excessive drinking. 'I have seen a journalist, and one very severe upon the vices of the poor, drink eight shillings worth of whiskey and soda in an evening, and do his work correctly . . . But the average poor labourer of the slums would be mad on a quarter of the liquor.' *Merrie England* (Journeyman, 1976 edn) pp. 72–3. Jack London agreed: 'Not only is this beer unfit for people to drink, but too often the men and women are unfit to drink it.' *The People of the Abyss* (Arco, 1963 edn) p. 176.

12. *The Times*, 2 August 1898.

13. *The Times*, 16 August 1898; *Reynolds's News*, 2 October 1898; *Manchester Evening News*, 15 August 1898.

14. 'HOOLIGANS: Street Fights in Chelsea', *The Daily Graphic*, 18 August 1898.

15. *The Times*, 16 August 1898; *News of the World*, 21 August 1898.

16. *The Daily Graphic*, 23 August 1898, 26 August 1898, 27 August 1898, 26 September 1898; *The Daily Mail*, 1 August 1898 and 15 August 1898; *The Sun*, 6 August 1898; *News of the World*, 25 September 1898.

17. *South London Chronicle*, 24 September 1898.

18. W. Besant, *East London* (Chatto & Windus, 1901) p. 177.

19. *Reynolds's News*, 7 August 1898; *South London Chronicle*, 20 August 1898.

20. *South London Chronicle*, 20 August 1898; *Reynolds's News*, 7 August 1898.

21. *South London Chronicle*, 27 August 1898.

22. *The Daily Graphic*, 6 October 1898; *South London Chronicle*, 1 October 1898 and 8 October 1898.

23. *Illustrated Police News*, 9 July 1898.

24. *South London Chronicle*, 15 October 1898; *Illustrated Police News*, 1 October 1898; *Reynolds's News*, 2 October 1898.

25. *News of the World*, 9 October 1898. This is probably the killing remembered by Arthur Harding in R. Samuel, *East End Underworld* (Routledge & Kegan Paul, 1981) pp. 13, 292.

26. *The Daily Mail*, 15 August 1898; *News of the World*, 14 August 1898; *The Evening News*, 13 August 1898.
27. R. Blatchford, *Dismal England* (Walter Scott, 1899) p. 37.
28. *News of the World*, 24 July 1898; *Illustrated Police News*, 30 July 1898.
29. *South London Chronicle*, 5 November 1898. *News of the World* (30 October 1898) described the convicted murderer as 'a youth of the Hooligan type'; but *The Evening News* (21 July 1898 and 26 July 1898) thought the incident arose out of gang rivalries and reprisals against a 'copper's nark'.
30. R. Samuel, 'East End Crime', Conference on Sociology and History, University of Essex, December 1979.
31. *Report of the Commissioner of Police of the Metropolis 1899*, Cd. 399 (HMSO, 1900); *Royal Commission on the Duties of the Metropolitan Police*, vol. 2, Cd. 4260 (HMSO, 1908) qu. 79; Public Record Office, MEPO 2/531 and MEPO 2/570.
32. *The Sun*, 3 August 1898.
33. *The Daily Mail*, 13 August 1898.
34. *News of the World*, 9 October 1898; *The Daily Mail*, 19 August 1898; *Bicycling News*, 10 August 1898.
35. *Reynolds's News*, 9 October 1898; *Manchester Evening News*, 10 September 1898 and 13 September 1898; and 'RAILWAY OUTRAGES . . . WHO IS THE WRECKER?', *News of the World*, 11 September 1898.
36. Public Record Office, Metropolitan Police, MEPO 2/362.
37. *South London Chronicle*, 13 August 1898 and 15 October 1898; Public Record Office, MEPO 2/467.
38. *Illustrated Police News*, 16 July 1898.
39. *South London Chronicle*, 13 August 1898 and 3 September 1898.
40. *South London Chronicle*, 27 August 1898; *Illustrated Police News*, 20 August 1898; *The Evening News*, 26 July 1898.
41. *South London Chronicle*, 6 August 1898.
42. The singing seems no more than a harmless jest about Miss Powers walking out with her young man. But the insult may have been more pointed if, as seems likely, the chant had been adapted from a current Music Hall number that described another 'lydy' who also worked at bottling ginger-beer and who had been 'doing some overtime' with the foreman:

> Woa, Charlotte! aint yer goin' strong,
> What with your dress and yer fancy bonnet
> And all yer stylish ribbons upon it.
> I can't make out why you look so sublime,
> But she can't kid me she's been doin' some overtime.

Quoted in 'Hooliganism and the Halls', *The Times*, 26 September 1898.

43. Public Record Office, Home Office Papers, HO 45/9723/A51956.
44. C. E. B. Russell, *Manchester Boys* (Manchester University Press, 1905) p. 51.
45. A. Devine, *Scuttlers and Scuttling* (Guardian Printing Works, 1890) p. 7.
46. R. Roberts, *The Classic Slum* (Penguin, 1973) p. 155.
47. J. Wright, *English Dialect Dictionary*, vol. 4 (Frowde, 1903).
48. Cf. *Comic Cuts*, 2 July 1898 where, as the police are sighted, Chokee Bill remarks, 'I would 'ave given worlds for an 'arf-brick, Mr. Edditer, when I saw them two blues.' *Comic Cuts* was making its contribution to law enforcement at this time by awarding 'Chokee Bill Medals' to regular readers. D. Gifford (ed.), *Victorian Comics* (Allen & Unwin, 1976) collects together some of Area Sneaker's contemporaries: the Terrible Twins, the Big Budget Kid, the Three Beery Bounders, the Ball's Pond Banditti, Orfis Boy and other Victorian precursors to Denis the Menace, Billy Whizz *et al*.
49. H. Mayhew, *London Labour and the London Poor*, vol. 1 (Dover, 1968) p. 51.
50. A. Morrison, *A Child of the Jago* (Penguin, 1946 edn) pp. 37, 105, 123.
51. *The Sun*, 6 August 1898; *The Echo*, 6 August 1898; *The Times*, 16 August 1989; *The Spectator*, 27 August 1898; *The Daily Mail*, 16 August 1898; *News of the World*, 14 August 1898; *Illustrated Police News*, 13 August 1898.
52. Quoted in N. D. McLachlan, *Larrikinism* (Melbourne University MA thesis, n.d.) p. 18. Cf. Ajax, 'Larrikinism', *Sydney Quarterly Magazine*, January 1884; A. Pratt, ' "Push" Larrikinism in Australia', *Blackwood's Magazine*, vol. MXXIX, July 1901; N. Gould, *Town and Bush* (Routledge, 1896) pp. 99–117; W. Tallack, *Penological and Preventive Principles* (Wertheimer, 1896) p. 114; C. M. H. Clark (ed.), *Select Documents in Australian History 1851–1900* (Angus & Robertson, 1955).
53. Devine, *Scuttlers and Scuttling*, p. 2.
54. Besant, *East London*, pp. 176–7.
55. Samuel, *East End Underworld*, pp. 116–23, 151–2, 190.
56. *The Daily Graphic*, 7 June 1897 and 6 July 1897; *Reynolds's News*, 6 June 1897.
57. *News of the World*, 16 October 1898; *Illustrated Police News*, 5 November 1898.
58. Public Record Office, MEPO 2/1162. The police had been tipped off by an anonymous letter, written in a wobbly hand and signed 'From one who is affraid'.
59. *Hansard*, 14 September 1893.
60. Public Record Office, MEPO 2/1044.
61. Rudyard Kipling, *Selected Verse* (Penguin, 1977 edn) pp. 160–1.
62. *The Clarion*, 12 November 1898.

63. N. B. Weissman, 'Rural Crime in Tsarist Russia: The Question of Hooliganism, 1905–1914', *Slavic Review*, vol. 37, no. 2, 1978, pp. 228–9. 'Hooligan' was already said to be 'part and parcel of the Russian language' in *Notes and Queries*, 10th Series, no. 1, 13 February 1904, p. 125. The confusion with redskins probably stems from the 'Apache' gangs of Paris, said to be 'more violent than the Hooligans over here owing to the lamentable custom of carrying a pistol or a dagger' by someone who clearly did not believe that Hooligans were armed. *Royal Commission on the Metropolitan Police*, qu. 45779.

64. Urwick, *Studies of Boy Life*, p. 295.

65. A. Freeman, *Boy Life and Labour* (King, 1914) p. 88.

66. *Report of the Inter-Departmental Committee on Physical Deterioration*, vol. 2, Cd. 2210 (HMSO, 1904) qu. 3665.

67. J. Springhall, *Youth, Empire and Society* (Croom Helm, 1977); J. A. Mangan, *Athleticism in the Victorian and Edwardian Public School* (Cambridge University Press, 1981).

68. Opening remarks to R. Baden-Powell, '"Boy Scouts" in connection with National Training and National Service', *Royal United Services Institute*, vol. LV, 1911, p. 584.

69. R. Baden-Powell, *Scouting for Boys* (Horace Cox, 1908) pp. 339–40.

70. *The Pall Mall Gazette*, 12 February 1901.

71. R. Buchanan, 'The Voice of the Hooligan', *Contemporary Review*, vol. 76, December 1899, pp. 774–89.

72. Kipling, *Selected Verse*, p. 162.

73. Urwick, *Studies of Boy Life*, p. 265.

74. T. Holmes, *Known to the Police* (Arnold, 1908) pp. 169–70.

75. Russell, *Manchester Boys*, p. 53.

76. R. Baden-Powell, 'Boy Scouts', *National Defence*, vol. 4, August 1910, p. 440.

77. Ibid, pp. 446–7.

78. J. O. Springhall, 'The Boy Scouts, Class and Militarism', *International Review of Social History*, vol. 17, 1972, pp. 138ff.

79. P. Green, *How to Deal with Lads* (Arnold, 1911) p. 19.

80. Urwick, *Studies of Boy Life*, p. 302.

81. Springhall, *Youth, Empire and Society*, p. 80.

82. Ibid, p. 138.

83. Springhall, 'Boy Scouts, Class and Militarism'.

84. Boy Scouts Association, *Our Aims, Methods and Needs*, 1920, p. 3. Cf. the fierce attack in a penny pamphlet, *Baden-Powell Exposed!* (Young Communist League, 1927).

85. *Scouting for Boys*, pp. 28, 313–4, 332, 342.
86. *National Defence*, 1910, p. 441.
87. *Royal United Services Institute Journal*, 1911, p. 592.
88. Quoted in A. Summers, 'Militarism in Britain before the Great War', *History Workshop*, no. 2, 1976, p. 114.
89. R. Blatchford, *My Life in the Army* (Clarion Press, 1910) pp. 133–9. Cf. the denunciation of Blatchford in 1915 as a 'vulgar jingo' in V. I. Lenin, 'British Pacifism and the British Dislike of Theory' in *On Britain* (Lawrence & Wishart, 1964) p. 440.
90. *National Defence*, 1910, p. 438.
91. A. Marwick, *The Deluge: British Society and the First World War* (Macmillan, 1965).
92. From 1900 to 1914 birchings ran at around 2,000 per year. In 1915 there were 3,514 ordered in the courts, rising to 4,864 in 1916, reaching a peak in 1917 of 5,210. From thereon, accompanying disenchantment with the war, birchings began to fall away rapidly. In 1921 only 661 were ordered, in 1927 the figure was 247, and with the exception of 1935 birchings never again rose above the 200 mark in peacetime. In 1938, when the Cadogan committee recommended that judicial corporal punishment should be totally abolished, there were a mere 48 birchings ordered in magistrates' courts. With the outbreak of the Second World War a similar, although much less pronounced, increase in birchings occurred. *Criminal Statistics for England and Wales*, Cmd. 5520 (HMSO, 1936); *Report of the Departmental Committee on Corporal Punishment*, Cmd. 5684 (HMSO, 1938); *Corporal Punishment*, Cmnd. 1213 (HMSO, 1960).
93. R. Baden-Powell, *Aids to Scoutmastership* (Jenkins, 1919) p. 9.
94. J. Butterworth, *Clubland* (Epworth, 1932) pp. 21–2; S. F. Hatton, *London's Bad Boys* (Chapman & Hall, 1931). 202–3. These can be contrasted with the sickly enthusiasm of R. Holmes, *My Police Court Friends with the Colours* (Blackwood, 1915).

Chapter 6   A New Variety of Crime

1. *The Times*, 6 February 1899.
2. W. Tallack, *Penological and Preventive Principles* (Wertheimer, 1896) pp. 111–15.
3. *Punch*, 6 April 1881; 30 April 1881; 21 May 1881; 25 March 1883; 1 July 1882; 30 September 1882.
4. *Punch*, 19 February 1881; 16 April 1881; 6 August 1881; 26

November 1881; 10 December 1881; 'Civilisation of the Rough', *Punch's Almanack for 1882*, 6 December 1881.

5. Public Record Office, Home Office Papers, HO 45/9629/A22415; HO 45/9625/A19890; HO 45/9636/A30742; HO 45/9638/A32518.

6. Public Record Office, Metropolitan Police Commissioner, MEPO 2/163.

7. *Punch*, 23 July 1881; *The City Jackdaw* (Manchester) vol. 1, no. 41, 25 August 1876; A. Ritchie, *King of the Road* (Wildwood, 1975).

8. M. Arnold, 'Democracy' in *Democratic Education* (Michigan University Press, 1962) p. 16.

9. M. Arnold, *Culture and Anarchy* (Cambridge University Press, 1960) pp. 77, 193.

10. Ibid, p. 80.

11. Ibid, p. 76.

12. M. Ignatieff, *A Just Measure of Pain* (Macmillan, 1978).

13. A. G. L. Shaw, *Convicts and the Colonies* (Faber, 1966).

14. D. D. Cooper, *The Lesson of the Scaffold* (Allen Lane, 1974).

15. P. W. J. Bartrip, 'Public Opinion and Law Enforcement: The Ticket-of-Leave Scares in Mid-Victorian Britain' in V. Bailey (ed.), *Policing and Punishment in Nineteenth Century Britain* (Croom Helm, 1981).

16. *Hansard*, 7 June 1855; *The Times*, 2 January 1863.

17. *Punch*, 6 December 1862 and 7 February 1863.

18. *The Times*, 1 January 1863.

19. *Culture and Anarchy*, p. 193.

20. G. Stedman Jones, *Outcast London* (Oxford University Press, 1971) part III.

21. Anon, 'The Science of Garotting', *Cornhill Magazine*, vol. 7, 1863, p. 79.

22. *The Spectator*, 19 July 1862; *The Observer*, 23 November 1862.

23. C. Dickens, 'The Ruffian' in *The Uncommercial Traveller* (Oxford University Press, 1958) p. 303.

24. *The Times*, 14 November 1856.

25. *The Times*, 1 December 1862.

26. *The Daily News*, 9 December 1862, 19 December 1862, 24 December 1862; *Reynolds's Newspaper*, 17 May 1863.

27. T. R. Gurr *et al.*, *The Politics of Crime and Conflict* (Sage, 1977) p. 188.

28. *Punch*, 20 December 1862.

29. *The Times*, 10 June 1863.

30. *Punch*, 5 July 1856 and 9 August 1856.

31. *Punch*, 27 December 1856.

32. *The Times*, 14 November 1856.

33. M. D. Hill, *Suggestions for the Repression of Crime* (Parker, 1857) p. 152.

34. *The Times*, 14 November 1856; *The Daily News*, 22 December 1862; and *Reports from Select Committees on Transportation, 1856*, British Parliamentary Publications (Irish University Press, 1969).

35. For example, *News of the World*, 7 August 1898; *The Lancet*, 20 August 1898; and the running battle on the 'flogging mania' in the pages of *The Echo* throughout August 1898. It testifies to the persistence of the Garotter's Act myth that the government reports of 1938 and 1960 still found it necessary to repudiate this 'common belief'. *Report of the Departmental Committee on Corporal Punishment*, Cmd 5684 (HMSO, 1938) p. 83; *Corporal Punishment*, Cmnd 1213 (HMSO, 1960); *Corporal Punishment* (Howard League, 1953) p. 4.

36. J. Davis, 'The London Garotting Panic of 1862' in V. A. C. Gatrell, B. Lenman and G. Parker (eds), *Crime and the Law* (Europa, 1980) p. 191.

37. *Reynolds's Newspaper*, 23 November 1856.

38. Cf. Herbert Spencer on 'The Morals of Trade' (1854), reprinted in *Essays: Scientific, Political and Speculative* (Williams & Northgate, 1868).

39. *Hansard*, 11 March 1863.

40. *Hansard*, 11 March 1863 and 6 May 1863.

41. *Hansard*, 11 March 1863.

42. *Report . . . Corporal Punishment* (1938) p. 7.

43. *Hansard*, 24 February 1863.

44. *The Times*, 30 December 1862 and 16 February 1863.

45. *The Times*, 30 December 1862.

46. I. Gibson, *The English Vice* (Duckworth, 1978).

47. *Reynolds's Newspaper*, 17 May 1863.

48. H. Cotton, 'Corporal Punishment in India', *Humane Review*, vol. 6, 1906; H. Cotton, 'Corporal Punishment in India', *The Humanitarian*, October 1910; H. Cotton, 'Whipping in India', *The Humanitarian*, April 1914.

49. B. Semmel, *The Governor Eyre Controversy* (MacGibbon & Kee, 1962).

50. *The Daily News*, 6 January 1866 quoted in *The English Vice*, p. p. 169.

51. *The English Vice*, p. 169.

52. *The Governor Eyre Controversy, passim.* Semmel argues that the vindication of Eyre's atrocity against the 'inferior' people of the

West Indies harmonised with ruling-class fears and resentment of working-class agitation on the home front during the 1860s. Britain's imperial instincts have often been prominent when whipping is on the agenda. For example, the *Punch* (21 December 1878) cartoon showing Britannia flourishing the birch-twigs against the 'childish' Ameer of Kabul during the Afghanistan crisis of 1878 (see p. 151). Or the debate on the 'White Slave Bill' in 1912 when flogging was introduced for the offence of procuring when it was alleged that men 'almost entirely of foreign origin' were decoying white girls into prostitution. 'London has become the dumping ground from countries all over the world', one MP thought and more than one Member rejoiced in the prospect of deporting the offenders 'with the hall-mark of some British muscle on his back', *Hansard*, 1 November 1912, cls 768, 769, 786, 791.

53. *Reynolds's Newspaper*, 19 July 1863 and 26 July 1863.
54. *The Times*, 13 July 1863.
55. *The Times*, 13 July 1863.
56. *The Daily News*, 31 December 1862.

Chapter 7   The Artful Chartist Dodger

1. M. Arnold, *Culture and Anarchy* (Cambridge University Press, 1960) p. 19.
2. C. Dickens, *Oliver Twist* (Penguin, 1966) and *Barnaby Rudge* (Oxford University Press, 1954). Cf. P. Collins, *Dickens and Crime* (Macmillan, 1964).
3. M. Jenkins, *The General Strike of 1842* (Lawrence & Wishart, 1980) p. 219.
4. *Report on the Sanitary Condition of the Labouring Population of Great Britain, 1842*, ed. M. W. Flinn (Edinburgh University Press, 1965).
5. F. Engels, *The Condition of the Working Class in England* (Panther, 1969) pp. 159–61.
6. H. Worsley, *Juvenile Depravity* (Gilpin, 1849) *passim*.
7. G. Pearson, *The Deviant Imagination* (Macmillan, 1975) pp. 160ff.
8. Worsley, *Juvenile Depravity*, pp. 93, 192; T. Beggs, *An Inquiry into the Extent and Causes of Juvenile Depravity* (Gilpin, 1849) pp. 7, 131; A. Thomson, *Social Evils: Their Causes and Their Cure* (Nisbet, 1852) p. 6; A. Thomson, *Punishment and Prevention* (Nisbet, 1857) p. 181; B. Rotch, *Suggestions for the Prevention of Juvenile Depravity* (Court, 1846).
9. Beggs, *An Inquiry*, p. 2.

10. Thomson, *Social Evils*, p. 29.
11. W. Buchanan, *Remarks on the Causes and State of Juvenile Crime in the Metropolis* (Taylor, 1846); Beggs, *An Inquiry*, pp. 49–51.
12. *Hansard*, 28 February 1843.
13. Ibid.
14. Ibid.
15. Ibid.
16. *The Times*, 1 March 1843 and 6 March 1843. The culmination to this episode was that the government's Factory Bill foundered amidst squabbling between different factions of the churches as to who should control the promised factory schools and bestow the benefits and blessings of Christian privilege upon the poor. Cf. J. L. and B. Hammond, *Lord Shaftesbury* (Penguin, 1939) pp. 86–7.
17. *Report on the Sanitary Condition*, ed. Flinn, p. 267.
18. 'On Sunday last a meeting was held on the hills near Accrington . . . there must have been 26,000 people present . . . They say they may as well die by the sword as by hunger.' *Liverpool Mercury*, 1842 quoted in T. Newbigging, *History of the Forest of Rossendale* (Rossendale Free Press, 1893) p. 325.
19. D. Williams, *The Rebecca Riots* (Wales University Press, 1971) pp. 199, 222, 232. Williams could only trace one occasion on which Rebecca broke the Sabbath. There is an illuminating discussion of the role of Christianity in early nineteenth-century politics in E. P. Thompson, *The Making of the English Working Class* (Penguin, 1968) ch. 11. For the organisation of working-class politics, see J. Foster, *Class Struggle and the Industrial Revolution* (Weidenfield & Nicolson, 1974).
20. Thompson, *The Making of the English Working Class*, p. 439. The double-edged morality of Christianity also troubled American slave-owners in the antebellum South. Some hoped that religious instruction would produce more obedient slaves. Others complained that it made slaves lazy, proud and 'saucy', and encouraged insurrectionary ideas. A. J. Raboteau, *Slave Religion* (Oxford University Press, 1980) pp. 123, 164, 209, 290–318; E. D. Genovese, *Roll, Jordan, Roll* (André Deutsch, 1975) pp. 161–8.
21. Beggs, *An Inquiry*, p. 152.
22. Worsley, *Juvenile Depravity*, p. 207.
23. C. F. Cornwallis, *On the Treatment of the Dangerous and Perishing Classes of Society* (Smith, Elder & Co., 1853) p. 344.
24. Thomson, *Social Evils*, p. 132.
25. M. Hill, *Juvenile Delinquency* (Smith, Elder & Co., 1953) p. 3.
26. Thomson, *Social Evils*, p. 1; *Punishment and Prevention*, p. 153.

27. Beggs, *An Inquiry*, p. 23; S. P. Day, *Juvenile Crime* (Reeves, 1858) p. 287.
28. Worsley, *Juvenile Depravity*, pp. 6, 9, 10.
29. Cornwallis, *On the Treatment of the Dangerous . . . Classes*, p. 352.
30. J. Adshead, *On Juvenile Criminals, Reformatories, etc.* (Harrison, 1856) p. 10; Engels, *The Condition of the Working Class in England*, p. 160.
31. Cornwallis, *On the Treatment of the Dangerous . . . Classes*, p. 410; Worsley, *Juvenile Depravity*, pp. 78, 94; Beggs, *An Inquiry*, p. 97.
32. Hill, *Juvenile Delinquency*, p. 39.
33. Beggs, *An Inquiry*, pp. 72–3.
34. Worsley, *Juvenile Depravity*, p. 79.
35. Ibid., pp. 53, 192, 211–2, 215. Cf. Beggs, *An Inquiry*, p. 149; 'Judges have repeatedly given expression to their feelings, that if it were not for intemperance their office would be a sinecure.'
36. Worsley, *Juvenile Depravity*, pp. 79–81, 95.
37. Beggs, *An Inquiry*, p. 96.
38. Hill, *Juvenile Delinquency*, pp. 9, 35.
39. Quoted in M. May, 'Innocence and Experience: The Evolution of the Concept of Juvenile Delinquency', *Victorian Studies*, vol. 17, no. 1, 1973, p. 7.
40. *Oliver Twist*, p. 100.
41. *The Union*, January 1843. Quoted in S. Smiles, *Character* (Murray, 1879) p. 60.
42. Worsley, *Juvenile Depravity*, pp. 28, 43, 50–1, 62.
43. J. P. Kay-Shuttleworth, *The Moral and Physical Condition of the Working Classes*, 1832 (Cass, 1970 edn) p. 48.
44. *Children's Employment Commission. Second Report. Trades and Manufactures*, 1843, British Parliamentary Papers (Irish University Press, 1968) p. 165.
45. *Report on the Sanitary Condition*, ed. Flinn, pp. 306ff.
46. Worsley, *Juvenile Depravity*, pp. 81–6.
47. Ibid, pp. 91–3.
48. M. Ignatieff, *A Just Measure of Pain* (Macmillan, 1978) pp. 114–15.
49. Hill, *Juvenile Delinquency*, pp. 11–24, 139.
50. T. Plint, *Crime in England* (Gilpin, 1851) p. ii.
51. Ibid, pp. 32–3, 80–100.
52. Ibid, pp. 32–4, 80–100, 159–72.
53. M. J. Wiener, *English Culture and the Decline of the Industrial Spirit, 1850–1980* (Cambridge University Press, 1981).
54. Hill, *Juvenile Delinquency*, p. 18; Adshead, *On Juvenile Criminals*, p. 11; Day, *Juvenile Crime*, pp. 283–5.
55. For how Manchester appeared to these distinguished visitors, see

S. Marcus, *Engels, Manchester and the Working Class* (Weidenfeld & Nicolson, 1974) pp. 28—66.

56. Quoted in ibid, p. 46.

57. For example, *The Responsible Society* (Conservative Political Centre, 1959) p. 60 which rejected the view that criminals 'are the victims of their environment', while pointing to 'before the war when unemployment and bad housing offered greater excuses than they do now'. Or, Sir Thomas Moore who described how in the 1930s 'unemployment was rife and . . . people committed crimes of violence with robbery as a possible or inevitable consequence', but now did it 'almost for the fun of doing so'. *Hansard*, 17 December 1959.

58. Cornwallis, *On the Treatment of the Dangerous . . . Classes*, p. 408.

59. Beggs, *An Inquiry*, p. 66 Chadwick to Home Secretary, 1843, Public Record Office, Home Office Papers, HO 45/454.

60. Thomson, *Punishment and Prevention*, p. 168; *Report of the Commissioners on Establishing an Efficient Constabulary Force* (HMSO, 1839) p. 67.

61. J. Kingsmill, *Serious Crime in England* (Longman, 1856) p. 24.

62. Day, *Juvenile Crime*, p. 32.

63. Hill, *Juvenile Delinquency*, pp. 28, 101.

64. Worsley, *Juvenile Depravity*, p. 198.

65. Ibid, pp. 191, 212.

66. Plint, *Crime in England*, pp. 41—79, 83.

67. J Clay, 'On the Effect of Good or Bad Times on Committals to Prison', *Journal of the Statistical Society of London*, vol. 18, 1855, pp. 74—9.

68. M. D. Hill, *Suggestions for the Repression of Crime* (Parker, 1857) p. 109.

69. *Report of the Select Committee on Criminal and Destitute Juveniles*, 1852, British Parliamentary Papers (Irish University Press, 1970), qu. 391.

70. Ibid, qu. 817.

71. M. Carpenter, *Juvenile Delinquents* (Patterson Smith, 1970 edn), pp. 1—2.

72. M. Carpenter, *Reformatory Schools* (Woburn, 1968 edn) p. 83.

73. *The Times*, 6 March 1843.

74. *Report of the Proceedings of a Conference on the Subject of Preventive and Reformatory Schools* (Longman, 1851) p. 33.

75. Cornwallis, *On the Treatment of the Dangerous . . . Classes*, p. 398.

76. *Punishment and Prevention*, pp. 174, 420; Beggs, *An Inquiry*, p. 4.

77. M. Foucault, *Discipline and Punish* (Allen Lane, 1977); Ignatieff, *A Just Measure of Pain*.

78. Carpenter, *Reformatory Schools*, p. 75.

79. Ibid, p. 337.
80. Ibid, p. 321–2.
81. Ibid, p. 74. Mary Carpenter, well tutored in Nonconformist philosophy by her father, was also something of an intellectual magpie. Here she was almost certainly echoing John Brewster, *On the Prevention of Crimes*, 1792: 'There are cords of love as well as fetters of iron.' Quoted in Ignatieff, p. 74.
82. J. Manton, *Mary Carpenter and the Children of the Streets* (Heinemann, 1976) pp. 43–5.
83. J. S. Mill, *Principles of Political Economy* in *Collected Works*, vol. 3 (Toronto University Press, 1965) pp. 760, 763. Mill had added the chapter 'On the Probable Futurity of the Labouring Classes' after the revolutionary convulsions of 1848 in Europe. Cf. J. S. Mill, *Autobiography* (Oxford University Press, 1969) pp. 139ff.
84. There are, of course, observable differences between Mill and Carpenter. Mill considered that 'the poor have come out of leading-strings, and cannot any longer be governed or treated like children' (*Principles*, p. 763). Whereas Carpenter's paternalistic (or should one say 'maternalistic'?) emphasis required that the object of reform should be, precisely, to return the unruly to the condition of childhood. Even so, the question of 'rule by consent' has continued to be intimately bound up with crime preoccupations. Cf. the analysis of Britain's contemporary 'law-and-order' movement as evidence of the 'exhaustion of consent' during the periodic crises of the 1970s in S. Hall *et al.*, *Policing the Crisis* (Macmillan, 1978) and the account of the authoritarian tendency in E. P. Thompson, *Writing by Candlelight* (Merlin, 1980).
85. Quoted in D. Jones, *Chartism and the Chartists* (Allen Lane, 1975) p. 41.
86. Beggs, *An Inquiry*, pp. 51–2, 134.
87. Cornwallis, *On the Treatment of the Dangerous . . . Classes*, p. 334.
88. Thomson, *Punishment and Prevention*, pp. 148, 157.
89. *Report on the Sanitary Condition*, ed. Flinn, pp. 266, 268, 335.

Chapter 8   Merrie England and its Unruly Apprentice

1. *The Complete Works of Thomas Shadwell* (Fortune Press, 1927) p. 122.
2. Cf. A. Macfarlane, *The Justice and the Mare's Ale* (Blackwell, 1981) pp. 1–26 for an attempt to reconcile the conflicting viewpoints.
3. M. Ignatieff, *A Just Measure of Pain* (Macmillan, 1978) pp. 179ff.

4. E. Irving, *The Last Days: A Discourse on the Evil Character of these Our Times* (Seeley & Burnside, 1829) pp. 78, 81.
5. Ibid, pp. 79, 84, 86–7.
6. Ibid, pp. 73, 78.
7. Ibid, p. 73.
8. W. B. Sanders (ed.), *Juvenile Offenders for a Thousand Years* (North Carolina University Press, 1970); A. M. Carr-Saunders *et al.*, *Juvenile Offenders* (Cambridge University Press, 1942) pp. 1–2; *Report from the Committee on the State of the Police of the Metropolis*, 1817, Order Paper 233, p. 17.
9. First Report of the Philanthropic Society, quoted in M. D. George, *London Life in the Eighteenth Century* (Penguin, 1966) p. 221.
10. Ignatieff, *A Just Measure of Pain.*
11. J. Hanway, *Solitude in Imprisonment* (Bew, 1776) pp. 3, 10, 13, 15.
12. D. Defoe, *The Complete English Tradesman* (Rivington, 1738) p. 93.
13. H. Fielding, *An Enquiry into the Causes of the Late Increase of Robbers* (Millar, 1751) pp. xi, xv, 1, 3.
14. George, *London Life*, pp. 41–55; G. Rudé, '"Mother Gin" and the London Riots of 1736' in *Paris and London in the 18th Century* (Fontana, 1970).
15. Quoted in H. Amory, 'Henry Fielding and the Criminal Legislation of 1751–2', *Philological Quarterly*, vol. 50, no. 2, 1971, p. 187.
16. Fielding, *An Enquiry*, p. 80.
17. D. W. R. Bahlman, *The Moral Revolution of 1688* (Yale University Press, 1957).
18. L. C. Jones, *The Clubs of the Georgian Rakes* (Columbia University Press, 1942); T. S. Graves, 'Some Pre-Mohock Clansmen', *Studies in Philology*, vol. 20, no. 4, 1923; W. C. McDaniel, 'Some Greek, Roman and English Tityretus', *American Journal of Philology*, vol. 35, no. 137, 1914.
19. Richard Braithwaite, *An Age for Apes*, 1658, quoted in Graves, 'Some Pre-Mohock Clansmen', p. 405.
20. Shadwell, *The Scowrers*, p. 92.
21. *The Plays of John Gay*, vol. 1 (Chapman & Dodd, n.d.) p. 12.
22. *Virgil: The Eclogues and Georgics*, ed. R. D. Williams (Macmillan, 1979) p. 3: 'Tityre, tu patulae recubans sub tegmine fagi.' Or, very roughly, 'Tityrus, you lie beneath the spreading beech.' The First Eclogue's pastoral lament was concerned with land confiscation in northern Italy after the Battle of Philippi in BC 42 which prompts speculation on whether the 'Tityre Tu' gangs were influenced by land enclosures in their own time in the choice of their title. An

alternative line of reasoning suggests that 'Tityre Tu' was derived from 'Tittery Whoppet', an old English slang word for the pudendum, and that it was an afterthought by 'some Virgilian wag in the spirit of irony' who placed the 'Tu' in 'Tityre Tu'. Cf. McDaniel, 'Some Greek, Roman and English Tityretus', pp. 65–6.

23. E. P. Thompson, 'The Moral Economy of the English Crowd in the Eighteenth Century', *Past and Present*, no. 50, 1971; E. P. Thompson, *Whigs and Hunters* (Allen Lane, 1975); D. Hay *et al.*, *Albion's Fatal Tree* (Allen Lane, 1975); J. Brewer and J. Styles, *An Ungovernable People* (Hutchinson, 1980).
24. Hay *et al.*, *Albion's Fatal Tree*; Thompson, *Whigs and Hunters*.
25. E. P. Thompson, 'The Crime of Anonymity' in *Albion's Fatal Tree*, pp. 300, 326, 330.
26. A. Smith, *The Wealth of Nations* (Penguin, 1970 edn) p. 226.
27. Ibid, pp. 222ff.
28. J. Rule, *The Experience of Labour in Eighteenth Century Industry* (Croom Helm, 1981) pp. 114ff.
29. Defoe, *Complete English Tradesman*, p. 143.
30. Rule, *The Experience of Labour*, pp. 101ff. and note 21 p. 120.
31. S. R. Smith, 'The London Apprentices as Seventeenth Century Adolescents', *Past and Present*, no. 61, 1973.
32. C. Hill, *The World Turned Upside Down* (Penguin, 1975) pp. 63, 188–9, 366.
33. George, *London Life*, p. 272.
34. Jones, *Clubs of the Georgian Rakes*, p. 27.
35. O. J. Dunlop, *English Apprenticeship and Child Labour* (Unwin, 1912) p. 189.
36. Ibid, pp. 191ff.
37. George, *London Life*, p. 269.
38. Quoted in P. Laslett, *The World We Have Lost* (Methuen, 1971) p. 3. For a sustained attempt at a comparison of age-structures in different epochs, see J. R. Gillis, *Youth and History* (Academic Press, 1974).
39. L. Stone, *The Family, Sex and Marriage in England 1500–1800* (Weidenfield & Nicolson, 1977).
40. George, *London Life*, pp. 262–92.
41. E. P. Thompson, 'Time, Work-Discipline and Industrial Capitalism', *Past and Present*, no. 38, 1967.
42. D. A. Reid, 'The Decline of Saint Monday, 1776–1876', *Past and Present*, no. 71, 1976.
43. P. Burke, *Popular Culture in Early Modern Europe* (Temple Smith, 1978); K. Thomas, *Religion and the Decline of Magic* (Penguin, 1978) pp. 54ff; E. K. Chambers, *The Mediaeval Stage*, vol. 1

(Oxford University Press, 1903); E. P. Thompson, 'Patrician Society, Plebeian Culture', *Journal of Social History*, vol. 7, no. 4, 1974.

44. E. Le Roy Ladurie, *Carnival: A People's Uprising at Romans 1579—1580* (Scolar, 1980) p. 175.

45. Burke, *Popular Culture*, pp. 203—4; N. Z. Davis, 'The Rites of Violence: Religious Riot in Sixteenth Century France', *Past and Present*, no. 59, 1973; B. Scribner, 'Reformation, Carnival and the World Turned Upside Down', *Social History*, vol. 3, no. 3, 1978.

46. P. Stubbes, *Anatomy of the Abuses in England* (New Shakespeare Society, 1877 edn) pp. 145, 155, 184; Burke, *Popular Culture*, p. 212.

47. Le Roy Ladurie, *Carnival*, p. 191.

48. S. Butler, *Hudibras*, ed. J. Wilders (Oxford University Press, 1967) p. 143.

49. T. Hardy, *The Mayor of Casterbridge* (Macmillan, 1974) p. 302.

50. E. P. Thompson, ' "Rough Music": Le Charivari Anglais', *Annales Economies Sociétés Civilisation*, vol. 27, no. 2, 1972; N. Z. Davis, 'The Reasons of Misrule: Youth Groups and Charivaris in Sixteenth Century France', *Past and Present*, no. 50, 1971; Chambers, *Mediaeval Stage*, pp. 152—3.

51. Butler, *Hudibras*, p. 144. Cf. *Hogarth, The Complete Engravings* (Thames & Hudson, 1968) plates 88 and 103 which portray Butler's Skimmington.

52. *Poems and Letters of Andrew Marvell*, vol. 1 (Oxford University Press, 1927) p. 150. A Skimmington also appears on stage in Thomas Heywood's *The Witches of Lancashire*, 1634, in *Dramatic Works*, vol. 4 (Russell & Russell, 1964) p. 234. Shakespeare's reference to 'A wisp of straw . . . To make this shameless callet know herself' in Part III of Henry VI, Act 2, Scene 2 alludes to the twist of straw sometimes used as the badge of a scolding woman in the Skimmington. *Complete Works* (Collins, 1951) p. 674.

53. N. Z. Davis, *Society and Culture in Early Modern France* (Duckworth, 1975) p. 140.

54. E. P. Thompson, *The Making of the English Working Class* (Penguin, 1968) p. 446; S. P. Menefee, *Wives For Sale* (Blackwell, 1981) pp. 5—7.

55. Chambers, *Mediaeval Stage*, p. 152; Davis, *Society and Culture*, p. 147; Rule, *Experience of Labour*, pp. 111, 187—8.

56. Public Record Office, Home Office Papers, HO 52/35. Cf. *Report of the Commissioners on Establishing an Efficient Constabulary Force* (HMSO, 1839) p. 44.

57. Public Record Office, HO 45/454 and HO 52/35.

58. HO 52/35; *Report on a Constabulary Force*, p. 44; D. Williams,

The Rebecca Riots (Wales University Press, 1955) p. 54. This was certainly not the first time that an informer was dealt with in this way. From Marlborough in 1753 we hear than an informer's effigy 'was hung in a Tree and burnt'. P. B. Munsche, *Gentlemen and Poachers* (Cambridge University Press, 1981) p. 98.

59. R. W. Malcolmson, *Popular Recreations in English Society 1700—1850* (Cambridge University Press, 1979) pp. 39—40. For a football match designed to destroy mills, cf. Thompson, 'Moral Economy of the English Crowd', p. 116.

60. Williams, *The Rebecca Riots*, p. 241.

61. *Reynolds's Newspaper*, 9 November 1856.

62. *Reynolds's Newspaper*, 9 November 1856.

63. Cf. Public Record Office papers quoted in note 5, Chapter 6.

64. R. Samuel, 'East End Crime', Conference on Sociology and History, University of Essex, December 1979.

65. *Clarion*, 12 November 1898.

66. I. and P. Opie, *The Lore and Language of Schoolchildren* (Paladin, 1977).

Making Sense of 'Law-and-Order' Myth

1. *Report of the Moss Side Enquiry Panel to the Leader of the Greater Manchester Council*, 30 September 1981, para. 31.1.

2. G. Ryle, *The Concept of Mind* (Penguin, 1963) p. 10.

3. F. Hill, *Crime: Its Amounts, Causes and Remedies* (Murray, 1853) pp. 19—20.

4. J. J. Tobias, *Crime and Industrial Society in the Nineteenth Century* (Penguin, 1972).

5. *The Guardian*, 26 April 1978 and *The Daily Telegraph*, 26 April 1978.

6. *Report of the Commissioner of the Police of the Metropolis 1898*, C. 9449 (HMSO, 1899) p. 8.

7. T. R. Gurr *et al.*, *The Politics of Crime and Conflict* (Sage, 1977) p. 111.

8. T. Plint, *Crime in England* (Gilpin, 1851) p. 12.

9. Hill, *Crime*, p. 19.

10. M. Carpenter, *Reformatory Schools*, 1851 (Woburn, 1968 edn) pp. 4—6.

11. D. Phillips, *Crime and Authority in Victorian England* (Croom Helm, 1977) p. 133.

12. *The Times*, 4 January 1937 and 25 October 1937.

13. A. E. Morgan, *The Needs of Youth* (Oxford University Press, 1939) p. 167.

14. L. Page, *Crime and the Community* (Faber, 1937) p. 278.

15. D. H. Thorpe *et al.*, *Out of Care* (Allen & Unwin, 1980) table 1.3; N. Tutt (ed.), *Alternative Stragegies for Coping with Crime* (Blackwell, 1978) table 4.

16. J. A. Ditchfield, *Police Cautioning in England and Wales* (HMSO, 1976).

17. From 1968 to 1977, there was a slight fall in those found guilty by courts from 22,018 to 20,929, but the numbers cautioned trebled from 13,435 to 42,154. J. Paley and C. Green, *Intermediate Treatment Research Project: Interim Report* (University of Lancaster, 1978).

18. *Criminal Statistics for England and Wales 1977*, Cmnd 7289 (HMSO, 1978) p. 20.

19. L. Radzinowicz and J. King, *The Growth of Crime* (Hamilton, 1977) p. 49. Cf. J. Ditton, *Part-Time Crime* (Macmillan, 1977); J. Ditton, *Natural Sociology* (University of Glasgow, 1982); S. Henry, *The Hidden Economy* (Robertson, 1978); F. Pearce, *Crimes of the Powerful* (Pluto, 1976).

20. *The Poems of Matthew Arnold* (Oxford University Press, 1926) p. 137.

21. Quoted in *The Times*, 1 March 1843.

22. Cf. the Marplan survey, *Law-and-Order in Britain*, conducted for *The Sun*, 22 June 1976; G. Pearson, *Public Attitudes Towards Vandalism* (Bradford City Police Crime Prevention Panel, 1978); G. Pearson, 'Leisure, Popular Culture and Street Games: A Broken Dialogue between Youth and Age', *Youth in Society*, no. 30, August 1978.

23. R. Sparkes *et al.*, *Surveying Victims* (Wiley, 1977); N. Colston and R. Mawby, *Crime and the Elderly* (University of Bradford, 1979); M. Ramsay, 'Mugging: Fears and Facts', *New Society*, 24 March 1982.

24. E. Irving, *The Last Days* (Seeley & Burnside, 1829) p. 73.

25. A. Cameron, *Circus Factions* (Oxford University Press, 1976) p. 222.

26. W. B. McDaniel, 'Some Greek, Roman and English Tityretus', *American Journal of Philology*, vol. 35, no. 137, 1914.

27. Cameron, *Circus Factions*, p. 226.

28. *Criminal Statistics for England and Wales 1977*, p. 84.

29. K. Lorenz, *On Aggression* (Methuen, 1967) p. 34; J. Sayers, *Biological Politics: Feminist and Anti-Feminist Perspectives* (Tavistock, 1982).

30. *The Daily Mirror*, 28 October 1977.

31. N. Z. Davis, 'Women on Top' in *Society and Culture in Early Modern France* (Duckworth, 1975); J. Walter, 'Grain Riots and Popular

Attitudes to Law' in J. Brewer and J. Styles (eds), *An Ungovernable People* (Hutchinson, 1980); E. P. Thompson, 'The Moral Economy of the English Crowd in the Eighteenth Century', *Past and Present*, no. 50, 1971, pp. 115–16.

32. M. Ignatieff, *A Just Measure of Pain* (Macmillan, 1978) pp. 218–20.
33. M. Midgley, *Beast and Man* (Harvester, 1978).
34. J. Swift, *Gulliver's Travels* (Penguin, 1967) p. 85.
35. Quoted in M. Howard, *War and the Liberal Conscience* (Oxford University Press, 1981) p. 15.
36. Midgley, *Beast and Man*.
37. R. Williams, 'Problems of Materialism' in *Problems in Materialism and Culture* (Verso, 1980); M. Midgley, 'Rival Fatalisms' in A. Montagu (ed.), *Sociobiology Examined* (Oxford University Press, 1980).
38. J. Oldham, *A Satire* (1682) quoted in T. S. Graves, 'Some Pre-Mohock Clansmen', *Studies in Philology*, vol. 20, no. 4, 1923, p. 420.
39. R. Williams, *Culture and Society 1780–1950* (Penguin, 1961); R. Williams, *The Country and the City* (Paladin, 1975); C. Wright Mills, 'The Professional Ideology of Social Pathologists', *American Journal of Sociology*, vol. 49, no. 2, 1943; G. Pearson, *The Deviant Imagination* (Macmillan, 1975) ch. 7.
40. J. P. Bean, *The Sheffield Gang Wars* (D & D Publications, 1981); *The Sun*, 2 August 1898 and Chapter 5 above.
41. Williams, *Culture and Society*; M. J. Wiener, *English Culture and the Decline of the Industrial Spirit 1850–1980* (Cambridge University Press, 1981).
42. I. Taylor, *Law and Order: Arguments for Socialism* (Macmillan, 1981); *Crime: A Challenge to Us All* (Labour Party, 1964).
43. G. Pearson, 'Sociology and Social Work: Who put the "Social" into Social Work?', British Sociological Association, University of Lancaster, April 1980.
44. H. Mannheim, *Social Aspects of Crime in England Between the Wars* (Allen & Unwin, 1940) ch. 5.
45. Wiener, *English Culture and the Decline*.
46. *New Standard*, 1 July 1981.
47. Pearson, *The Deviant Imagination*.
48. *Crime Knows No Boundaries* (Conservative Political Centre, 1966) p. 11.
49. M. D. George, *London Life in the Eighteenth Century* (Penguin, 1966) p. 126.
50. The Irish associations of the name 'Hooligan' are clear enough, although I do not know that the accusation was ever directly levelled against the London Irish population that they were responsible for the Hooligan outrages of 1898. While confessing its ignorance of

the origins of the term 'Hooliganism', *The Clarion* (15 October 1898) observed that 'its adoption has not been influenced by the preponderance of Irishmen in the ranks of the rowdy communities, as might have been supposed'. Even so, in south London where the 'Hooligans' were sometimes said to have originated, there was a substantial Irish settlement. See also note 3, Chapter 5.

51. 'WHITELAW ACCUSES PARENTS', *The Daily Telegraph*, 8 July 1981; 'SEARCH FOR THE MASKED MEN' and 'EXTREMISTS' MASTER PLAN FOR CHAOS', *The Daily Mail*, 7 July 1981 and 10 July 1981. Unquestionably, the most spectacular of the conspiracy theories was the *New Standard* headline of 10 July 1981: 'FOUR BEHIND THE RIOTS'.

52. *The Times*, 10 November 1856.

53. C. Leeson, *The Child and the War* (King, 1917) p. 15.

54. Ibid, p. 25; C. E. B. Russell, *The Problem of Juvenile Crime* (Oxford University Press, 1917); *Report of the Board of Education 1916–1917*, Cd. 9045 (HMSO, 1918) p. 4; C. Chapman, *The Poor Man's Court of Justice* (Hodder & Stoughton, 1925) p. 279; National Council of Public Morals, *The Cinema* (Williams & Northgate, 1917); H. Mannheim, *War and Crime* (Watts, 1941) pp. 120–8; A. Marwick, *The Deluge* (Macmillan, 1965) pp. 118–19; and note 92, Chapter 5 for the birching craze.

55. Mannheim, *War and Crime*, p. 133; E. Smithies, *Crime in Wartime* (Allen & Unwin, 1982); A. Calder, *The People's War* (Panther, 1971) p. 389.

56. 'THE DEAD ROBBED. Jewelry Stolen from Raid Victims', *The Times*, 9 January 1941; 'OUTBURST OF LOOTING AT SHEFFIELD', *The Times*, 4 March 1941; 'LOOTING FROM DAMAGED PREMISES: COURT-MARTIAL FOR SIX SOLDIERS', *The Times*, 30 October 1940; and *The Times* 14 January 1941, 16 January 1941, 18 January 1941, 13 February 1941, 25 March 1941, 20 May 1941 and 6 November 1940, etc.

57. *Criminal Statistics England and Wales 1939–1945*, Cmd. 7227 (HMSO, 1947) pp. 22–5; *Hansard*, 26 June 1941, cls 1082–3.

58. C. E. B. Russell, *Manchester Boys* (Manchester University Press, 1905) p. 1.

Index

Adderley, C. B.   148, 152
Adshead, Joseph   164
'affluence' as cause of crime
      16—17, 20—1, 57—8, 166,
      173—5, 186—7, 208, 233—4,
      240
'Americanisation'   19—21, 25—8,
      31—2, 124, 168
Anderton, James   6, 213, 218
Apache gangs   260 n63
   see also youth cultures
apprentices   190—4
   see also boy labour question;
      youth cultures
Arnold, Matthew   124—6, 128,
      156, 219
arson   89—90, 106, 160, 180,
      189—90
Ashley, Lord (Earl of Shaftesbury)
      159—61, 176, 219
assaults
   on football referees   30, 64—5
   on immigrants   18, 76, 82,
      100, 195, 236, 249 n40
   on old people   9, 35, 84,
      100, 122, 129, 188, 220
   on police   36—8, 74, 85—9,
      100, 124, 188, 214, 241
   on underground rail system
      122, 125
Atkins, Tommie   106, 109
   see also military service; war
Avison, N. H.   54

Baden-Powell, R. S. S.   34, 44,
      56, 69, 71, 108, 110—15,
      249—50 n52

bag-snatches   35—6
   see also muggings; street
      robberies
Bank Holidays   62, 65—6, 74,
      202, 221
   see also holiday disturbances
Barnett, Mary   55
Beggs, Thomas   156—7, 163—6,
      177, 182
Besant, Walter   84, 102
bicycle craze   66—9, 124,
      254 n47
   see also hit-and-run cycling
      accidents; women cyclists
biology and violence   223—8
birching   12—14, 18, 28—9,
      35—6, 55, 104—6, 115,
      240—1, 248 n32, 261 n92
   see also flogging
Blatchford, Robert   86, 115,
      257 n11
   see also Clarion Clubs
Boer War   56, 61, 72—3, 111,
      240, 251 n8
Bonfire Night   38, 106, 201
Booth, Charles   58
boy bishops   195—6, 201
   see also youth cultures
boy labour question   58—60,
      107, 252 n21
Boy Scouts   34, 41—2, 44, 69,
      110—15, 249—50 n52
Boys' Brigade   112
boys' club movement   39—40, 57,
      108, 111—12, 116
Bosanquet, Helen   55, 59—60,
      66

Boyson, Rhodes 5, 9, 27, 34
Braithwaite, W. J. 57
British Medical Association, views
    on crime 15–17, 66, 77
British way of life 3–9, 13, 16,
    19, 25–6, 53–4, 62, 70–3,
    75–6, 130–2, 187, 209,
    225–6, 229ff
Bryan, H. S. 41–2
Bryant, Arthur 15
Buchanan, Robert 109
Buchanan, Walter 159
Butler, R. A. 13, 18, 27
Butler, Samuel 197–8
Butterworth, James 39–42, 48,
    116

Calvert, R. and Calvert, T. 28
Cameron, Alan 222
Campagnac, E. T. 57
carnival disorders 195–7, 202
    see also Bank Holidays; holiday
    disturbances
Carpenter, Mary 175–7,
    179–81, 215, 268 n84
Casson, Herbert 44–5
ceffyl pren 199–201
    see also Rebecca Riots; Riding
    the Stang; Skimmington
Chadwick, Edwin 157, 173, 182
Chambers, E. K. 199
Charity Organisation Society 128
Chartism 156–7, 159–62, 181,
    230
Children and Young Persons Act
    1933 34, 46–7, 216
Children and Young Persons Act
    1969 47, 217
Christianity 158–9, 161–3,
    265 n19, 265 n20
Church attendances 28, 48, 69,
    235
Church Lads' Brigade 112
cinema as cause of crime 13, 27,
    31–3, 63–4, 208
    see also Music Halls; newspaper
    sensationalism; penny gaffs;
    popular amusements;
    television

Clarion Clubs 68, 79–80, 104
    see also bicycle craze;
    Blatchford, Robert
Clay, Rev. John 175
Conservative Party 5, 12–15,
    235, 267 n57
Continuation Schools 40, 59,
    108
Cornwallis, C. F. 163–4, 173,
    177
cosh boys 21
    see also street robberies; Teddy
    Boys
costermongers 98
Cox, C. B. 27
crime waves 12–14, 35, 46–7,
    145, 164, 186–7, 208–9,
    214–18, 240–1
    see also criminal statistics;
    newspaper sensationalism
Crimean War 201
criminal statistics 35–6, 46–7,
    54, 144, 209, 213–19, 224
Critchley, T. A. 7

Dagos 22
    see also youth cultures
'dark figure' of crime 218–19, 224
Davis, Jennifer 144
Davis, Natalie 198
Day, Samuel Phillips 164, 173–4
Dead Boys 188
    see also youth cultures
Defoe, Daniel 186, 191
democracy 61–2, 68–9, 126,
    179–81, 230–1, 237–8,
    268 n84
Detention Centres 12–13, 217
    see also drill; short, sharp,
    shocks
Devine, Alex 96
Dewey, John 43–4, 184
    see also educational standards;
    permissiveness; progressive
    education
Dickens, Charles 131, 156, 167
Dors, Diana 10
drill 12–13, 44, 113, 179–80
    see also military service

drunkenness   39, 75, 165—6,
    194—5, 257 n11

educational standards   10, 26—7,
    43—6, 107, 161, 176, 208,
    239, 242
election rowdyism   248—9 n37
    see also political violence
Eliot, T. S.   26—7
Elkin, Winifred   28
Engels, F.   157, 164
Ensor, Ernest   65

factory system   167—71, 194
    see also Industrial Revolution
Faithfull, Baroness   10
Falkland Islands   143
family breakdown   28, 34, 55—7,
    70—1, 165—7, 184—6, 191,
    194, 210—11
Fielding, Henry   33, 186—7
firearms   38, 73, 76, 101—6, 124,
    138, 259 n58
First World War   43, 53, 115—16,
    240
flogging   9, 12—14, 18, 35—6,
    77—8, 107, 127—8, 132,
    143—52, 227—8, 263 n35,
    263—4 n52
    see also birching
food riots   189, 199, 225
football disorders   29—31, 64—5,
    71, 108, 193, 196, 200—1,
    202, 221—2, 247 n16
    see also assaults on football
    referees
Fountaine, Andrew   17—18
freedom of youth   28, 48, 57—8,
    107, 160, 165—7, 191—4, 208
Freeman, Arnold   107
Fyvel, T. R.   16—17

Gale, George   4
garotters   128—46
    see also street robberies
Garotter's Act 1863   143—53,
    263 n35
    see also flogging

Gatrell, V. A. C.   54
Gay, John   188
generation gap   15, 28, 53,
    219—24
George, Dorothy   193
girls   17, 60, 89—92, 96, 129,
    160, 198—9, 225
    see also women; working
    mothers
Gorst, Sir John   57
Governor Eyre controversy
    150—2, 263—4 n52
graffiti   40, 90
Graham, Sir James   161
Green, Rev. Peter   111
Grey, Sir George   134, 143, 149
Gurr, T. R.   54

Hadden, T. B.   54
Hanway, Joseph   186
Hardy, Thomas   197
Hatton, S. F.   39—42
Heathcote, C. G.   54—5
Henriques, Basil   41
Hill, Frederic   213, 215
Hill, Matthew Davenport   143,
    167, 175
Hill, Micaiah   163, 167, 175
hit-and-run cycling accidents
    67—8
Hobsbawm, E. J.   62
Hoggart, Richard   19—20, 31
holiday disturbances   38, 65—6,
    74, 82, 84, 100, 192, 195,
    202, 221, 253 n40
    see also Bank Holidays; carnival
    disorders
Hooligan: origins of word   74—9,
    83—4 *and especially* 255—6
    n3
Hooligans
    dress-style   92—101
    firearms   101—6, 260 n63
    in Russia   106—7
    see also youth cultures
Hopwood, Charles   104

ideologies of crime   230—41

street fights 18, 30, 38–9, 76, 81–6, 88, 90–2, 94–6, 102–3, 110, 153–5, 188, 192, 201
street gangs *see* Mohocks; Nickers; Skeleton Army; street robberies; Tityre Tus; youth cultures
street robberies 18, 21, 34–6, 84, 122, 128–30, 186–8
  see also bag-snatches; garotters; Hooligans; muggings

Tallack, William 121–2
Taylor, A. J. P. 31
Teddy Boys 17–23, 74, 94, 100, 144
  see also youth cultures
television as cause of crime 13, 17, 21, 33, 62, 208, 242
  see also cinema; Music Halls; penny gaffs; popular amusements
Thatcher, Margaret 5, 11, 237
  see also democracy; family breakdown; leniency; permissiveness; reformative principles; rule by consent; sentimentalism; unemployment; war; working mothers
Thompson, Denys 27, 43
Thompson, E. P. 189, 265 n19, 268 n84, 272 n59
Thomson, Alexander 163–4, 173, 177
Tityre Tus 188, 269–70 n22
  see also Dead Boys; Mohocks; Nickers
trade unions 24, 61, 163, 191, 230, 232–4
transportation 127, 143
  see also Falkland Islands
Treason Act 1842 148
  see also flogging; Garotter's Act
Turpin, Dick 33, 165, 178

unemployment 34, 43, 59–60, 146, 174, 233–4, 236–9, 267 n57
unemployment disturbances 38
upper-class hooliganism 153–5, 188
urbanisation 61–2, 69–73, 110, 121, 163–4, 166, 168–75, 186–7
  see also factory system; Industrial Revolution; social change
Urwick, E. J. 107, 110, 112

Vagrancy Act 1824 148
  see also flogging
vandalism 18, 39, 89–90, 100, 188–9, 192, 217–18
Velvet Cap Gang 83, 94
  see also youth cultures
Victorian standards 9, 22, 54–5, 122–6, 146–55
vigilantes 14, 77, 133, 138, 142, 240

war 43, 109–11, 113–16, 201–2, 227, 239–41, 249 n40
Webb, Sidney 58–9
whipping *see* birching; flogging
White Slave Bill, 1912 263–4 n52
  see also flogging
Whitehouse, J. H. 57
wife-beating 197–200
women 17, 61, 68, 85, 90, 198–200, 225, 235, 241, 254 n47
  see also girls; working mothers
women cyclists 68, 254 n47
Woodcraft Folk 113
working mothers 15, 165, 208, 240
Worsley, Rev. Henry 157–8, 163–6, 168–70, 174, 179

Ikes 96
  see also youth cultures
immigration and crime 4, 131, 209, 225–6, 236–9, 263–4 n52, 274–5 n50
imperialism 109, 150–2, 263–4 n52
Industrial Revolution 163–4, 167–75, 183, 191, 194
Irving, Rev. Edward 183–5, 220

Jebb, Joshua 134, 145
Jenkin, Patrick 8
jingoism 72–3, 111, 115, 201
  see also war
Joseph, Sir Keith 5, 8
juvenile delinquency 28–9, 39–42, 46–7, 54–5, 184–5, 216–18, 223–4, 240–1
  see also freedom of youth; generation gap; youth cultures

Kay-Shuttleworth, James 168
Kingsmill, Rev. Joseph 173
Kipling, Rudyard 106, 109–10
Knacker's Act 1786 148
  see also flogging; Garotter's Act
Knights, Philip 5

Labour Party 11, 61, 233–5
laissez-faire 59–60, 168–9, 189, 191
Larrikins 98–100, 110
  see also youth cultures
Le Mesurier, Lilian 46
Leavis, F. R. 27–8, 31
Leavis, Q. D. 27
leniency 3, 13, 28–9, 41–3, 47–8, 76, 79, 84, 121–2, 127–8, 133, 143, 146–9, 153–5, 186–7, 189, 208, 216–17, 227–8, 237–8
  see also birching; drill; educational standards; flogging; permissiveness; sentimentalism

Locke, John 194
London, Jack 72, 157 n11
looting 36, 38, 241

McIntyre, Patrick 77
McLintock, F. H. 54
Mafficking 72–3, 111
  see also jingoism
Mannheim, Hermann 241
Mark, Sir Robert 6–7, 36–7
Marvell, Andrew 198
Marx, Karl 166
mass media *see* cinema; newspaper sensationalism; television
Mass Observation 21–2, 39
Masterman, Charles 71
Mayhew, Henry 98
militarism 113–15
military service 22, 24, 61, 108–16, 246 n24
  see also drill; war
Mill, John Stuart 152, 181, 268 n84
Misrule 195–7
Mods 74, 227
  see also youth cultures
Mohocks 188
monkey parade 63, 91–2, 98, 101
  see also youth cultures
Moore, Sir Thomas 14, 18, 267 n57
Morgan, A. E. 28, 32, 216
Morgan, Patricia 10
Mosley, Oswald 9, 248–9 n37
Mother Folly 195–201
muggings 9, 20, 130
  see also bag-snatches; street robberies
Music Halls as cause of crime 33, 58, 63, 74–5, 86, 208, 258 n42
  see also cinema; penny gaffs; television

Nabarro, Gerald 14
National Council of Public Morals 31–2